Mexico

A Concise Illustrated History

John W. Sherman

ROWMAN & LITTLEFIELD
Lanham • Boulder • New York • London

Executive Editor: Susan McEachern
Assistant Editor: Katelyn Turner
Higher Education Channel Manager: Jonathan Raeder

Credits and acknowledgments for material borrowed from other sources, and reproduced with permission, appear on the appropriate pages within the text.

Published by Rowman & Littlefield
An imprint of The Rowman & Littlefield Publishing Group, Inc.
4501 Forbes Boulevard, Suite 200, Lanham, Maryland 20706
www.rowman.com

6 Tinworth Street, London SE11 5AL, United Kingdom

Copyright © 2020 by The Rowman & Littlefield Publishing Group, Inc.

All rights reserved. No part of this book may be reproduced in any form or by any electronic or mechanical means, including information storage and retrieval systems, without written permission from the publisher, except by a reviewer who may quote passages in a review.

British Library Cataloguing in Publication Information Available

Library of Congress Cataloging-in-Publication Data

Names: Sherman, John W., 1960- author.
Title: Mexico : a concise illustrated history / John W. Sherman.
Description: Lanham : Rowman & Littlefield, [2020] | Includes bibliographical references and index.
Identifiers: LCCN 2019047115 (print) | LCCN 2019047116 (ebook) | ISBN 9781538137833 (cloth) | ISBN 9781538137840 (paperback) | ISBN 9781538137857 (epub)
Subjects: LCSH: Mexico—History.
Classification: LCC F1226 .S517 2020 (print) | LCC F1226 (ebook) | DDC 972—dc23
LC record available at https://lccn.loc.gov/2019047115
LC ebook record available at https://lccn.loc.gov/2019047116

Contents

Preface		v
Note about the Cover Image		xi

Part I: Ancient Civilizations

Chapter 1	Great Pyramids in the Highlands	3
Chapter 2	The Maya of Yucatán	13
Chapter 3	Olmecs, Téenek, Aztecs	23
Chapter 4	Conquests	35

Part II: Colonial Centuries

Chapter 5	The Creation of New Spain	47
Chapter 6	Mid-Colonial Economics	57
Chapter 7	Mid-Colonial Society	69
Chapter 8	Late Colonial Reform and Revolt	79

Part III: Independence and Modernity

Chapter 9	The Insurmountable Divide	91
Chapter 10	Showdown with the Americans	101

| Chapter 11 | Juárez, War, and the French | 113 |
| Chapter 12 | Age of the Railroad | 123 |

Part IV: The Age of Rebellion

Chapter 13	Twilight of the Porfirians	137
Chapter 14	The Season of Rebellions	147
Chapter 15	Return of the Strong Arm	157
Chapter 16	The Limits of Idealism	167

Part V: Structures of Power

Chapter 17	Miguel Alemán—Legacy President	181
Chapter 18	PRI-Eminence	191
Chapter 19	Bombast, Boom, Bust	203
Chapter 20	Crises and Control	213
	Afterword	225
	Suggestions for Further Reading	231
	Index	241

Preface

This book provides a short, easy-to-read introduction to the broad sweep of Mexican history, from precontact civilizations to (nearly) the present. It is primarily concerned with political processes, though economic factors figure prominently as well. It largely comprises narrative, with a chronicle of events built around several politically important persons. Narrative evokes images, works our imagination, and typically sticks in the mind more readily than explanatory and analytical material. This image-feeding approach is particularly useful for the newly initiated student of any given historical subfield, in that it fixes and engrains certain seminal events in the mind. The emphasis here is on lucidity, with a minimum of proper names, acronyms, and terms. This is *not* a text in the traditional sense of reflecting a synthesis of ongoing scholarship by academics. That book already exists: *The Course of Mexican History* from Oxford University Press, regularly updated, is a thick and thorough scholarly text. Several other all-encompassing textbooks are also available for those seeking a weighty compendium.

One of the features of the discipline of history, which makes it so diverse and enticing, is that historians differ on their fundamental approaches to studying the past. Since World War II, the narrow confines of traditional political and economic history have been broadly and beautifully stretched by inroads into social and cultural history. Even within the realm of political history, a postwar engagement of "history from below" has swept the profession. Driven by the epistemological concept of *agency*—the notion that peoples subordinate in overarching power structures can still exercise volition and shape their own historical destiny—this interpretative approach has challenged and enriched the discipline. In this context, I readily acknowledge that, as a historian, I am a bit anachronistic. I overwhelmingly read and write narrative, and in terms of power structures I am highly skeptical of the notion of agency. To put it another way: I am old school. This is not to say that my approach is correct, much less to disparage the approaches of others. Indeed, at the end of the day—if objective truth exists (another hotly debated topic)—perhaps my interpretative methodology is less perceptive than theirs. But awareness of my approach will likely influence your decision to buy, assign (if an instructor), or read this book.

This is a lively, traditional narrative history of Mexico. It addresses political power brokers, who historically have been mostly lighter-skinned males. Because of its focus on elite-driven politics, few women take center stage. Many social and cultural historians will undoubtedly use this book as a supplementary reader, leaving it to address the political narrative as they teach social and cultural material. Unlike with other all-encompassing and detailed texts (which incorporate social and cultural history), there is no awkward overlap between the book and such course content.

While I have largely refrained from challenging conventional interpretations regarding top-down political history, in three major debates regarding the twentieth century I take minority positions. First, this book downplays the meaning and significance of the 1910 Revolution, in the tradition of such authors as Ramón Ruíz. Second, with regard to the postwar era, it argues that Mexico should be identified as an oligarchy rather than a one-party state that maturates into a democracy with the election of the "opposition" in 2000 (scholars have long collectively acknowledged that late twentieth-century Mexico was undemocratic, but many have seen in the 2000 election a step into genuine democracy). Third, I contend that Miguel Alemán (not Lázaro Cárdenas) is the most important midcentury political figure in the nation's history, in that he was integral to creating what I term the PRI fraternity (so-named after the dominant political party), which has continued to exercise decisive political power in Mexico even to this day. Alemán and his friends undid nearly all of Cárdenas's political projects, and he was the key figure in turning postwar Mexico into an oligarchy. This interpretation is indebted not so much to my own earlier work on Cárdenas but to several scholars studying Mexico in the 1940s, most notably Stephen Niblo. An afterword addresses some political processes currently at work—this is certainly an engaging time to study Mexico's political history, given at least the possibility of an authentic democratic transformation.

And now, some mechanical issues: In terms of wording, please note that I use *Americans* to refer to residents of the United States, *America* for the United States as an entity, and *American* as a referencing adjective. I acknowledge that Mexicans regard themselves as *Americanos*, and typically in contrast call U.S. citizens *Norte Americanos*. Again, a combination of clarity and brevity dictates this stylistic preference. Playfully, for the thoughtful benefit of my fellow U.S. citizens, I refer to three American states in Spanish: *Tejas*, *La Florida*, and *Nuevo Mexico*. With regard to language, I have translated almost all Spanish terms, sometimes a bit liberally (e.g., *científicos* as positivists rather than *scientists*) in order to make this book accessible to readers without any knowledge of Spanish. Select, exceptionally well-known Spanish terms (such as *lucha libre*) are defined upon introduction but then retained. A few others are translated into English but then follow with Spanish in parentheses. I do periodically use the Spanish possessive *-ista* to denote a group, such as *Villistas*, partisans of the revolutionary Francisco Villa, or *Callistas*, loyalists of President Plutarco Calles. I have, however, avoided the awkward term PRI-*ista*—for partisans of the Institutional Revolutionary Party. In namesakes, I have opted to refer to sons as "Jr." in the English usage rather than work with the Spanish paternal-maternal combination of last names.

In countless references to persons and events throughout this simple book, I have declined to employ conditioning words and phrases, which quickly become burdensome to the reader and distract from the major point being made. Of course in knowledge there are constant questions of degree of certainty. We are not absolutely sure, for example, that the Aztecs of Tenochtitlán were struck by a smallpox epidemic in 1520. Yet in mentioning this event (in chapter 4) I have stated it decisively, rather than insert the word *probably*. In myriad places throughout the book, a more technical conditioning would dictate countless insertions of *maybe*, *likely*, *we think*, *might have*, *almost certainly*, and so on—all of which would make for tedious reading.

The structure of this book is simple: It comprises twenty chapters in groups of four. Part I addresses pre-contact native civilizations and their subjugation. It does so in an order determined by geography and importance rather than via chronology—a novel approach that offers, I believe, a more cogent narrative. Predictably, in these chapters social and cultural dimensions are more preeminent than elsewhere in the book. Part 2 (chapters 5–8) overviews the three-hundred-year colonial era. It does so more by topic than chronology, though there is a primary focus on the sixteenth century in chapter 5 and an emphasis on the eighteenth century in chapter 8. Part 3 (chapters 9–12) addresses the nineteenth century, part 4 (chapters 13–16) the first half of the twentieth century, and part 5 (chapters 17–20) the late twentieth century. Though the afterword speaks to some contemporary (mostly political) phenomena, I have dutifully refrained from addressing recent events in detail so as to defer to the expertise of history's sister disciplines.

From the start of this project I was keen to include photographs, and I am grateful to Rowman & Littlefield for accommodating this desire. Photographs add another layer to a survey and greatly enliven it. The photographs herein are a mix of archival and on-the-ground originals, almost all shot by myself with professional-grade equipment, then screened and edited as needed by Professor Spencer Cunningham of the University of Findlay (Ohio). We have not modified the photographs, generally, except for issues of light and shadow. The frequency of photographs increases later in the book, a reflection of the generally limited options (i.e., artists' portraits and headshots) for especially the colonial and early nineteenth-century material. Almost all archival photos are duplicates photographed from museum collections.

Like any author, I am indebted to a wide array of colleagues and associates—though I take responsibility for any shortcomings herein. Besides Spencer, whose studious eyes ensured great photographs, several historians read selective chapters and made useful recommendations, most notably my decades-long friend Peter Henderson (Emeritus, Winona State University). I thank the four thoughtful reviewers engaged by Rowman & Littlefield's veteran acquisitions editor, Susan McEachern, two of whom were later identified—Michele McArdle Stephens at West Virginia University and Steve Lewis of Chico State. I have participated for thirty years in the Rocky Mountain Council of Latin American Studies (RMCLAS), the oldest professional organization in the United States with regard to Latin America, where I enjoy several collegial friendships. Of special note is Monica Rankin of (UT Dallas), Steve Bunker (University of Alabama), and Jay Harrison (Hood College), a trio of exceptional scholars who stay grounded even while thriving in the Ivory Tower. I count Friedrich Schuller (Portland State), Peter Linder (New Mexico Highlands), Susan Deeds (Emeritus, Northern Arizona), Don Stevens (Drexel University), Jonathan Truitt (Central Michigan), Ward Albro, Shannon Baker, and Alberto Rodríguez (all of Texas A&M–Kingsville) as friends who engage history with such zest so as to continue to inspire. This communal thread via RMCLAS has been key to keeping me connected to Mexican history even as I have pursued a second historical subfield, genocide studies. I want to acknowledge my colleagues at Wright State, where I have taught for a quarter century, in the context of the awful developments there in 2018–2019, as I wrote this book. Forced into an impossible situation by an opportunistic administration, in winter 2019 the unionized faculty went on strike—and in the process I came to realize anew how much I appreciate and respect my teaching colleagues, and how much I admire those eleven fellow historians who stayed on the picket lines until we preserved tenure and at least a modicum of commitment to education over money making.

I found critical inspiration for this book from the Mexican people. I traversed Mexico in three major trips to shoot photographs, venturing from Oaxaca to Mexico City (via Puebla), from Mexico City to San Luis Potosí (via Pachuca), and from San Luis Potosí to Ciudad Juárez (via Zacatecas and Durango), while taking two shorter trips to Yucatán and Tijuana. Some things never change. The friendliness and warmth of Mexicans, especially away from the heavily touristed regions, is unflappable, even in difficult times. Whether it was the rancher who gave me a lift on his *moto* in stifling summer heat as I hiked to the archeological site of Tamtoc or the taxi driver who waited patiently as I photographed the ruins of Saturnino Cedillo's house and visited his tomb, in a desert frequented by the Zeta drug cartel (as a lookout scouted us from a nearby ridgeline)—Mexicans exude an amicable spirit that cannot help but draw us back. What a wonderful people and an amazing country!

Note about the Cover Image

A Jaguar Warrior vanquishes a Bird Warrior in the mural of the epic battle at Cacaxtla. Since its discovery in 1974, the sixty-foot-long mural has perplexed scholars: Is it referencing a real battle, or is it a metaphor of struggle between good and evil? Either way, the arresting brilliance of this twelve-hundred-year-old work of art, dominated by exquisite displays of Maya Blue, is undeniable.

PART I

ANCIENT CIVILIZATIONS

CHAPTER ONE

Great Pyramids in the Highlands

So awed by what their distant ancestors had constructed, the Aztecs called it "The Place Where Men Became Gods." Today we know it as *Teotihuacán*, an archeological site thirty-five miles northeast of Mexico City that locals still commonly refer to as the *Pyramids*. Tourists flock here to see massive structures rivaling those of ancient Egypt. Undeniably one of the world's great wonders, Mexico's pyramids have fascinated and intrigued for centuries. But what can we know of their creators, of a people who left us such works of grandeur, yet no written history?

The pre-contact period of Mexican history—before Spaniards arrived along the Gulf coastline in the 1510s—is unlocked by the disciplines of archeology and anthropology. Archeology, the study of material remains of past human life, goes hand in hand with anthropology—the study of humans, especially when the later focuses on origins and the nature of primitive peoples. Both disciplines arose in the mid-nineteenth century, when pondering questions of human origin was vogue. The Enlightenment of the eighteenth century had challenged conventional explanations provided by Christianity. If God did not create a unique first couple (with Adam and Eve's sons and daughters then marrying each another), from where did the human species come?

The geographic division of "Old" and "New" worlds further complicated the question of origin. When Europeans explored the Americas in the early sixteenth century, they encountered vast numbers of natives on two continents, separated from the rest of humanity for millennia. Where did *they* come from? How could the Christian God allow a large segment of humanity to be separated from the efficacious message of the gospel? These questions perplexed minds into the mid-nineteenth century. One imaginative American, named Joseph Smith, contended that the Native Americans were in fact Jews, comprising the fabled Lost Tribe of Israel!

With the rise of the professional disciplines of archeology and anthropology, the search for a scientifically deduced link between Old and New World peoples began in earnest. In 1932, archeologists discovered a spearhead near Clovis, New Mexico. It had a distinctive shape, a beveling at the lower edges similar to those found in Asian Siberia. When Mexicans unearthed an ancient skeleton at a construction site in Mexico City fifteen years later, academics noted that it had certain Mongol-like features. The combination of these discoveries gave credence to a theory that the Americas' native population originated in Asia. Terrestrial study of the Bering Sea, and the understanding that it had been dry land during the last interglacial age, seemed to confirm an Asia-to-the-Americas migration.

In the difficult study of a far-distant past, nothing is ever quite certain. Using fluorine analysis (fluorine from ground water gradually replaces calcium in the bones, allowing for a computation of age), scholars determined that the skeleton found in Mexico City dated from around 9000 BCE. Earlier specialists had declared the remains male. Now, with ever-improving techniques, it appears that perhaps this *female* dates from around 5000 BCE. Other skeletal remains in South America suggest much earlier migratory patterns. In the 1990s, the recovery of arrowheads in southern France, also resembling that found at Clovis, sparked debate about a possible trans-Atlantic migration. But all new factors considered, the thesis of long-distant Asiatic origins of the earliest inhabitants of the Americas still holds weight. DNA patterns (the tracking of an acid molecule present in all living organisms), and a disproportionately common blood type among Native Americans, have left a genetic footprint that points back to Asiatic Mongolians.

Where Men Became Gods

Even in 1521, when the Spaniards subdued the Aztecs in their capital to southwest, hundreds of Native Americans still lived among the pyramids at Teotihuacán. Within months of the conquest, Spaniards saw the structures and marveled, but they did not attempt to settle in the vicinity of this "heathen" site. For the breadth of three centuries, when Mexico was a colony under Spanish rule, the pyramids remained little more than a curiosity. But in the mid-nineteenth century, with the rise of the discipline of archeology and tales of jewel-laden inner chambers in the pyramids of Egypt, the curious began to explore the site in earnest. They (wrongly) named the largest pyramid that of the "Sun," and a nearby smaller one after the moon. In the late nineteenth century, after Mexico had gained its independence, the government designated an official National Archeologist to investigate the nation's ancient patrimony. Unfortunately, the president at the time appointed an untrained antiquities dealer to the position. Leopoldo Batres did great disservice to many of Mexico's still largely untouched archeological sites. At Teotihuacán, he stripped the Pyramid of the Sun of still-intact murals, most of which then inexplicably disappeared—apparently sold off to private collectors. Batres also tore away much of the protective cut-stone exterior of the weathered structure and incorrectly began rebuilding it with five—instead of the original four—platform levels. A good portion of the dirt-filled pyramid washed away before he could complete the task, and ultimately the entire

Figure 1.1. Mexicans first seriously explored their antiquities in the late nineteenth century, unfortunately under the supervision of an ill-trained cadre of opportunistic government officials. The creation of a highly professional National Institute of Anthropology and History came in the 1930s. Here, an excavation crew pauses for a photographer at Cempoala, Veracruz, in 1891. Cempoala was the first indigenous city visited by the Spanish conqueror Hernán Cortés when he landed in Mexico in 1519.
Source: Fototeca, Instituto Nacional de Antropología e Historia, Pachuca.

exterior had to be rebuilt. What tourists excitedly climb atop today, as an "ancient pyramid," is in fact a heavy reconstruction from the late nineteenth century.

We do not know the original measurements of the pyramid, as Batres neither recorded them nor documented his excavation procedures. The present structure reaches 213 feet in height, with a base 746 feet wide, and is comprised of one million cubic yards of dirt, sand, and adobe (hardened clay), along with a (heavily restored) cut-stone surface mortared with a cement-like lime-sand mix. It is probably a bit larger than the original, but of course much of the interior is still authentic. The original pyramid was built around 200 CE as a singular, one-time project; it would have dominated the cityscape much as the rebuilt one does today. Residents must have regarded it as special—the symbol of their great city. A small subterranean cavern beneath the pyramid, detected in 1971, suggests that it might be tied to the cult of Tlaloc, a fearsome, white-fanged rain god whose abode lay beneath the earth in a watery underworld. Digs deep within the Sun Pyramid in 2008 revealed skeletal remains, including those of four children. Were these innocents sacrificed for the pleasure of Tlaloc?

In the mid-twentieth century, trained scholars began to systematically study Teotihuacán. A team from the University of Rochester under archeologist René Millon canvassed it in the 1950s, computerizing data on five thousand designated sectors while gathering 1.3 million objects—mostly pottery shards. The Sun Pyramid sits to the east of a series of large plazas collectively termed the Avenue of the Dead (a dramatic earlier misnomer reflecting an ultimately vain search for tombs). At the northern terminus of this linear "avenue" is the Moon Pyramid. The combination of these two features presents a long-baffling mystery: their axis is oriented slightly off due north (by 15°25′), despite the fact that the North Star is easily identifiable. Why is this so? One recent theory posits that this alignment is based on a 260-day calendric cycle, corresponding to the location of stars as they appear on our dates of August 12 and April 30.

The Moon Pyramid, unlike the Sun, is relatively authentic. At 120 feet in height, also earth-filled with an outer shell of cut stone, it was enlarged several times by the original inhabitants. The initial structure probably dates from the time of Christ. Archeologists in the last fifteen years have found burials in the Moon—decapitated skeletons along with eagle, jaguar, and rattlesnake remains, all likely sacrifices to bless reconstruction and rededication. Of particular interest has been what is designated Site Number 5, where there have been found ornaments, greenstone beads, and pendants deposited in patterns similar to Mayan burials in the distant Yucatán peninsula. Mayan lords likely visited Teotihuacán, bringing gifts of honor.

A quarter mile south of the Sun Pyramid, yet also to the east of the Avenue of the Dead, is the sprawling "Citadel." In the last decade the most exciting excavations have been carried out here, in an enclosed courtyard around what is known as the Feathered Serpent Pyramid. Only seventy feet high and two hundred feet wide, this pyramid seems an unlikely candidate for significance, but its location suggests great importance. The Citadel around it could have held one hundred thousand standing people. A second pyramid, directly in front of it, features a platform clearly designed to allow for viewing the Feathered Serpent Pyramid's elaborate façade. On the façade, in high relief, is the Feathered Serpent God himself, undulating, amidst seashells, in the watery underworld. Wearing a headdress, the sign of the calendar, he is among other attributes the deity who controls time, the one who determined Teotihuacán's destiny. Recent digs at the Pyramid have uncovered two hundred skeletal remains around its base—all males between thirteen and fifty years old, in sets of thirteen and twenty (when multiplied, equal to the 260-day count of the sacred cyclical calendar). Some of these victims have cranial deformities and were buried in a kneeling position, their wrists tied behind their backs. Seashells, slate discs, and obsidian arrowheads accompanied them into the realm of unknown time. Nearby, artisans' workshops abounded, and digs within these structures have turned up ceremonial clay figurines. There is no doubt the Feathered Serpent Pyramid held great religious significance, and that the Citadel was the center of an important religious cult.

Today's visitors to Teotihuacán are of course viewing only the surviving foundations of myriad structures, some of which were built of stone, others of wood, and still others of a combination of materials. A malleable, porous volcanic rock was the most common component. The foundations themselves create puzzles: superimposed reconstruction over many centuries make for multiple levels of decayed ruins, often several feet deep. Excavations near the Avenue of the Dead, for example, have revealed the base of stairs flanked by two split-tongued snakeheads, sculpted of gray quarry stone and covered with painted stucco, much of it tinted pink. Where did this lead? The entire city at its height would have been filled with color, murals nearly everywhere. A very few remaining stone reliefs on one base platform of the Sun Pyramid show Feathered Jaguars, complete with painted paws. Dozens of murals from Teotihuacán's administrative center have been uncovered and preserved, shedding light on both religious convictions and daily life.

At its height Teotihuacán probably had a population of some 150,000, perhaps more. In the fifth century, when the city reached its apogee, it was almost certainly the largest metropolis on earth. Elites dwelt in the center, with lower classes living on the periphery, crowded into small apartment-like rooms. To keep warm during the coldest months people stayed in close proximity, sleeping side by side. A middle class of skilled artisans manned workshops, honing tools for cooking and farming, some from green obsidian mined in the area. Others crafted a fine, thin, orange-tinted pottery. This was traded widely; pieces have been discovered in places as far away as present-day Guatemala. Though the lower classes had a limited diet of maize and beans, the elite enjoyed sumptuous fare, including fowl from nearby lakes. Teotihuacán thrived in apparent peace, retaining its grandeur for centuries, with little in the way of militarism—a hallmark of what has long been termed the Classic Period of the pre-contact era, dating from roughly 200 BCE to 900 CE. Yet around the eighth century there are signs of distress: charred roof beams indicate large fires and a partial destruction; signs of a hastily constructed, crude wall appear, suggesting external dangers. Indeed, brutish migrants from the north threatened the great city, terrorizing its inhabitants. There was ecological decline as well, deforestation and soil exhaustion taking an environmental toll in the surrounding broad valley. In slow decline during the ninth century, one hundred years later Teotihuacán was a ghost of its former self, and soon after nearly abandoned.

More Great Sites and Discoveries

Teotihuacán was not alone in its Classic Period glory. Seventy miles to the southeast another city arose at Cholula. This archeological site's history belies the meaning of its name, which translates as "The Place of Those Who Fled." In fact, people occupied Cholula as early as 500 BCE, but perhaps there was an influx of refugees at some later point. Here we find the largest pyramid ever built—at least by the size of its base. The Great Pyramid is 1,150 feet wide (and square), and 218 feet high. Started around 200 CE, it was enlarged multiple times over nine centuries. Not neatly restored like the Sun Pyramid at Teotihuacán, it draws far fewer tourists, though Cholula as a site is much more authentic. Both cities flourished during the middle centuries of the Classic Period, when Cholula both emulated and rivaled Teotihuacán. Many of the same architectural techniques and motifs appear at both places, while the Cholulans' pantheon of gods included Tlaloc, a cult likely imparted by the Teotihuacanese. Otherwise, the Cholulans reserved their highest devotion for Huehueteotl, the God of Fire. And no wonder!

From atop the Great Pyramid one clearly sees the oft-smoking hulk of Popocatépetl, Mexico's eighteen-thousand-foot monster volcano.

Study of the Great Pyramid began in 1931 under the supervision of Mexican archeologist Ignacio Márquina. Penetrating the massive hill with five miles of tunnels by the early 1950s (some of which tourists trek through today), Márquina and his team confirmed that natives built this structure with better techniques than those used at Teotihuacán, solidifying much of the interior dirt into rock-hard adobe. The exterior was stripped of its limestone-and-painted stucco surface long ago, but it must have once been truly spectacular. After the conquest, Spaniards leveled off the top of the pyramid and stuck a large wooden cross on it, which was subsequently destroyed by a fire sparked by a lightning strike (was Huehueteotl angry?). After lightning destroyed a second cross, they erected a church at this place where, according to a sixteenth-century friar, many idols to the devil were found.

Those destroyed "idols" undoubtedly included wonderful examples of Cholulan pottery. Cholula as a site is interesting because, unlike Teotihuacán, its habitation persisted for a full two centuries into the Post-Classic, an era that dates roughly from 900 CE to the time of the Spanish conquest. Typical features, including militarism, surface in this pocket of time, while the quality of Cholulan pottery actually gets better (the Post-Classic, otherwise, is a period of consistent degeneration and decline). Post-Classic pottery from the environs of Cholula is known by the name Mixteca-Puebla. Featuring dark finishes, flat foundations, and curved sides, many pieces are clearly utilitarian and resemble modern-day cereal bowls. What makes Mixteca-Puebla pottery so exceptional is its geometrical precision. Polychromatic, most have red interiors, but otherwise are made of black, orange, or white clay. One artistic feature is the "solar band," with an orange ring close to the vessel's rim and emanating red vertical lines and hooks designed to represent the sun. Even the conquering Spaniards—disinclined to praise anything originating from the natives—lauded Mixteca-Puebla pottery as exemplary.

The Cholulan elite celebrated life through extravagant feasts and drinking. Banquets held religious connotations. Some exquisite pottery pieces were specially designed for the sacred consumption of pulque, a fermented cactus juice used by priests and drunk by nobles at a fête (commoners, in contrast, were only allowed to indulge on their deathbeds). When archeologists excavated an area just south of the Great Pyramid in 1969, they found a 185-foot-long, 8-foot-high mural of just such a festival. "The Drinkers" is the longest preserved pre-contact mural yet found. It shows 164 different people in various states of ecstasy and inebriation, with several crossing the line to penance—they are vomiting.

Figure 1.2. In the late Post-Classic, native lords traveled long distances to undergo surgical procedures in Cholula. Here, as portrayed in a facsimile of a page in a sixteenth-century codex, a Cholulan priest prepares to perforate his patient's nasal septum (the cartilage separating the nostrils), so that he can wear a bar through the nose that will confirm his important status.
Source: Museo Regional de Cholula, Cholula.

Crafting mammoth murals seems to have been all the rage among native peoples in the Post-Classic. Twenty miles north of Cholula, artists rendered a work that can only be described as exquisite. Digs at Cacaxtla in 1975 revealed the priceless treasure, which nearly twelve centuries earlier had been carefully covered with sand, then soil, before undertaking new construction atop it. "The Battle" is an amazing wall of paintings portraying a mammoth struggle between Jaguar and Bird Warriors. Is this memorialized fight mythical or real? Is it a metaphysical depiction of good versus evil, and a tribute to the Jaguar cult, connected in turn to the moralistic Feathered Serpent God? Whatever its intention, as the pictures progress, it is clear that the Jaguar Warriors are victorious, mutilating and decapitating the vanquished. The mural at Cacaxtla is astounding in part because of its state of preservation. Twelve hundred years old, it is still largely intact, unlike Cholula's badly fragmented "The Drinkers." It features five colors: white, yellow, black (in small bits), red, and blue. The red, which is common to highlands murals, has a soft purplish shade to it, clearly created from soils with iron and magnesium. The richly toned blue—termed Maya Blue by archeologists because the Maya seem to have first developed it—is predominant, made from soil with silicates of aluminum.

As Teotihuacán and Cholula flourished, yet another impressive culture prospered in the broad Valley of Oaxaca, in the distant mountains of southern Mexico. The Zapotecs were descendants of natives who crafted the earliest form of writing in the Americas, symbols in low relief etched on stone slabs, at around 600 BCE. In the 1920s, a talented Mexican archeologist named Alfonso Caso began a lifelong study of the Zapotecs and their great administrative center at Monte Albán. Though off the beaten path and less visited than sites in Yucatán and central Mexico, Monte Albán is arguably the most breathtaking of all. Perched on a plateau thirteen hundred feet above a valley floor, with rugged mountains as a backdrop, it features a main plaza reconstructed under Caso's direction in the 1950s. Villages emerged in this area ten thousand years ago, while settlement at Monte Albán itself

Figure 1.3. Over centuries, the weathering process naturally reduces pyramids in size and shape. In more temperate climates, brush and trees grow from sediment in ever-widening cracks. Here at Monte Albán, with its drier climate, wind is more of an issue. In this photograph from a heavily rebuilt North Platform, we can see reconstructed stone walls in the foreground, but parts of System IV structures have otherwise been left in a relatively raw state.

began at around 500 BCE. It was not a logical place for habitation. For centuries, water had to be carried up to the site—only later were reservoirs dug to collect rainfall. Even in its heyday, Monte Albán drew upon the broader valley for food (mostly maize), and hence was more of a cultural center than a city. At its height in the early Classic Period it was probably home to about twenty-five thousand people, most living in small one-room huts, hundreds of which were constructed in close proximity using the "wattle and daub" method that employs sticks as a frame for adobe.

Though Monte Albán was probably a distinctive plateau from the beginning, the main plaza was further flattened and expanded by the Zapotecs again and again, over many centuries. Here stood administrative and ceremonial buildings of import, many themselves rebuilt and expanded over the course of nearly a millennium. Among these we find Monte Albán's much celebrated *danzantes*. Three hundred of these stone carvings exist, almost all of people in unnatural, dance-like poses. As charming as they appear, inspiring scores of restaurants and commercial products named Danzante, one of the latest theories is that these images actually portray ill-fated slaves and prisoners. On several, genitals are visible—a stigma of denuded captives. One danzante has a severed head, and a couple of others appear to show sexual mutilation and flowing blood.

Monte Albán long thrived in relative isolation, but in the eighth century it was abandoned, as primitive newcomers encroached upon Zapotec domains. Among these, ultimately consolidating their own mini-empire in a region to the immediate northwest, were the Mixtecs, whose beautiful pottery fused with that of the Cholulans. A relatively peaceful Post-Classic culture that married its nobility into preexisting kingdoms, the Mixtecs eventually came to dominate most of the former Zapotec population centers. At Monte Albán they buried an illustrious leader in the fourteenth century, slaying his entourage of personal servants upon his death (a common practice, which undoubtedly inspired many servants to be highly attentive to their master's health and well-being). They enshrined his corpse with a magnificent array of artifacts. The cache that Caso and his team uncovered at so-called Tomb Seven in 1932 is the greatest ever found in the Americas. Thousands of beads made of gold, pearl, coral, and human teeth littered the floor. Astounding turquoise objects testified to the exceptional talents of Mixtec craftsmen. Yet, as if this and all the discoveries in the highlands were not enough, other great cultures left equally impressive legacies in the lowlands of the Gulf coast, foremostly the Maya in Yucatán.

CHAPTER TWO

The Maya of Yucatán

An early account tells us that, when the Spaniards first landed in Mexico, on a large eastern peninsula, they asked the natives, "What do you call this place?" Not understanding Spanish, the natives predictably responded, "What are you saying?" In their language, this sounded roughly like *Yuc-eth-thon*, and so the peninsula was thus named. Home to the indelible Maya, Yucatán is a distinctive part of Mexico. Centuries after the first encounter here, for very different reasons, foreigners still flock to its shores. Tens of millions of visitors annually sunbathe on the beaches at Cancún or along the so-called Mayan Riviera. Many venture to the manicured lawns of the rather *faux* Mayan ruins at Tulum, or inland to the spectacular but still liberally restored archeological site of Chichen Itzá.

The focus of impressive archeological research, the ancient Maya continue to intrigue and perplex. For sources, we have the chronicles of Spaniards who first made contact, most notably those of Catholic friars. Critical is the work of Diego de Landa, a zealous Franciscan who lived among the Maya in the mid-sixteenth century and learned to speak a Yucatecan language fluently. His *Relation of the Things of Yucatán* is a meticulous accounting by a man sensitive to detail. But Landa is a mixed blessing to those who would know the ancient Mayan world, for he was also instrumental in destroying most of the indigenous texts that could have unlocked many more unknowns. These book-like texts were bound, oversized parchment sheets made of deerskin or tree fiber. When folded out they revealed hieroglyphs or pictographs—pictures but not fully words, a mix of images and symbols. Michael Coe, the foremost Mayanist scholar with both archeological and anthropological training, has called these symbols strange. To Landa, they were expressions of the devil. Frustrated by the apparent inability (or unwillingness) of the Maya to comprehend the mysteries of the Catholic faith, he seized all the books he could find, gathered the Mayan lords, and burned the texts in front of them as rubbish. Great, we are told, were the cries and sorrow of the elders.

Only three of the books are known to have survived Landa's purge. The best dates from 1178 CE and is now called the Dresden Codex (after the city in which it is stored—German collectors having bought the ancient script in the eighteenth century from a Hapsburg contact in Vienna). In 2010 archeologists found important murals at Xultún, a site in Guatemala. These

Figure 2.1. Stele Number 5 from the Mayan site of Sayil features such excellent detail that it is on display at the National Museum of Anthropology in Mexico City. Intricate carved stone shows a priest-lord dancing while holding a staff in his right hand and a leather shield in his left. Other symbols indicate that he has great power through a dynastic lineage. This and seven other stelae at Sayil were discovered in 1895.
Source: Museo Nacional de Antropologia, Mexico City.

painted walls date from the ninth century but have calendric numbers similar to those found in the Dresden Codex. This discovery and other advances have allowed for bits of the Codex to be deciphered, though many hieroglyphs are still largely incomprehensible. Had more survived, of course, the odds of an interpretative breakthrough would be much greater. Stone stelae with similar writings have been discovered at several archeological sites, as have many more painted and etched hieroglyphics on stone walls, many inevitably in advanced states of decay.

After the destruction of the sacred texts, native elders tried to recreate them. They recalled what they could and spoke to missionary-trained, Spanish-educated youth. Written in Spanish, though with some paltry attempts at restoring some picture-symbols, the secret undertaking ultimately produced the late sixteenth-century *Books of Chilam Balam*. Fourteen of these are known to exist, the most famous being the *Popul Vuh*, which features a series of creation stories. Predictably, though, these are a mesh of polytheistic tales blended with post-conquest Christian theology. Anyone familiar with the biblical Book of Genesis will recognize some features, though the god-characters are a mass of contradictions, with varied motives and rival personalities not unlike that of the Greek pantheon. The Popul Vuh tells us that the earliest gods arose from a watery void, peopled the earth, and then drowned in a great flood. Twins born to an early couple, brothers called the Maize Gods, played too loudly in a ball court; summoned to the Underworld, they were tortured to death by angry elders. But in death these empowered gods turned their rivals into monkeys, who in turn became deities of music and dance. Miraculously they also had post-mortem offspring. Their sons, the Hero Twins, slew malicious gods, including those who spewed fire (from volcanoes) and needlessly shook the ground (with earthquakes). The Hero Twins had their greatest triumph by bringing their own father back to life, the divine Maize God. Many rituals among the Maya thus followed the cycles of corn planting, growth, and harvest.

From Tikal to Chichen Itzá

The Maya inhabited a vast territory, stretching across the isthmus of what is now northern Central America, through the Guatemalan highlands, across the Petén (northern Guatemalan lowlands and parts of present-day Belize), down along the Pacific coastlands, and ultimately through the two-million-year-old limestone shelf that is Yucatán peninsula. We know very little about what is dubbed the Pre-Classic, the time before 300 BCE when far-flung villages took form, many ultimately featuring small temples atop modest platforms. Clay pottery emerged around 900 BCE. Nomadic hunter-gatherers had settled down, growing maize and manioc (a tuber), slowly domesticating other crops, and celebrating the accomplishments of their Olmec ancestors to the west. Indeed, the Olmecs (see chapter 3) were akin to the Romans in the European Dark Ages. The Maya shared a diffused linguistic heritage from them, inherited a 260-day calendar, and otherwise knew of their earlier greatness.

As the Olmec civilization declined, that of the Maya arose, especially in the Petén. The Proto-Classic, a period from roughly 350 BCE to 250 CE, saw the Petén-Maya perhaps briefly advance ahead of the great cultures of central Mexico in a remarkable fluorescence. The city-state of Tikal grew notably during this time, its massive pyramids with intact stone temples atop them when discovered in the early nineteenth century. Tikal's so-called Temple IV, at 210 feet with a steep incline, is the archetype of a giant pyramid protruding above a dense jungle canopy, howler monkeys playfully screeching in the early dawn hours below, to the delight of tourists.

Tikal's significance for the Mayan Classic Period (from 250 CE to 900 CE) is certain, but Yucatán Maya were also in ascent. Indeed, the Classic Period saw robust growth everywhere, with concentrated populations in big cities. The Maya built large structures of stone. At Cobá, temple pyramids similar in design and size to those at Tikal emerged, connected via a series of elevated masonry paths, which were perhaps used for pilgrimage to this likely religious site. Great cities, such as Uxmal, Mayapán, and Chichen Itzá, featured multi-tiered and complex societies, group relations largely defined by kinship as determined by both patriarchal and matriarchal lineage, though males appear to have had monopolized political and economic power. Like at Tikal, a hereditary elite ruled from a royal court. Here hundreds of influential lords lived in close proximity, the king and his extended family serviced by courtiers and guarded by gatekeepers. The priests (also likely hereditary) exercised their skills in writing, music, architecture, art, and war. Bureaucrats managed affairs of state, with teams of accountants tallying cacao beans (used as a form of money) to ensure the collection of taxes. Entertainers, including the deformed and dwarfs, performed for religious purposes and for leisure, while a small army of manual laborers cleaned, cooked, assisted the royals—and swept the floors. As in so many societies around the world (Japan, Egypt, and elsewhere), the elite spoke a higher form of the language, which separated and privileged them from the masses.

Political loci of power rose and fell in the Classic Yucatán. In the late eighth century, much authority rested in the hands of a king called Black Jaguar, in the city of Ek Balam. He and his predecessors ruled the heart of

Yucatán from atop a magnificent acropolis. To see the lord, one had to pass through the giant teeth and jawbone of a white stucco frieze—approaching him must have been like walking toward the Wizard of Oz! The frieze was largely intact when uncovered from layers of dirt in the 1980s, meaning that visitors to this site behold plasterwork that is 1,200 years old. When Black Jaguar died in 814 CE, his body was laid on a jaguar's coat, and his spirit was sent off to the netherworld with a collection of coveted objects, including an imported golden frog from Panama. Atop a nearby capstone, Mexican archeologists found a hieroglyphic text linking him to the cult of the Maize God.

Thirty miles to the southwest, during the reign of Black Jaguar, the great city of Chichen Itzá continued to rise. Like with Ek Balam, its central location on the peninsula facilitated political dominance, and by the mid-800s it began a centuries-long primacy. Though the Classic Period wound down, and other Mayan cities declined, Chichen Itzá flourished. Its lords awed their

Figure 2.2. The acropolis at Ek Balam. From here in the late eighth century, a much admired king named Black Jaguar ruled central Yucatán. The site today is on the "Maya Trail" and is undergoing aggressive restoration. Maya archeological tourism is big business. In 2019 the Mexican government announced plans for a "Maya Train" rail system in the Yucatán. But to what degree should tourism inspire a sanitized rebuilding of sites, some features of which can become quite speculative?

citizens and opponents by building magnificent religious structures in what was effectively a Mayan Mecca. But something dramatic and important happened here in the late tenth century, when invaders called Toltecs arrived from the central Mexican Highlands. After defeating the Maya in a great battle of canoes off the coast, these aggressive warriors reached Chichen Itzá itself, and in a vicious flurry of fighting installed their lord, the Feathered Serpent Prince, as king in 987 CE. He ruled for many years, with the help of collaborating Maya nobles, as a just and reasonable leader. His reputation throughout the peninsula elevated him to god-like status—the great Kulkulkán. To ensure his authority, he saw that the potential rival city of Ek Balam was abandoned.

Over the next two centuries, the Toltec rebuilt and expanded Chichen Itzá (though some hold-out Maya scholars stubbornly continue to deny the Toltec presence). Hence, today's visitors wander a new and old city. The Toltec center, to the north and east, features dramatic but heavily reconstructed works, including the huge Pyramid of Kulkulkán, object of a nighttime light show. Hundreds of stone columns parallel large stone structures to the east—pillars that once supported wooden roofs in porticos of houses and markets. The blending of architectural styles in New Chichen Itzá confirms the presence and influence of highlanders. On many walls we find an abundance of Toltec art. Images of warriors, heart-devouring eagles, and serpents adorn the base walls of a series of platforms, including the so-called Temple of Venus. Nearby, on the large *Tzompantli*, or Platform of the Skulls, we find exceptionally ghoulish imagery alongside precision stonework. The proximity of this platform to an enormous ball court—at 480 feet by 122 feet the largest of ancient ball courts in the Americas—suggests the possibility (now deemed remote) that the losers of this game incurred the death penalty.

One place of sacrificial death was the nearby sacred *cenote*, or water pool. Yucatán has a distinctive topography, all but devoid of surface creeks and rivers. Erosion in the great limestone shelf has instead produced sinkholes. Numbering 2,500 throughout the peninsula, these of course have held great practical importance as sources of water, though they vary greatly in size and accessibility. Water pools were believed to be access points to the underworld, where dwelt the souls of the dead. Chichen Itzá's sacred pool is rounded and picturesque, with steep limestone walls above its emerald-green, darkened waters. In the late Classic, when Yucatán Maya struggled with a centuries-long cycle of drought, they attempted to appease the rain god, Chaac, by casting valuables and human victims into this hole. The depths here were thus assumed to hold great treasure. In the early twentieth century, an enterprising American diplomat serving in Mérida arranged to dredge

Figure 2.3. This bas relief on Chichen Itzá's *Tzompantli* (Platform of the Skulls) shows a priest in headdress. Clearly both a man of status (carrying a scepter) and a warrior (three arrows in his left hand), he is ominously holding the decapitated head of his victim in battle. Surrounded by snakes, he is in the service of the God-King Kulkulkán.

the pool. Edward Thompson was ultimately disappointed with his recovery efforts, which produced (from his perspective) too many bones and copper bells, and too few gold and silver objects. His pillaging of the national patrimony is still a sore point with Mexicans, as noted in a critical plaque on the walls of the modern visitor's center. Thompson eventually donated most of his recovered objects to Harvard University.

One final and important structure in the Toltec sector is the Temple of the Warriors. Here, wall paintings and frescoes showed images of battle, including that of the "navies" along the coast. The structure itself, restored in the 1920s, is very similar to a pyramid in the Central Highlands city of Tula, capital of the Toltec, though with superior craftsmanship. And most intriguingly, within its bowels were discovered a throne room, with a series of parallel seats for both Toltec and Mayan lords. Clearly the invaders were able to co-opt local elites after their conquest; perhaps they even had the benefit of treacherous spies and rebels, making their invasion easier. Alongside the Temple of the Warriors is an even larger structure, eminently Toltec, surrounded by the misnamed Thousand Columns. Atop it are two of many chacmools, the reclining figure so readily associated with Chichen

Itzá. These, too, originated in Tula. Though assumed to be a repository for sacrificed human hearts (atop the table supported by the reclining figure's bent knees and elbows), the chacmool's use and significance is not absolutely certain.

What is termed "old" Chichen Itzá, several hundred yards to the southwest, is less visited, yet more authentic. Although even the untrained eye can see architectural differences in these more modest yet ornately decorated structures, we predictably know less about their significance. The so-called Observatory might well have served as a high platform for studying the stars (niches in the stone suggest alignment with certain heavenly bodies), but its unusual circular structure atop is not the ancient planetarium it seems to resemble. The stately Red House is so named simply because bits of red paint were found within. Chichen Itzá's eye-catching grandeur draws hordes of modern-day visitors, but our knowledge of what each foundation, column, and pyramid meant to the ancient Maya will always be limited.

The Mayan Livelihood

Though great archeological sites inspire, and books and documentaries celebrate the varied accomplishments of this mysterious ancient culture, ultimately on any given day the Maya lived for one purpose: to find food and eat. Like nearly all primitive peoples, life could be reduced to a daily struggle for food and shelter—the latter not nearly as essential in the tropical climate of Yucatán. The most prominent of the Mayan deities (116 known gods at the time of the Spanish conquest) were tied to crops, harvesting, or essential factors such as rain, while a two-symbol numeric system was undoubtedly invented for the marketplace. That system is vigesimal, or based on the number twenty. Early Spanish friars noted the common practice of twenty Maya working in a *milpa*, or cornfield—twenty more or less the sacred number of Mayan religion.

The number twenty also figures prominently in the much-celebrated 260-day Mayan calendar, which cycled in accordance with planting and harvesting crops. But the Maya also had a Calendar Round, based on the solar year, very similar to our own. They multiplied *this* calendar by twenty and extended the "long count" in thirteen cycles, priests playing with mathematically large numbers. When projected onto our calendar, the long count from an initial date in 3114 BCE ended in 2012. Throughout much of the world, including the United States, many people became convinced that, in 2012, the world might end. This hysteria was in truth a misperception of the Mayan concept of time. While the long count ended, a new cycle began.

The Maya did not have a concept of the end of time, either in their sacred calendars or in their religion.

Over many centuries, the Maya domesticated new crops, and their diet diversified. By the time the Spanish arrived, they were eating a wide range of food, varieties of squash and beans, along with the ever-present manioc and vital maize. Corn was not pounded into *tortillas*, as is so common in the Hispanic world today. Instead, it was eaten as a cornmeal paste, flavored with chili pepper, or sometimes consumed as a drier dough. Natural fruits and nuts were harvested throughout Yucatán, supplementing the diet, while its animal life, foremostly fowl and deer, were hunted with blow guns and, later, bow and arrow. Dogs were domesticated, some of them fattened with corn gruel and eaten as a delicacy. In lagoons along the coast, Maya fished with rope-twine nets. They preserved fish with salt from highly prized deposits on the northern coast. Elite Maya probably ate more meat than commoners and surely enjoyed the much-coveted cacao (chocolate beans) mixed in their drinks, though this was an expensive habit.

For whatever reasons, in the twelfth century Chichen Itzá and other remaining northern population centers began a noteworthy decline. Two hundred years later there were no major concentrations of Maya, to the vexation of the arriving Spaniards. Though counterintuitive, the droughts that had long plagued the region lifted in the Post-Classic Period; overall population continued to be robust, while commerce may have actually increased. Archeology reveals an abundance of widely dispersed objects before the conquest. The lords of the declining cities lost their monopolies on trade, and an entrepreneurial free-for-all inspired more interaction. The Maya never had anything akin to roads in the flora-thick Yucatán, only narrow paths, difficult to traverse with a cargo of any size. Hence, they turned to the sea, and by the fourteenth century had built up an impressive system of coastal commerce, in long canoes. Docking and "port" facilities, at places like Tulum, thrived. In 1502 Christopher Columbus encountered one of these coast-hugging canoes, its crew frozen in fear as the strange white men came aboard and rifled through its cargo. When the Spaniards inadvertently spilled some cacao beans, the natives sprung to life, scrambling to carefully pick each one up.

Unfortunately for the Spaniards, while a daily quest for food consumed the Maya, their one legitimate pastime was always war. For most of the twentieth century, scholars embraced the image of the peace-loving, Classic Period "noble savage" in Mexico, the Maya especially celebrated as a stargazing, high-minded people. But in fact, the evidence is overwhelming—in countless hieroglyphic walls and frescoes, in stelae and through defensive walls found at sites like Ek Balam—the Maya were almost at constant war with each other. Defeated nobles were beheaded, their charges enslaved. This internecine violence weakened the Maya, yet at another level prepared them to at least be able to contest their subjugation by newcomers. The Post-Classic warriorhood cult corresponded with that in other parts of Mexico, where Toltec, Aztec, and other tribes embraced war as an expression of collective identity and even faith in the divine.

CHAPTER THREE

Olmecs, Téenek, Aztecs

Mexico is a land awash in great archeological sites. The pre-contact period saw ancient kingdoms rise and fall over three millennia, creating a mosaic of native cultures that fills in much of a modern-day map of central Mexico. Though the population is now overwhelmingly a mix of dark-skinned native and white European (the brown-skinned *mestizo*), most Mexicans can claim some native heritage, especially in rural areas of the mountainous south. Thus far, we have focused our attention on the Classic Period and its immediate aftermath, an era from roughly 200 CE to 1100 CE when several large cultures reached their apogee. We now turn our attention to a range of pre-contact cultures both before and after the Classic Period, in diverse geographic regions, in order to fully appreciate the great Native American mosaic of ancient civilizations.

Mayan Ancestors and Cousins

In 1925 a Danish archeologist and an American anthropologist, roaming through coastal jungle, discovered the ruins of what became known as *La Venta*. At first they and others were convinced that it was Mayan, but within years they came to realize that they had stumbled upon something very different. La Venta was in fact *Olmec*, the patrimony of a great people who had lived much earlier than other native cultures. From a stele here, with a decipherable calendar, and new procedures developed later (most notably radio carbon dating in the 1950s—which allows for age computation of any formerly living object, namely wood), they eventually concluded that the Olmec flourished from roughly 1200 BCE to 400 BCE, making it the grandfather civilization of Mexico's native peoples. Exploration and digs continued through the mid-twentieth century and turned up an even earlier Olmec site at San Lorenzo. Here, and in the vicinity of La Venta as well, archeologists uncovered the defining artistic treasure of the Olmec people: giant stone heads. Fifteen of these were eventually found, ranging in height from four feet to ten feet, always made of basalt, an igneous black-gray rock that sometimes turns brown or reddish through weathering. The basalt had to come from mountains some sixty miles away, meaning that Olmec society was complex enough to produce large labor pools under hierarchical management. But what was the purpose of these heads? They had fairly uniform features: rotund cheeks, broad noses, raised irises, fleshy lips, and, most strangely, helmet-like coverings. Even more perplexing was the deliberate mutilation of some around 900 BCE. Pounded with a great but unknown force, perhaps pendulum-swinging tree trunks, many of the heads were badly damaged and then buried. Was this activity tied to a religious cult that had somehow been discredited?

Figure 3.1. A mother culture to the Maya, the Pre-Classic Olmecs are a continued focus of debate and some puzzlement. Of the great colossal stone heads that they produced, only one—buried deep in the ground—escaped significant damage. Recovered at San Lorenzo, this pock-marked eight-footer is typical of the remainder. One of the largest heads, weighing twenty tons, it was moved to the National Museum of Anthropology in Mexico City on a flatbed truck.
Source: Museo Nacional de Antropologia, Mexico City.

Besides the mysterious giant heads, Olmec sites turned up an array of delightful pottery. Artists worked not just in clay, but with seashells, animal bones, and rare stones. Among the latter, they favored turquoise and jade. The use of jade is particularly impressive, as it is exceedingly hard and difficult to shape with stone tools. Jade was valued for its resonant jade-on-jade clapping sound; royalty wore it and were often buried with jade pieces. Olmec pottery represents humans, most typically seated, and embraces a surprising realism, often portraying the deformed or overweight. The Olmecs were fond of depicting animals, predictably giving special attention to the jaguar, the largest carnivorous cat in the Americas. They regarded the jaguar as a deified ancestor, a hunter like themselves. In time, a deeper meaning emerged, as they began to associate it with certain events and concepts, including rain and fertility. Sometimes in their pottery, the Olmecs fused human and animal together, creating imaginative creatures of supernatural potential.

The great Olmec culture presaged that of the Maya, and its decline roughly coincides with the initial rise of the Maya, especially in the Petén, in present-day northern Guatemala. The Olmecs were the precursors, the seedlings of peoples throughout the coastal lowlands of what would become Mexico. By patterns of influence and migration, lowland cultures differed from those in the highlands—environmental contrasts and resources made altitude very significant. Lowland natives taken into the highlands during the early colonial period invariably felt as though they had crossed into some strange netherworld. In ancient, pre-contact Mexico, altitude often held more importance than geographic distance.

Just as the Olmecs were something of a midwife to the Classical Maya, some very early Maya spawned the native culture that would dominate what would become northeastern Mexico. The very first natives lived in the lush Panuco region as early as 1600 BCE (in the environs of the present-day coastal city of Tampico, and west into an area called the Huasteca Potosina). They ate tubers, especially those of yucca and manioc, peeling them with obsidian chips, which have been found by the hundreds in digs near ancient villages. Around 1100 BCE a noteworthy influx of newcomers arrived, peoples known as the *Huasteca*, or today more commonly called *Téenek*. We do not actually know the meaning of these terms (the old theory that *Téenek* is a contraction of Te'Inik, or "people from here"—which in itself is hardly revealing—has been proven false), but the language of these natives is related to Mayan, indicating their ultimate origin. Back in the late nineteenth century some linguists posited that the Téenek migrated from the north and then went south, multiplying robustly to become the Maya themselves, but the Olmec discoveries and more recent conclusions about the earliest Maya

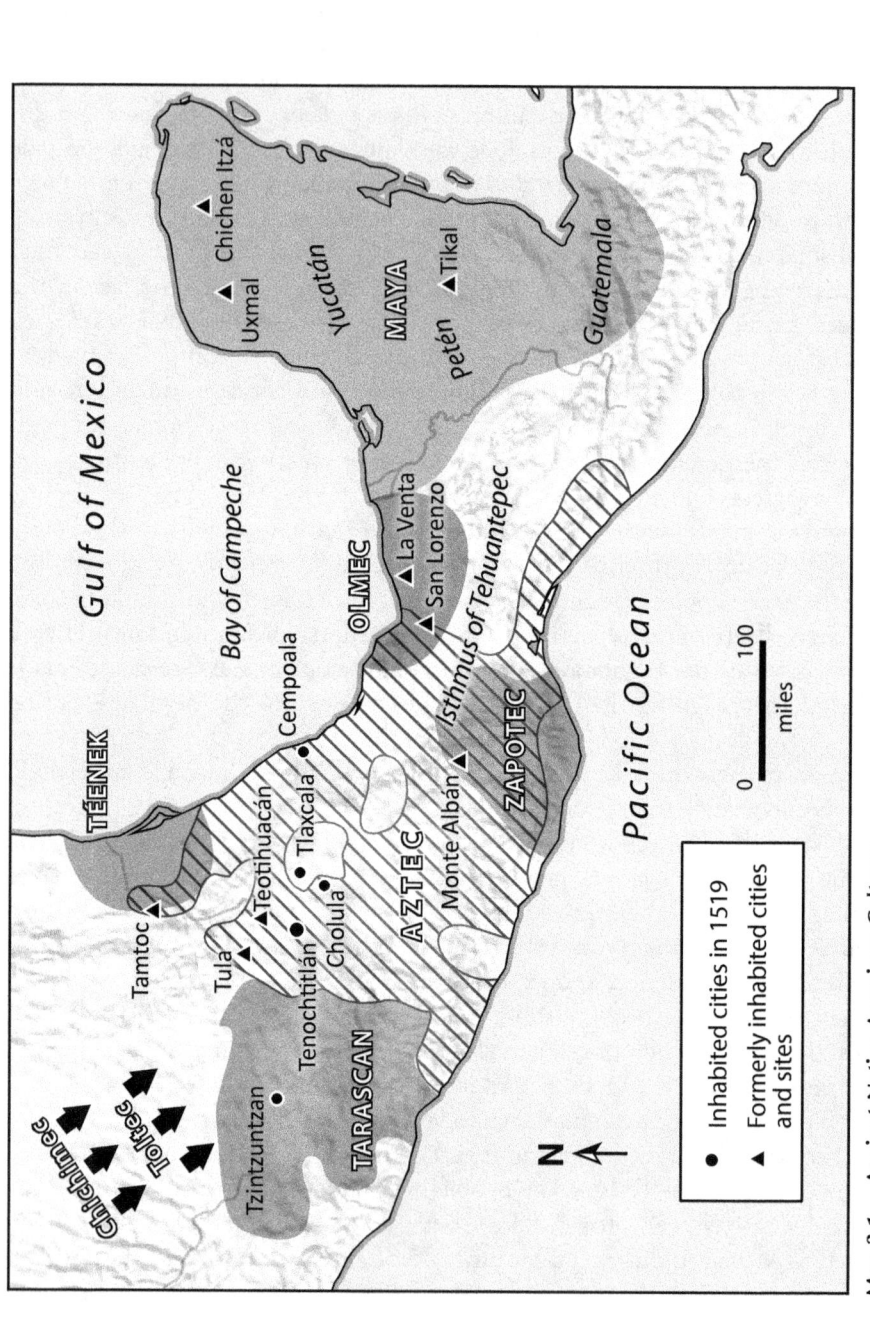

Map 3.1. Ancient Native American Cultures

indicate that the movement was south to north, whether by canoe or (more likely) by overland migration spread across several generations. After this movement northward, other natives interposed themselves along the coast, severing direct links between the Téenek and the Maya. Hence, the northeasterners altered their language, which over hundreds of years became quite distinctive from their Mayan mother tongue.

The Téenek remained in relative isolation for some 1,500 years. Despite living along one of Mexico's few navigable rivers, their world was a bubble. That river system quickly becomes a web of cascading creeks as one ascends into the eastern Sierra Madre, which with its formidable heights discouraged the Téenek from connecting with the densely populated highlands. The strange, cold, and inhospitable cactus-ridden plateau beyond the *Huasteca Potosina* also gave them little reason to venture westward. Not able to sail the seas, the Téenek were effectively cut off to the east. There is little evidence of persistent migration down the coast from Texas, where native populations were quite thin, while movement to the south was prohibited by largely hostile tribes and the rugged landscape of the Sierra Madre's foothills.

In such isolation (a factor accounting for the distinctive evolution of their language), the Téenek unfortunately developed much slower than other cultures. By the time of the Spaniards, they were particularly ill-equipped to adjust and resist. The Aztecs, who knew of their existence, regarded them as grossly inferior, appalled that they lived stark naked, males not even covering their genitalia. Despite their limitations, the Téenek did develop a wideranging diet, expanding from the tuber-eaters of their distant past to a people fond of beans, peppers, squash, and tropical nuts and fruits. Corn came late to them, and they never fully adopted it—it grows poorly in this region—as much inclined to use the stalks as wrappers and cobs as novelties than eat the kernels. Though we know little about the Téenek until the second millennium, we do know that they overwhelmingly resided in modest villages, even at the time of the Spanish arrival. One apparent exception was a religious and cultural center called *Tamtoc*.

Tamtoc, "The Place of Water Clouds," is located in a bend of the Tampaón River where, predictably, it is shrouded in dense fog each morning on this unforgivingly hot and moist coastal plain. First explored in the 1890s, it was studied in the 1930s and again in the 1990s before opening to visitors in 2006. It was a ceremonial center, its population likely in the low thousands as it prospered, beginning in the tenth century, for over four hundred years. Dozens of structures, mostly earthen-filled, partly stone terraces and platforms, dot the landscape. The so-called East Base is sixty feet high and likely the foundation of an important temple tied to astronomy and a

28 Chapter Three

Figure 3.2. Off the beaten path, and in a region of Mexico notorious for cartel activities, the Téenek archeological site of Tamtoc has fallen into disuse over the past decade. Visitors who make it here can expect to have its relatively modest (by Mexican standards) earthworks to themselves. Probably more of a ceremonial center than a political capital, Tamtoc prospered for several hundred years.

religious cult. An even higher platform nearby reaches nearly one hundred feet. Yet compared to other Mexican archeological sites, Tamtoc is modest, with little creative detail or stonework. Archeologists have detected a network of irrigation canals, though, and they have also uncovered a strange, thirty-ton lunar calendar made of rock, which may have predated habitation of the site. Tamtoc also has an unusual preponderance of female remains; 90 percent of the burials here are those of women. Funerary offerings include elaborate ceramics, some recovered from a nearby lagoon. Were the Téenek once matriarchal? Female images dominate in Tamtoc pottery, though animals also figure prominently. The fantastic, too, appears—for example, human-serpent combinations—with many pieces paying homage to *Ehecatl*, god of the wind. This god was important to the Téenek, who built circular temples in his honor. Evidence suggests that his cult transferred from the Téenek to the Aztec—quite unusual, given the disdain in which the later held these people. Predictably, for a society living in mostly grass huts, Ehécatl could be a benign deity (a cool breeze is much valued along the coast), but also a malicious one.

Northern Invaders and the Aztecs

While the Téenek multiplied in relative isolation along the northeastern coast during the Post-Classic, momentous change gripped native cultures in the central highlands. As the great city of Teotihuacán declined (see chapter 1), it was overrun by migrating waves of primitive natives, sweeping southward across the central plateau of present-day Mexico, between the great eastern and western mountain ranges of the Sierra Madre (see map 3.1). Eventually, a more militarized and violent culture than that at Teotihuacán coalesced. The *Toltecs*, with a far less impressive urban center at Tula, ruled the highlands for several generations. In time, they themselves were inundated by still more wild northern savages. These originated from what is today the southwestern United States, where a dry and precarious climate, along with cold winters, encouraged southward migration. Archeological study of present-day Colorado and northern New Mexico indicate that, between the twelfth and fourteenth centuries, populations there increased fifteen-fold. These nomadic hunter-gatherers moved southward slowly, over many generations, intermingling along the way—the process is not neat and tidy. Sedentary central highlands residents in the fourteenth century called this great second wave of newcomers the *Chichimecs*, or literally "Dog-Descended People." They seemed so crass, so animal-like, and so avaricious that they reminded their host cultures of dogs.

Naturally, so despised, the migrants first lived on marginal lands among the well-established peoples. Many subgroups or tribes comprised the collectively designated Chichimec, though we know few of their names. At the end of the thirteenth century, one modest tribe found itself stuck on a muddy tract of land along the shores of a big lake. The Aztecs ate snakes and lizards, and they clung stubbornly to primitive ways. Working as mercenaries for richer natives, they made war central to their lifestyle. In time, they worshipped a god of war, named Huitzilopochtli. In reality, the early Aztecs were probably not unusually brutish or crass. But after they became a great people, they promulgated myths about their distant past, including in accounts provided to the Spanish who later subdued them. By playing up excesses, they could distinguish themselves as an exceptional people—and thereby assuage, perhaps, some of the pain of their humiliating defeat. According to Aztec lore, their forefathers sought from Huitzilopochtli a sign for the location of their own city. When they saw an eagle perched on a prickly pear cactus, devouring a snake, their supplications were answered.

Until the mid-fifteenth century, greatness eluded the Aztecs. Although steadily increasing in numbers, their city of Tenochtitlán played second fiddle to Texcoco, a prosperous center on the other side of the lake, which also bore its name. A wise king named Nezahualcóyotl, or Hungry Coyote, long ruled in Texcoco. An engineer and poet, he cautiously negotiated with the Aztecs and kept them at bay for decades. But after his death, Tenochtitlán rose to further prominence. Warring on outlying tribes, the Aztecs levied tribute, or taxes, on other peoples and grew rich. In the year 1515 they imposed their own puppet ruler in Texcoco, just four years before the Spanish arrival. Hence, the much-celebrated Aztec Empire was very young when the Spanish arrived, built upon a network of tribute-paying underlings. Though millions of natives inhabited the central highlands, the Aztec themselves only numbered in the hundreds of thousands. On the top of a political pyramid, they had proverbial targets on their backs—invaders from beyond the seas would find ample Aztec-hating natives with whom to conspire.

Aztec culture was certainly violent, and reflective of the Post-Classic Period as a whole. Cosmology and religion were intertwined. More than

Figure 3.3. An artist's rendition of the Aztec capital of Tenochtitlán, complete with some overly dramatic flat-top mountains in the background. The two-temple Great Pyramid is clearly visible in the city center. At the time of its conquest, Tenochtitlán was at least three times larger than Toledo, its counterpart in Spain, and much cleaner and safer besides.
Source: Museo de la Ciudad de México, Mexico City.

seeing Tenochtitlán as a political capital, the Aztecs viewed their city as the spiritual center of the universe. The four cardinal directions of east, west, north, and south were deemed important, and Tenochtitlán was accordingly divided into quadrats. A fifth zone, its center, was preeminent: the seat of imperial government and temples that denoted Ground Zero for the entire world. A Great Pyramid dominated this zone. Begun around 1390 CE, it was enlarged seven times over the next century, eventually reaching a height of 150 feet. Atop it were dual temples, one to Tlaloc (god of rain and fertility, a deity handed down from the Teotihuacanese), and the other to Huitzilopochtli. Temple entrances faced west—in the direction of the setting sun. The Aztecs believed that four suns had previously existed, and that they lived in the age of the Fifth Sun. Though God of War, Huitzilopochtli also raised the sun each day, tossing it across the sky from east to west.

The Aztecs were a feared but also fearful people, believing that the gods were inclined toward anger and periodically destroyed their own creation (a comprehensible view, given the frequency of earthquakes and the proximity of several volcanoes). Their task was thus to propitiate the gods, lest their wrath burn so feverish that they destroy the Fifth Sun. Each day, Huitzilopochtli was cajoled to raise the sun through human sacrifice. When the temple itself was dedicated in 1487, after its seventh expansion, the Aztecs reputedly sacrificed four thousand persons in order to honor their two most powerful gods. For although they had a cyclical view of time based on fifty-two-year-long centuries, they were not completely convinced that the Sixth Sun would come—the idea of an "end" of time troubled them. The passing of each century was a momentous event. In the entire Aztec realm, all fires were extinguished and all dishes were broken at nightfall (which was not a great loss—Aztec utilitarian pottery was bland, typically in colors of orange and black). Then came the much-anticipated rising of the sun at dawn, the New Fire ceremony, and the rekindling of flame throughout the empire, so vital to life in cooking and warmth.

That Aztec religion was violent is beyond doubt. In 1978 Mexicans began to excavate the site of the Great Pyramid in downtown Mexico City (alongside the cathedral); in 2015, digs turned up a skull rack similar to that found at Chichen Itzá, with celebratory symbols of violent death. And no culture in history was so committed to the idea of sacrificing humans to appease the gods—a concept the Aztecs expanded upon from the gruesome Toltecs and other precursor cultures. A celibate priesthood oversaw the ritual itself. A bare-chested victim was held face-up, spread-eagled, buttocks resting on the drum-like sacrificial stone (visible today in Mexico City's National Museum of Anthropology). With four strong priests holding limbs firmly, a fifth equipped with an obsidian blade sliced the abdomen open vertically, then plunged under the rib cage and upward, into the chest cavity, to retrieve what was hopefully a still-palpating heart. Hearts piled up in a sacrificial canister designed as a Jaguar (also visible in the museum), for the pleasure of the gods. The Jaguar was central to the cult of warriorhood, a symbol of masculinity. A special feast prepared for the gods was that comprised of the hearts of brave warriors captured in battle. The elite special forces of the Aztec Empire were the Jaguar Knights, young men skilled with javelins, spears, and slings, while trained in hand-to-hand combat. Yet women could also obtain an afterlife through the Huitzilopochtli-Jaguar cult by dying in childbirth. Indeed, the Aztecs viewed excruciating parturition as an act of war!

For all other Aztecs, death was final. No reincarnation or other avenues to eternal life existed. And although bleak, cosmology and religion were only one slice of the Aztec world. The Aztecs loved flowers. They filled their city with a fragrant array of floral displays and celebrated their variety and colors. In gender relations they were more progressive than the conquering Spaniards. Women played prominent roles in society, managing markets and working as merchants and artisans. Sometimes they exercised lower-level political authority. The female goddesses of Aztec religion were benign, even friendly; the beloved Corn Goddesses gave humanity its life-sustaining crop. Atop Aztec society was a nobility of skill and sophistication. Living in two-story stone houses in the central district, they ate duck, pheasant, turkey, and a wide variety of fruits and vegetables. The emperor came from the nobility but was selected by priests for his qualifications. Tenochtitlán was an orderly and well-managed metropolis, with lagoon-gardens of mud and seaweed that yielded several times more food than the normal land-based fields (what Spaniards mistakenly called "floating gardens"). It had one thousand garbage collectors, and its residents bathed regularly—it was likely cleaner and healthier than any European counterpart. It even had a zoo, where the star attraction was jaguars.

By the time of the Spanish arrival, Tenochtitlán had taken shape on an island in Lake Texcoco, connected to the mainland by three long causeways. It was a Venice of sorts, with hundreds of canoes negotiating both the lake and the narrow canals crisscrossing the city. Commoners lived in kinship groups, in crowded complexes of huts around big courtyards, in the four outlying quadrants. Though variations of work abounded, the ultimate duty of every male commoner was to prepare for war. The dream of most Aztec boys was to become a brave warrior and to capture four opponents in battle, thereby receiving an invitation to become a Jaguar Knight. Commoners very rarely glimpsed the emperor, who was considered semi-divine (no one could look directly at him—and no servant could turn around in his presence). In 1502 Moctezuma II ascended to the throne, an accomplished warrior himself, but otherwise a strangely pensive man. Many years passed before his sages divined troubling signs. In 1519 he received word of perplexing events on the endless lake to the east. Soon after, white-skinned god-men appeared on its shores.

CHAPTER FOUR

Conquests

In 1517 the first Spaniards arrived in Mexico. When the boats of an exploratory expedition under Francisco Hernández de Córdoba scouted the northern coast of the Yucatán, Maya aboard canoes greeted them, beckoning them to come ashore. Córdoba dispatched a landing party, which disembarked on a nondescript beach and then entered the nearby jungle. Soon it was surrounded by natives, the sudden hiss of arrows signaling the start of an ambush. Closing ranks, the Spaniards in the landing party fought and forced their way into a nearby plaza, where during the night they rested and rummaged through a native temple and discovered small pieces of gold. Heartened by the find, with men whose injuries seemed only mild, the party returned unmolested to the sea, the flotilla proceeding further west over the next three weeks.

The size of Maya coastal towns grew larger as the Spanish fleet progressed. But alas, the arrow wounds also enlarged and festered, flint having shattered upon impact with bone, producing an ugly flesh wound that often led to a slow, painful death. Hernández himself led a new and larger landing party in search of water, but it was quickly surrounded by hordes of Mayan warriors and forced to hunker down for a sleepless night. At dawn, surrounded by thousands, it was attacked. Nearly all the Spaniards were struck by arrows or stones, and some had to fight off bold natives, armed with clubs, at close quarters. Reaching their boats with difficulty, the Spaniards returned to their colonial base in Cuba, woefully parched in the Caribbean heat. Dozens succumbed to their wounds, including Hernández, yet word of a great land filled with abundant people and gold stirred their compatriots' souls. A new expedition was soon underway.

The Spain That Encountered Mexico

Spanish attitudes toward Native Americans were shaped by a deep historical context. When the Prophet Mohammed crafted the tenets of the Islamic faith in the Arabian peninsula, he sanctioned *jihad*, or holy war, against the non-believer. Islam swept across North Africa in the century after his death, into a distant region known in the great cities of the Middle East only as *al-Maghreb*, or the Far West. Here, farming Berbers tilled the wet coastal valleys of what would one day become Algeria and Morocco. A Muslim convert among them, Tariq, led armies across the narrow strait at Gibraltar (literally *Jabal Tariq*, or Tariq's Mountain) to subdue the infidel Christians. Though ultimately defeated by Charles "The Hammer" Martel and his Franks, Tariq's victorious warriors occupied much of the Iberian peninsula of southwestern Europe. When the great Caliph Idriss established a Berber-Muslim kingdom in the late eighth century, it transcended the waters of the narrow strait. A caliphate largely answering to his son, who ruled from Fez in central Morocco, arose in the southern Iberian reaches, known as al-Andalus.

Thus penetrated by Moors, what would become "Spain" had indelible markings from the Muslim world. It was a time when Islam had significant material and technological knowledge—when Christians were the laggards. In the tenth century, Andalucía's city of Córdoba boasted the best universities and most advanced scholarship in Europe, though it still was not quite on par with Damascus. Its artisans and craftsmen elevated architecture to new heights, as exemplified in the construction of its Mesquita mosque. Designed to resemble a desert oasis, with its hundreds of columns imitating palm trees, the shrine could hold thirty thousand worshippers. The Moors gave Iberians cultural gems too, like the chess game, and dozens of words eventually absorbed into their romantic language (like *alforja* and *naranja*, and of course both the word and content of *algebra*). Muslim rule for centuries was benign, Christians and Jews allowed to intermarry while perpetuating and practicing their own faith.

In the twelfth century, however, more zealous Muslims called Almohads gained power in al-Maghreb. Purists who believed in the spiritual supremacy of Islam, they insisted on a cultural conformity that upset Iberia's myriad Christians. Whether it be square-shaped coins, in honor of the Kaaba in Mecca, or restrictions on certain non-Muslim rituals and music, Almohadian rule triggered a backlash, as Christians insisted on the preservation of their own religious culture. Heavy taxes and an official ban on Christianity (though not fully enforced) triggered fighting. A coalition of princes united under Alfonso of Castile, who in July 1212 nearly forced his way into Andalucía itself, marching his coalition force through an obscure mountain pass that allowed for the ambush of a larger Muslim army.

Religious lines drawn sharply, for the next three centuries Iberia saw intermittent war. Known to Christians—who dominated the northern half of the peninsula—as the Reconquest, this slow-burning struggle against the Muslim "infidel" gave rise to a cult of warriorhood. In time, Iberian Christians came to define manhood by the act of war and vanquishing the nonbeliever as an expression of the Christian faith (a strange twist, given Jesus's obvious repudiation of the sword). Chivalry and valor were found among the masculine camaraderie of battle-hardened warriors. The effeminate was of lesser value, and homosexuality was despised as an egregious spiritual offense. The resistant infidel could be enslaved, as the Kingdom of God of earth was subject to expansion by force. Indeed, Iberian Christianity had inadvertently internalized the earlier creed of Islam, that war and faith go hand in hand.

Consolidated and strengthening over time, the Christian kingdoms of northern Spain benefited from a unity of purpose and rarely warred against each other. In 1469, an eighteen-year-old princess named Isabella, of the sprawling interior kingdom of Castile, married a younger Prince Ferdinand of Aragón. Their union created "Spain," though Isabella's contested rule in Castile was not ensured until a decade later. Known as "The Most Catholic Monarchs," both aspired to complete the centuries-long Reconquest by toppling the last Muslim strongholds in Andalucía. The headlining event of the year 1492 was the fall of the great fortress of Alhambra, signaling the end of the southern caliphate. Fewer Europeans took note when a seaman dispatched by Isabella later reported finding new lands by a westward voyage across the ocean blue.

Cortés and the Conquest of Tenochtitlán

After Hernández's voyage to Yucatán, and a second coastal foray, the Spanish governor in Cuba sent a large expedition to Mexico under a ruddy-haired and strong-willed man named Hernán Cortés. An assistant to the governor who had earned his marks by enslaving natives in Cuba, Cortés possessed a restlessness that fueled deep ambition. Under him were hundreds of seasoned soldiers and sixteen horses—an animal returning to the mainland of the Americas for the first time in ten thousand years. Relatively disinterested in Yucatán, Cortés skirted its coast while pursuing rumors of a far greater inland kingdom. He had the good fortune, however, of retrieving a Spaniard shipwrecked among the Maya several years earlier. He also received, as a concubine and slave, the princess of a peace-seeking Mayan lord. Destined to become the most famous and notorious woman of Latin American history, *Malinche* ("The Betrayer") became the conquistador's lover and friend. Raised in the highlands, Malinche spoke both Aztec Nahuatl and a lowland language, which meant that she could communicate with the formerly shipwrecked Spaniard. Cortés had translators.

Hugging the coastline for hundreds of miles, the Spanish fleet finally made contact with friendly natives in territory dominated by the Aztecs. The Cempoaltecas, according to the foot soldier Bernal Díaz—famed chronicler of the conquest—had an overweight chief, one the machiavellian Cortés easily ran circles around. When tax collectors arrived from Aztec Tenochtitlán, Cortés insisted that the Cempoaltecas arrest them instead of paying further tribute. Then, secretly, Cortés released the prisoners, sending them home with a message of friendship to the Aztec emperor. From the Cempoaltecas, the Spaniard also learned about Tlaxcala, a kingdom outside of Aztec control. Cortés soon gathered his men and ascended the eastern Sierra Madre in search of the Tlaxcalans' fortress-like empire.

At first reluctant to befriend the newcomers, even engaging briefly in battle, the Tlaxcalans eventually welcomed them. Like the Cempoaltecas, they were awed by the weaponry of these white-skinned men (Spaniards typically caucasian), with their shiny breastplates and mysterious helmets, and dumbfounded by their incredibly loud (yet small) cannon. Even more bewildering were the enormous and powerful horses; when mounted, a man could tower above the tallest warriors and move rapidly, like some kind of supernatural being. Not merely a fighter, Cortés was a magnificent student of human nature, well versed in the Roman maxim of "divide and conquer." He was particularly anxious to hear all about the Aztecs and their emperor, Moctezuma, whom the Tlaxcalans visibly detested.* He expressed empathy for his hosts as they recounted decades-long Aztec treacheries. Once semicoordinated military training exercises, so-called Flower Wars in which each side vied to capture prisoners had spun badly out of control, and over decades the Aztecs and Tlaxcalans had become implacable enemies.

So too, the Tlaxcalans hated the nearby tribe of Aztec collaborators at Cholula. They were not far away. Cortés marched forth, now with an entourage of Tlaxcalan warriors alongside his own men. Though welcoming

---

* As noted in the previous chapter, the Aztec emperor at the time of the conquest was Moctezuma II, Moctezuma I having ruled decades earlier. For simplicity purposes, I am now referring to Moctezuma II as merely Moctezuma.

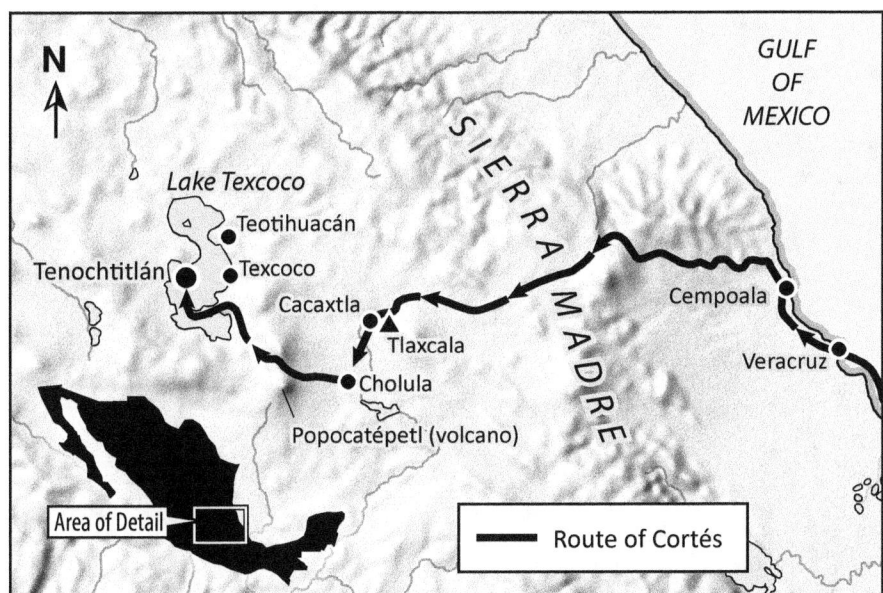

Map 4.1. Spanish Conquest of Mexico

Cortés in friendship, as he continued to exchange messages with the distant Moctezuma, the Cholulans were in fact instructed by the Aztec emperor to entertain and then slaughter the newcomers. The intrigues in Cholula played out over a couple of weeks, with Malinche informed by a Cholulan woman-friend of the devious plans. She in turn told Cortés, who struck first and struck hard. Luring unsuspecting Cholulan priests and nobles into his presence, his men sealed off courtyard exits and slew them wholesale. The Tlaxcalans gleefully joined in, though they were disappointed that the Spaniards had not first taunted their victims.

Hearing of the massacre, Moctezuma gave up hope of turning back Cortés. Weeks later, on a Lake Texcoco causeway, he welcomed him into Tenochtitlán. The Spaniards stayed in the royal palace as his guests. They wandered the great city, marveling at its sights—bustling markets, lakebed gardens, and its zoo. But other Aztecs watched these interlopers with increasing suspicion. Who were they? Why did the emperor never leave their presence? The more they saw of them, the less they looked like possible gods. When Cortés demanded the cessation of human sacrifice to Huitzilopochtli, many warrior-priests were incensed. Debates ensued among the Aztec elite about what to do. For those who wanted to challenge the Spanish presence, an apparent opportunity arose after several months, when Cortés and about half

Figure 4.1. The meeting of Hernán Cortés and Moctezuma was an encounter that altered Mexico's destiny. The conquistador realized this and later in his life urged that a church be built at the exact site. Today, Cortés's remains lie within this original mid-sixteenth-century wall; a modern tiled mural celebrates the meeting. As Cortés dismounted from his horse, Aztec servants refused to let him embrace the semi-divine emperor. What thoughts must have raced through Moctezuma's mind in those moments!

of his men departed for the coastal base of Veracruz. A second Spanish force had arrived there—the conquistador correctly surmising that it was sent by an antsy and potentially jealous Cuban governor. In Tenochtitlán, Spanish numbers were thus perilously reduced. Was a festival led by warrior-priests a prelude to an attack on this skeleton command? The nervous Spaniards took no chances. They preemptively massacred an assembly of Aztec nobles, just as Cortés had done so successfully at Cholula.

Cortés, meanwhile, met the arriving troops on the coast and incorporated them into his ranks, alluring them with promises of untold riches in the great Aztec capital. When he made his way back to Tenochtitlán, he discovered his remnant besieged in the palace compound. Forcing his way into the city to join them, he soon recognized the strategic hopelessness of the situation, with insufficient food and water to sustain his command. He ordered Moctezuma onto the palace rooftop, instructing him to settle the crowds and halt their attacks, with the promise that his "guests" would soon leave. But the restive populace was irreconcilable. Some began to throw stones at the emperor. One struck the elderly Moctezuma in the head; he died a couple of days later.

His protector gone, his position untenable, Cortés prepared to leave Tenochtitlán. On June 20, 1520, known in Spanish history as the Sad Night, the entire Spanish entourage snuck quietly out of the palace and made its way onto one of the causeways. But they were spotted. Watchmen blew conch shells, and the Aztec population stirred to life. Jaguar Knights attacked the Spanish column with reckless abandon. Anticipating their retreat, the Aztecs had removed the causeway's small wooden bridges, obligating Spaniards to swim. Some, weighted down with silver and gold, sank to the bottom of the lake. Others dumped their treasures and fled. Canoes of Aztec warriors harried them all, capturing scores. As Hernan Cortés and the survivors reached the mainland, they could hear their comrades' screams and cries—they were on their way to the sacrificial pyramid of Huitzilopochtli.

The Spanish plight in central Mexico would have been temporarily lost had not the Tlaxcalans and other tribes remained cooperative, focused on destroying the rival Aztecs. Tribal hatreds ran deep. Natives aligning with Cortés could not see that they sowed in collaboration the seeds of their own eventual declination. Preparations to war on Tenochtitlán took an entire year. Spaniards built small portable boats, which could be reassembled and used to take control of Lake Texcoco. Others scaled the daunting heights of Popocatepetl in order to retrieve sulfur for gunpowder. In the spring of 1521 tens of thousands of natives led by Cortés laid siege to the great city. The Aztecs had not fared well in the interim. Ravaged by a smallpox epidemic, inadvertently brought by Spaniards—who had comparative immunity to this Old World disease—they were weakened and demoralized. Even Moctezuma's successor had died of the perplexing ailment. A new emperor, just eighteen years old, took his place. Cuauhtémoc led his people in a brave but ultimately futile struggle, especially after the Tlaxcalans destroyed the network of hollowed logs that carried fresh water into the metropolis. When Cuauhtémoc attempted at last to flee by canoe, he and his bodyguards were easily captured. Cortés turned him over to Spaniards who wanted to torture him, believing that he might lead them to secret deposits of gold. Slowly burning his feet, they gained no such knowledge, the young emperor eventually dying in Spanish captivity.

Conquests beyond Tenochtitlán

Though the great Aztec capital had fallen, there were several peripheral regions yet to conquer. The most important secondary kingdom lay immediately to the west. The Tarascans were erstwhile adversaries of the Aztecs for decades, refusing to pay tribute and never submitting to their spears. The Aztecs called their kingdom *Michoacán*, or the "Place of the Fish Masters." The Tarascan king ruled from a terraced city along the shores of a large lake, and indeed, Tarascans seemed to be very fond of eating fish. But their society is otherwise striking for its dissimilarities with other native cultures. Their pantheon of deities omitted the widely and long-venerated Tlaloc and Feathered Serpent God, and they lacked the nearly universal 260-day calendar. Their tobacco-smoking priests married and interpreted the will foremostly of Kurikaweri, the Sun God, who required spectacular bonfires. Tarascan artisans crafted exceptional handiwork of turquoise, gold, and silver—there is a theory, in fact, that some of the objects attributed to the Mixtecs might be Tarascan. They also made weapons of copper, one reason even the aggressive Aztecs learned to leave them alone.

Tarascan copper was of little use against the Spaniards, accompanied by overwhelming numbers of native warriors who were allowed to pillage the Tarascan capital in a destructive conquest. Nearly all of Cortés's subordinates duplicated the cruelty they had seen in him, most without the concomitant finesse of his divide-and-conquer diplomacy. The reputation of the Spaniards preceded them—at least in central Mexico, where natives increasingly perceived resistance as futile. Still, degrees of relative cruelty exist, and with little doubt the most sadistic sub-conquest of all came at the hands of lawyer-turned-conquistador Nuño de Guzmán. Guzmán seemed to slaughter as many natives as he subdued in the far western regions, hanging thousands from trees and butchering villages wholesale. It took time to absorb and recover from such a sudden and horrendous brutality, but in 1540, Native Americans in the region revolted, laying siege to the Spanish town of Guadalajara. Only a thirty-thousand-strong army of Aztecs and Tlaxcalans, under Spanish direction, could suppress this rebellion, again with the collaborating natives permitted to seize women and possessions as they worked the Spanish will.

Everywhere the Spanish went, they used preexisting divisions among indigenous peoples as an avenue to power. But they mainly went where they believed "civilized" natives might have silver and gold, and when they wandered into an area with scant evidence of metallurgy, their interest quickly dissipated. Such was the case with Oaxaca, to the southeast, which also discouraged with its relatively small towns and mountainous, physically exhausting terrain. Competition among conquistadors drove expeditions into present-day Central America. In Guatemala, the rival Kaqchikel and K'iche' peoples were easily turned against each other. Honduras generated few signs of wealth and subsequently little interest—most of the isthmus of the Americas would eventually devolve out of Mexico's political orbit.

Figure 4.2. How could hundreds of Spaniards subdue hundreds of thousands of Native Americans? The Spanish conquered Mexico by playing off deep divisions among their hosts. In countless battles, orchestrated by the Spaniards, Native Americans killed one another. Hernán Cortés could not have defeated the Aztecs without the Tlaxcalans. At this baptismal font in 1520, he watched Tlaxcalan chiefs willingly receive the Catholic rite of baptism. The font sits in Tlaxcala's Cathedral, one of Mexico's oldest churches.

There were hopes for Yucatán, though the Maya had gained a reputation from the initial coastal encounters as a naturally treacherous and hostile people. In a first round of conquest on the peninsula things went badly, Spaniards frustrated in the overgrown jungle, weaving down disorienting paths too narrow for horses, sweating profusely in their heavy armor. The Maya would strike without warning, darts and arrows finding their mark, then drift back into the thick bushes before Spanish swords could reach them. But most of all, the Spanish failed in the late 1520s because they could not find the social cleavages essential to "divide and conquer." All the Mayan villages and chiefs seemed alike; there was no clear hierarchy or civic structure. There was also no substantial evidence of precious metals, so for several years the Spaniards went away.

When a second effort at conquest was undertaken, the Spaniards adapted better to the climate and terrain, donning light chainmail armor and operating with greater mobility. Most importantly, they slowly learned enough of the different languages and found enough tribal lines to foster at least a modicum of division. The Maya failed to coordinate their attacks, and yet they fought stubbornly in a war without quarter, even fouling their water pools and burning their beloved cornfields as the intruders established bases in the peninsula's interior. Ultimately, for the Spaniard, a lack of gold made the Maya themselves the prize—enslaving and coercing them into a tributary system in which Maya women were compelled to deliver their excellent handwoven cloth and other goods to white masters who settled in a ring of small coastal towns.

At least the Maya were able to offer some resistance. In the northeast, the sedentary but still primitive Téenek were the most vulnerable kind of native people. Lacking much of the militarism that defined other Post-Classic cultures, they were ill-prepared to even comprehend the forces that suddenly swallowed up their world, much less resist them. In 1522 Cortés himself arrived with an army of Tlaxcalans and Aztecs. Given license to plunder and kill, these natives annihilated the Téenek, while Spaniards saw to the decapitation of chiefs and priests, sometimes in front of their children. If that were not enough, the cruel Nuño de Guzmán arrived as an administrator years later, concluding that the only real use for the Téenek was enslavement. Tens of thousands were branded and shipped off to labor-hungry Cuba (where the indigenous population had been exterminated), generally at a price of one peso per adult male, or fifteen Téeneks for one horse. Surviving Téeneks refused to procreate, with childbearing all but ending and suicide by adults common. For this and other cultures like it, the Spaniards might as well have been creatures from outer space, so thorough and unfathomable were the apocalyptic consequences of their arrival.

PART II

COLONIAL CENTURIES

CHAPTER FIVE

The Creation of New Spain

Though the story of the conquest of Mexico has been endlessly rewritten and retold, one of the more fascinating pockets of Mexican history remains a relative enigma—the few years right after the Spanish triumph, when conquerors lived in and near Tenochtitlán, a recovering metropolis they rechristened Mexico City. Even the name is telling, though: *Mexica* was another name for the Aztecs; hence Cortés honored them in defeat, rather than rename their city after the king of Spain. In truth, the Spaniards' earliest rule depended on cooptation and finesse, not on raw power. How strange it must have been to have hundreds of white-skinned men in the environs of the great native city which they had so recently (along with their critical native allies) vanquished!

Outlying conquests and exploration did, of course, draw Spaniards away frequently, as they in effect became new masters atop a vast and unevenly integrated political (and eventually social) pyramid that governed for hundreds of miles in all directions. There has been much debate among scholars as to Mexico's indigenous population in the 1520s, which of course is exceedingly difficult to gauge. In the mid-twentieth century, academics generally worked with figures hovering in the range of ten to twelve million in the central highlands, with fifteen to twenty million in aggregate. In the late sixties and early seventies, scholars primarily at the University of California–Berkeley offered dramatically higher figures—numbers that attracted media attention and seemed politically charged in the context of the American Indian Movement. They claimed thirty-five million or more natives in what would become Mexico. Whatever the true number, there is no doubt that waves of epidemics—coupled with debilitating physical abuse over the course of the mid-sixteenth century—decimated the native population, collapsing it to around two and a half million by 1600.

The frenzy of conquest-era violence subsided quickly but also took its toll. For most indigenous people, life suddenly became much harder. The distant Spanish crown recognized Cortés's absolute authority in Mexico—it could not help but do otherwise—and within months the conquistador was assigning native laborers to his soldiers. Seized Aztec silver and gold were neither sufficient nor wholly satisfying to the ranks of fighting Spaniards, who aspired to live in comfort, obtain noble titles, and get rich. This process, of apportioning tributary payments and labor obligations by male head count, was called *encomienda*, and the holder an *encomendero*. It had been established in Cuba, where it was little more than chattel slavery in practice, though not in law. In the opening years of the *colony* of New Spain (also routinely called Mexico), abuses appear to have steadily risen as the Spaniards grew ever more certain of their control. In the very early years, though, prominent natives received grants of encomienda as well—telling evidence of the need to still divide in order to rule and co-opt native leadership. Tlaxcalans were exempted from encomienda for a long time, until Spanish power was definitive, when even they faced some limited obligations.

In the mid-1520s, the first Spanish bureaucrats arrived in Mexico City, establishing a governing body known as an *audiencia*. This five-member panel of administrators, with judicial, legislative, and executive authority, was the first attempt to directly establish crown prerogatives in New Spain—still an unstable political milieu of competing interests. One wild card was the constant arrival of lower-class Spaniards, who were not assigned many natives in encomienda and who railed against the "injustice" of a system that did not allow them to immediately become wealthy. In contrast, Cortés had withdrawn to the town of Cuernavaca south of Mexico City, where he built a palace and oversaw tens of thousands of his own encomienda charges. He and other leading conquistadors argued that encomienda should be granted in perpetuity by a crown grateful for services rendered. After all, they were the fighting men who courageously explored and subdued the new continent. With angst, they could see the writing on the wall—that in time their power would be usurped by soft-skinned bureaucrats and spoiled nobles arriving from the homeland. Even worse for the conqueror class, in the competition for political and social influence another player was about to enter the mix: the Roman Catholic Church.

Catholicism Comes to Mexico

In 1524, three years after the fall of Aztec Tenochtitlán, twelve priests arrived at Veracruz. In their first act, they removed their shoes and walked barefoot for two hundred miles to Mexico City, sharing the indignity, and physical pain, of the new colony's indigenous poor. These men were mendicants, vow-taking friars of the Catholic Church. Their order, established by Italian Francis of Assisi three centuries earlier, required oaths of chastity and poverty. The Franciscans played a dominant role in the quest to win the newly subservient native masses to Christianity. The Dominican Order, inspired by the life of a Spanish cleric nearly contemporaneous with Francis, also followed in their wake, its institutions already well established in the Spanish Caribbean (where even a nation would one day bear its name).

How did Spaniards, victorious in war, seek to convert their charges? To its credit, despite the cultural legacy of the Reconquest, the church held that faith could only be obtained through the willful choice of an inquiring soul. From the start, too, it perceived Native Americans as fully human and capable of belief, though only in child-like simplicity (hence natives could not be ordained). A priest who accompanied Cortés on the conquest attempted to convert Moctezuma, to no avail. Conversely, there is little

Figure 5.1. The Convent of San Bernardino de Siena de Sisal, constructed in the 1550s with Moorish architectural features, was the second-largest and one of the most important Franciscan houses in Yucatán. Unfortunately for the Maya, the Franciscan Fathers suspected them of backsliding into idolatry, and twenty years later they carried out a savage inquisition in which thousands were rounded up and systematically tortured.

evidence that early contact natives who accepted the ritual of baptism mentally understood even the basic tenets of the Christian faith. In many cases, polytheistic natives seemed to perceive the victor's god as merely a new deity, albeit a very powerful one. The Spaniards' apparent immunity to smallpox, as it ravaged the Mexica (Aztecs), convinced many that a mighty divine favored the newcomers. The Franciscans, more than the Dominicans and others, pressed their charges to accept baptism quickly, warning them through sermons (though language was frequently a problem), artworks, and even theatrical plays of the perils of eternal damnation should they refuse. As epidemic disease and hardship carried off millions, friars rushed to and fro with great evangelistic zeal, many embracing an end-of-time millennialism and convinced of Christ's imminent return.

Clerics observed pre-contact native religious practice and took liberties to fit the Christian faith into certain aspects of it—a process scholars term *syncretism*. Getting natives to suddenly reject all of their prior religious values was not realistic. The friars thus accommodated certain "acceptable" aspects of native belief. Could not polytheism speak to the multiplicity of Christian saints? Could not devotion to the Corn Mother mutate into a belief in the Virgin Mary? Protecting animal spirits became analogous to guardian angels. Many native holy sites retained their sanctity. In countless places, friars oversaw the construction of chapels and churches atop the pyramids and ruins of native temples and shrines. Sometimes, they left stones with native religious imagery exposed, facing outward, effectively affirming a continuity of faith. These tactics, more than conventional evangelization, wooed the masses. Many Catholic rituals were internalized by natives, who accepted the new methods (alongside older practices) as means of honoring the divine. But select earlier rites were completely abolished—most notably human sacrifice—and friars did displace native priests, invariably creating tension.

One attempt to defuse tensions was the heralded appearance of the Virgin Mary in Mexico, a dark-skinned mother who offered succor to the subjugated. In 1532, a Christianized Native American named Juan Diego reputedly encountered the Virgin on a hillside north of Mexico City. A good example of syncretism, she made her appearance near the site where indigenous peoples had long venerated a mother goddess named Tonantzin. Asking for proof of her existence, Diego received a bundle of roses, which he wrapped in his outer garment, or *sarape*. When he opened the cloth in the presence of the archbishop, he found that the flowers and petals had morphed into an image dubbed the Virgin of Guadalupe. In fact, this reputedly miraculous portrait at the time was known, among many clergy, to have been produced by Marcos Cipac, an accomplished native artist. Cipac used a tempera technique, a mixture of oil, gilding, and gouache (a mix of water and gum) to create a somewhat unique—but hardly mysterious—painting. Devotion to this cult was limited at first, but it came to life generations later, in the eighteenth century.

Certainly a more critical aspect of church-indigenous relations was the role of clergy in the face of encomienda abuses. There is no doubt that clerics, including the zealous Franciscans, frequently inserted themselves between the oppressed and the oppressor. Encomenderos often complained about clerical "interference," while friars sent copious letters to the crown documenting widespread disregard for safeguards and limitations. Mexico's first bishop, himself a Franciscan bearing the title "Protector of the Indians," intervened to remove several officials who sanctioned abuses that basically turned encomienda into slavery. And yet this same bishop had a native burned at the stake as a heretic. The church and its clergy thus had a mixed record in their treatment of natives, on the one hand as paternalistic protectors, on the other as forces for social conformity and cultural eradication.

Such contradictions are evident in the establishment of the College of Santa Cruz de Tlatelolco, a school for the sons of Native American nobles. This institution drew young boys away from their parents and, in effect, used them as lifelong tools for promoting Spanish values and beliefs. Yet the skills and knowledge that the students learned were broadly superior to those of native society and often empowered them economically and socially. Santa Cruz employed native artistic traditions rather than disparage them. Many teaching friars were not only tolerant but genuinely curious about indigenous ways and sought an exchange of knowledge. Associated with Santa Cruz was the gifted intellectual Franciscan Bernardino de Sahagún, who mastered Nahuatl, wrote in it (more than in Spanish), and astutely documented native society. Indeed, much of what we know about pre-contact Mexico comes from his authoritative *General History of the Things of New Spain*. He even recorded Native American remembrances of the conquest, capturing some of the sense of pain and loss triggered by the Spanish arrival.

Yet at other times Catholic clerics were cruel. One of the grimmest chapters in church history is the 1562 inquisition under Franciscans in the Yucatán. Upon discovering that Maya were still secretly appeasing their own gods, and reputedly even practicing human sacrifice, enraged friars led by Bishop Diego de Landa pursued a judicial inquiry that employed torture. Native Americans were hoisted up (their limbs dislocated), flogged bloody, doused with hot wax, and subjected to the cord and water (where pressure is applied, even as volumes of water are poured into the mouth to simulate drowning). Ultimately, friars tortured thousands, many dying or committing suicide in

Figure 5.2. A late colonial representation of the Augustinian Order's Saint Nicolás Tolentino. A thirteenth-century Italian mystic who helped the poor and criminals, Tolentino represented the Augustinian endeavor to minister to outcasts. Because of its theological roots in the works of St. Augustine, this order advocated a more benign conversion process, believing that merit could be found even in non-Christian religious traditions. Unfortunately for Mexico's natives, the Augustinians were comparatively minor players in post-conquest evangelization.
Source: Museo de las Culturas de Oaxaca, Oaxaca.

the process. Under duress, natives predictably confessed to idolatry, then scrambled to manufacture all the idols they claimed to possess—lest they fail to produce them and be tortured again. In a reversal of roles, encomenderos in the Yucatán defended the natives and pled that the inquisition be stopped by secular authorities lest it trigger a revolt.

In Michoacán in the mid-sixteenth century, in contrast, the church produced communes that were peaceful and prosperous, if not idyllic. Vasco de Quiroga, a bishop assigned to the old Tarascan domains of Michoacán, was a humanist influenced by Sir Thomas More's *Utopia*. Also mindful of communist tendencies in early Christianity—passages in the Book of Acts explaining that early believers "shared everything in common"—his governance stressed cooperation and equality. Men tilled fields, women worked in less physically demanding labor, and children attended school. Produce and benefits were dispersed according to need, with the surplus given to widows and orphans. Native Americans flocked to these church-run villages willingly (though it is fair to ask if they would have done so if conditions were not abusive elsewhere).

Establishing Royal Government

On the whole, the Catholic Church had more day-to-day influence on the lives of colonials than the state, at least until the eighteenth century. The line between church and state, however, was quite blurred. During the Reconquest, the pope had granted special prerogatives to Iberian princes. Known as Royal Patronage, the Spanish crown subsequently received the authority to appoint and recall bishops, draw diocesan boundaries, and manage missionary efforts. The state also collected a mandatory church tax, or tithe (of 10 percent), which gave it great influence over church affairs. Many crown bureaucrats were clerics, and the king's intimate advisors included priests and bishops.

Geography posed a dilemma to governing New Spain: How could the crown oversee a colony so far away? Sheer distance made the logistics nearly impossible; it took three months just to get a message from Spain to Mexico City. As a solution, the crown set up the office of *viceroy*, or vice-king. Mexico would, in effect, have its own monarch. Technically appointed for life, many viceroys returned to Spain after a limited tenure (the sixteenth-century average was seven years' service). In 1535 the first and ultimately most famous viceroy arrived. A personal friend of the king, Antonio de Mendoza was a sagacious choice. He exuded authority, reined in out-of-control conquistadors and overly demanding encomienda-seeking newcomers, and brought sound governance to the colony for fifteen years. He is renowned in history for his retort to the incessant and frequently ill-advised instructions emitted by bureaucrats in the Mother Country: "I obey, but I do not comply." Mendoza's sensitivity to local circumstances and administrative flexibility enabled him to negotiate the perils of rule in a vast, newly subjugated land (in contrast, ex-conquistadors murdered his pushy counterpart in Peru!).

Several tiers of government functioned under the viceroy. Ten audiencia courts oversaw sub-districts, with an eleventh assigned to the Philippines, an archipelago acquired via Spanish exploration (largely operating on its own—though technically this outpost on the other side of the Pacific Ocean was administered from Mexico). Governors ruled provinces within each audiencia district, and below them, about two hundred (colony-wide) *corregidores* administered smaller regions, both the corregidores and the governors appointed by the viceroy for terms of typically five years. To complicate matters, each level of officialdom had multiple roles—there was no separation of powers in the system. This dynamic predictably generated contradictory laws and confusion, effectively further empowering the viceroy atop the pyramid, who often arbitrated disputes. Many Spaniards used service in the colony as a springboard for better positions back home, so turnover throughout the bureaucracy was high. As he finally left office in 1550, Mendoza began an important administrative tradition: the *relación* was a report to one's successor, explaining conditions and seminal issues in the district. This provided a modicum of continuity, as did the Spanish tradition of the *residencia*, or judicial review of an outgoing official with an assessment of his time in office.

Below all of these crown-appointed officials was the *municipio* (municipality or town), which incorporated the nearby countryside, unlike its Anglo-American counterpart. Municipalities were governed by a *cabildo*, or town council, typically of five to fifteen members. Invariably those of economic means and social status controlled it, with councilors only nominally elected, often through a quasi-public meeting. Cabildos regulated markets, maintained common spaces (including fountains—for most citizens their source of water), oversaw public ceremonies, and settled local disputes as the court of first instance. Royal instructions for the establishment of towns stipulated that they be orderly and laid out as a grid of square blocks, with a main plaza set on the cardinal directions at a 1-to-1.5 ratio (rectangular in shape) with eight to ten emanating main streets. In Mexico locals often preferred the Nahuatl term *zócalo* to the Spanish *plaza mayor*.

Though the Spanish state and Catholic Church had arrived, in the sixteenth century colonial life was still overwhelmingly contiguous with pre-conquest times, instead of reflecting new conditions. Preexisting native boundaries determined most of the locations of the corregimientos, while even lower-level Spanish bureaucrats had relatively little direct contact with indigenous people. Hostility between various Native American cultures and tribes persisted—and despite an overarching political structure, the Spanish colony was hardly homogeneous. By 1570 there were just over sixty thousand (overwhelmingly white-skinned) Spanish colonists in New Spain, almost all living in towns and cities. Native villagers often went weeks without seeing one of them and of course still spoke their own languages. In lifestyle, pre-conquest norms endured. Native markets persisted, as did a village-based barter economy. Native Americans continued to sleep on mats, dress in trousers and skirts of cotton, wool, or maguey fiber, and eat primarily maize, though increasingly in the form of the tortilla (grounded and cooked), or sometimes as *atole* (a drinkable, gruel-like variation often flavored with honey or sugar). The arrival of domesticated fowl (chickens) and hogs introduced more meat into their diet, especially in the lowlands. Native Americans drank more alcohol after the conquest, mostly fermentations from the juice of the agave cactus called *pulque* and *mescal*.

Figure 5.3. One of the major tasks of municipal governments in colonial times was providing citizens with water. Fountains in plazas and streets were sometimes elaborate—and could be expensive. The town of Saltillo once spent three-quarters of its annual budget on a single fountain! This colonial masterpiece graces an intersection in Zacatecas, an exceptionally prosperous mining town.

What would strike any modern visitor to sixteenth-century Mexico is the predominance of the natural over the synthetic—our world of plastics and metal of course unknown. Even iron tools were rare, and European manufactures were almost exclusively restricted to the houses and workshops of the small Spanish minority. Nearly everything on the streets, in villages, and on farms was of natural origin: brooms of straw, baskets of hoop vine, utensils of plant fiber, plates of fired clay (Native Americans eating with their hands), and an abundance of objects made of leather and wood. Take, for example, fencing. With neither barbed wire nor modern post-digging techniques, colonials grew plants into position to set boundaries and control animal life.

In the lowlands, fast-growing flora like pengwin (wild pineapple) worked well; in the interior various cacti, though slow-growing, created fences that could last for a century. Though labor-intensive, low stone walls were also common.

As post-conquest populations dwindled in the far northern frontier, conditions were even more primitive. This part of the colony was dubbed *Nueva Vizcaya*, correspondent with the north-central region in Spain. Here, where the climate was more desert-like and dry, adobe huts predominated. The best adobe came from a combination of clay and sandy soil, with straw added for strength. With low rainfall these structures held up well. A lack of wood often meant roofing with shingle-like maguey cactus leaves or layers of twigs. The lack of arable land kept settlement sparse, making Nueva Vizcaya outposts vulnerable to Native American raiders. One of the ironies of colonial history is that the most primitive peoples resisted the Spaniards far better than the advanced and sedentary. The Chichimecs, nomadic hunters of the distant north, plagued Spanish colonists for centuries. Completely mobile, in the face of conquest they simply ran away. Unable to harness them as workers, Spanish officials moved docile sedentary natives into frontier towns. In San Luis Potosí, for example, hundreds of Tlaxcalans and Tarascans arrived to "civilize" the region and work the mines.

Near the end of his tenure, Viceroy Mendoza encouraged exploration of the unknown lands *beyond* Nueva Vizcaya, in what would eventually become the southwestern United States. Chosen to lead this well-equipped expedition was his friend, Francisco Vázquez de Coronado, who commanded four hundred mounted soldiers and hundreds of native scouts, servants, and cooks (with accompanying herds of cattle and horses). The Spaniards roamed into a no-man's-land, finding marvels that awed and perplexed. They weaved their way across the Painted Desert. They discovered what they termed the Divine Abyss, in present-day Arizona, a chasm so great that after three days of scaling its walls they abandoned all hope of traversing it. They encountered strange creatures, including a particularly nasty type of snake "with a castanet on its tail." The indigenous Pueblo in present-day northern New Mexico evoked little excitement, given the modesty of their huts and possessions, and when the Spaniards asked them about rumored cities of silver and gold, they told them, "Farther on, go farther on." Vázquez de Coronado and his troops eventually wandered into present-day Kansas, finding flat land as far as the eye could see, and nothing more than enormous herds of "shaggy cows." Turning back in despair, they eventually reached Mexico City, where a disappointed Mendoza refused to even meet with them. Spanish authorities were absolutely certain that nothing would ever come of the vast wasteland north of Mexico's frontier.

CHAPTER SIX

Mid-Colonial Economics

Demographics played a critical role in the three-century colonial era. Waves of epidemics ravaged the native population in the mid-sixteenth century, killing millions. The isolation of the Western Hemisphere had created a biological time bomb, as natives lacked immunity to a host of Old World diseases. Physical abuse, alcoholism, and despair also played a part in the numerical holocaust. New Spain profoundly changed as native numbers dropped by 90 percent or more, to a nadir around 1640, when only about one million pure-blooded Native Americans remained in the highlands. By that time, whites numbered 125,000, with tens of thousands of mixed-blood *mestizos* besides (the product of relations between white males and native females). White-skinned Spaniards were outnumbered by *creoles*, or whites born in the colony itself, as larger numbers of Spanish women arrived in the late sixteenth century, nearly all quickly married to Spanish men.

Labor and Land

Spaniards depended on native labor in the sixteenth century. With their masculinity defined by warriorhood, no proud Spaniard would have been caught tilling a field or planting seeds—work considered beneath their dignity. All wanted to be nobles. Tribute and labor from encomienda made many rich and allowed others to live relatively easy lives of gossip and petty pursuits in small towns. Most of the dying native masses lived in their own villages and for decades remained outside the cash economy. Things changed in 1549, when the government removed labor obligations from encomienda. Tributary payments actually rose in the wake of this supposed reform and increasingly became a cash payment, typically of one silver peso per family. Remaining encomiendas reverted to the crown upon the death of the encomendero, but this was of little advantage to Native Americans. Greedy corregidores often collected excess tribute, while also trapping them into acquiring the needed coinage (to make their legal payments) through forced purchases of goods they did not want or forced sales of their best livestock or possessions. Local merchants, working with the corregidor, participated in these actions and also profited. Burdens increased when officials were slow to adjust encomienda requirements for population loss. Unattached single males often moved into less-taxed villages, further skewing the collection of tribute and making some unfortunate areas even more destitute.

While there is little practical evidence that the Spaniards ever tempered or tamed the abusive institution of encomienda, despite an abundance of reforming regulations on the books, in time the demographic collapse of the Native American population *did* bring real change. In the 1560s and 1570s, as another devastating round of smallpox hit central Mexico, indigenous laborers became valuable simply by their declining numbers (vis-à-vis with the steadily rising numbers of labor-hungry whites). The crown replaced encomienda with a milder form of labor obligation called the *repartimiento*. In this practice, a judge summoned workers two or three times each year and portioned them out in labor drafts, including to the few hundred remaining encomenderos. Time of service was typically for two weeks, though the rich often bent the rules and extended the length of service. This system amounted to a rationing of labor and further empowered the crown at the expense of the encomenderos, since the state became the arbiter of the labor supply.

With the shift to a moneyed economy, a further change predictably happened. Wealthy whites lured Native Americans to work with cash payments. By the advent of the seventeenth century, free wage labor was displacing repartimiento, as the rich used cash to monopolize native labor. As the racial demographics continued to evolve, Spaniards and creoles found themselves in competition for labor, and mobility by Native Americans ensured that the highest payers won. Populations shifted around, too, as people sought out more favorable niches in the labor market. Conditions for the darker-skinned masses were at their very best in the first half of the 1600s, with skilled workers enjoying a degree of upward mobility. Even a few entrepreneurial Native Americans became well-to-do in the quasi-capitalist labor market.

This early seventeenth-century period coincided with another seminal economic change: the rise of the landed estate, or Mexico's famous *hacienda*. Although it is counterintuitive to us, from the time of the conquests until the early seventeenth century Spaniards had little interest in land. It was plentiful; native labor, not land, made men rich. But now, with the labor pool in sharp decline, land became a meaningful asset. As more Spanish colonists arrived and towns grew (even as native villages declined), haciendas arose to produce food, especially wheat—a staple of the Spaniard's diet. Indeed, a century or so after the conquest, *New Spain* was starting to look a bit like old Spain, in food, dress, and culture. Spanish finally displaced Nahuatl and other native languages.

Privileged and politically connected Spaniards acquired land through grants from the crown. Authorities combined decimated native village populations and through resettlement freed up large tracts of land for distribution. Some well-placed Native Americans also acquired grants—about 7 percent went to indigenous people. It is a common misconception that the hacienda arose everywhere in Mexico, when in fact it predominated only in the center and north, eventually extending into the semi-arid frontier lands of Nueva Vizcaya (see chapter 8). In the remote, mountainous south, with its inferior land quality and fewer Spanish towns, Native Americans largely retained their villages and traditional lifestyles. One of the most important areas of hacienda growth was to the northwest of Mexico City, in an oval-shaped region known as the *Bajío*. At a lower elevation than the capital, this relatively flat area became a nominal grain belt, supplying nearby silver mines and towns, as well as the viceregal capital.

The hacienda was commercial, producing wheat, beef, and other goods for profit, while generating income in coinage. But it also had feudal characteristics, gravitating toward self-sufficiency and even in the heyday of free wage labor exuding the lofty status of the proprietor, or *patrón*. As the population began to slowly recover in the mid-seventeenth century, labor again gradually became cheaper. In time, the stereotypical hacienda of old movies emerged: the distinguished, silver-spurred *hacendado* (owner) and his well-groomed family dwelling in a fine house, surrounded by the lowly brown-skinned (mestizo) peons, deferential to his every whim—until Pancho Villa comes along! This caricature is not far from the truth. By the eighteenth century, workers were increasingly ensnared in debt, especially in the far north of Mexico. They bought seed and rented farming implements at a company store, they were paid in script instead of money, and their sons inherited their financial obligations, effectively trapping them on the estate, much like serfs in Russia. Haciendas became nearly self-sustaining, with artisans'

Figure 6.1. The rise of the hacienda defined much of rural Mexico in the mid-colonial period. This great house at the Hacienda San Diego, about sixty miles southeast of San Luis Potosí, reflects the daunting power and status of the hacendado, or patrón. The eighteenth-century chapel alongside the hacienda testifies to the collaboration of the church in this exercise of power. Here, the hacendado might honor a faithful peasant by attending his wedding or funeral.

shops, mills, wagon trains, and even parish churches, while the hacendado exercised judicial authority similar to that of a feudal lord.

The Wealth of Kingdoms

Metallurgy was of course the paramount concern of the Spaniards. At first, in the wake of the conquests, they eagerly seized any silver and gold possessed by the Native Americans. They also quickly inquired as to the whereabouts of natural deposits. None of the native mining sites were large (Taxco, south of Mexico City, was the only substantial one), but the Spaniards soon discovered Mexico's unprecedented endowment in silver. In the Bajío, the mining town of Guanajuato arose, then flourished upon striking the ridiculously concentrated mother lode at *La Valenciana*—depending on one's definition of what constitutes a mine, it was arguably the greatest silver find in the history of the world. In mid-century, Spaniards stumbled upon a protruding vein on the extreme northwestern edge of the Bajío. Its location was distinctive, near a rock outcropping similar in shape to a coxcomb flower. The silver mecca of Zacatecas quickly took form on the valley floor below, and within ten years was the second-largest city in New Spain. It retained this status for decades, enriched locals building stately houses and churches constructed of

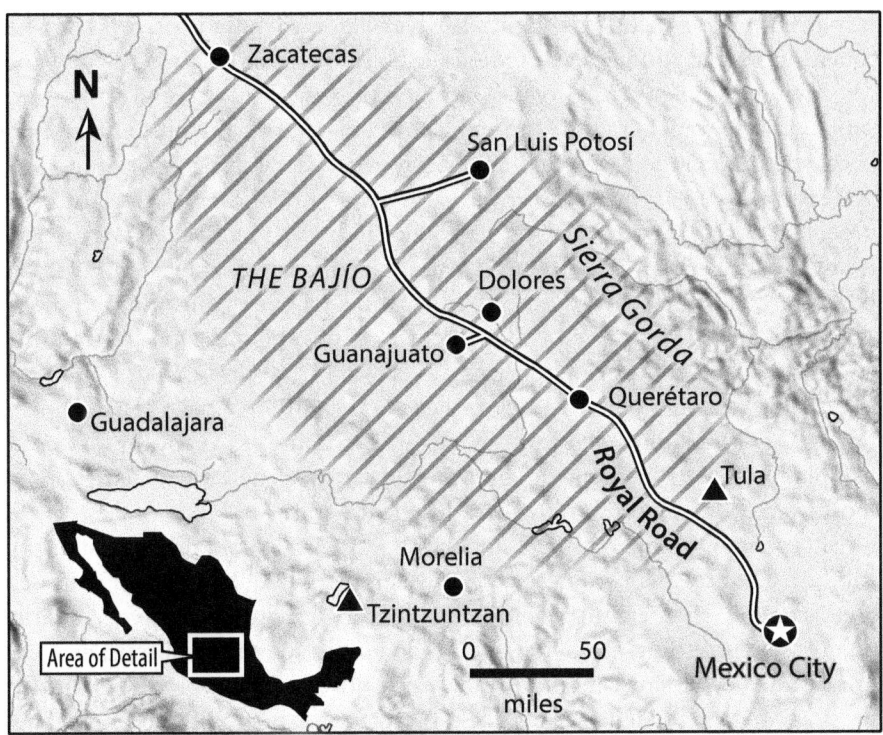

Map 6.1. Bajío Region

the region's distinctive pink-toned sandstone. Ultimately, Zacatecas's silver output nearly matched that of Guanajuato. A combination of smaller strikes in both silver and gold gave rise to San Luis Potosí, in the northeastern Bajío.

As colonials disgorged fabulous wealth from mines, only a relative few became rich. Mining was like a natural lottery, where random luck largely determined the winners—though one had to have enough political clout and legal resources to secure claims. For the rest, silver mining was anything but glamorous. Working in dark and dank tunnels, they chipped away at rock face with crude tools for endless hours and carried heavy loads up rickety ladders in baskets strapped to their backs. In the late sixteenth century, especially in remote settings like Zacatecas (which lacked sufficient native populations), mines used African slaves. Wage labor drew Native Americans into the business later, and these gleaned some economic benefits, with the eventual right to work overtime and keep a portion of the ore for themselves. Yet the silver industry was never labor-intensive; even at its height it employed fewer than fifteen thousand miners.

No matter how rich the vein, all silver-laden rock had to be processed. Smelting in lead furnaces was tedious, requiring enormous amounts of wood to generate sufficient heat—wood in much of New Spain in grievously short supply. In the mid-sixteenth century a colonial deduced an alternative: mercury, when combined with ore crushed to a powder (along with some copper or iron pyrites), broke down properties in a chemical reaction, thereby producing "quick silver." Mixing took place in large stone-walled vats, where natives served as walking spoons, stirring the concoction by pacing in circles barefoot. Of course, over time, they suffered mercury poisoning, with its symptoms of shaking, loss of teeth, and paralysis, before eventual insanity and death. The ratio of mercury to silver was six to one, making mercury itself a prized commodity. Mines in Peru and southern Spain provided sufficient quantities until the mid-seventeenth century via a royal monopoly. Coupled with a 10 percent tax and minting, it was the crown that profited most from Mexico's astounding metallurgical wealth.

Silver was typically 80 percent of the value of colonial exports to the Mother Country. The mines were prosperous, but owners never amassed great capital. In the mid-seventeenth century production slowed, mainly due to mercury shortages. Drainage problems also curtailed output, as older mines ran deeper into mountainsides and drew in more groundwater. As precious metals flooded into Spain, the crown squandered them on decades of war in a vain attempt to suppress Protestantism in northern Europe. Price inflation famously gripped Europe because of the influx of Mexican silver, further undercutting Spain's accumulated wealth. Could Spain have used colonial mining to become an enduring world power? It is unlikely. The Spaniards themselves were dealt a poor geographical hand. While it is true that Catholic Spain was resistant to the humanist ideas that fueled technological change, it also had very little in the way of rollicking streams (for water power), coal fields, or iron ore deposits like those that would turn Britain into an industrial power two centuries later. Iberia was semi-arid and could not generate a large surplus population. Mexican silver temporarily rained wealth on a Spanish crown that was destined to ultimately languish.

As the Kingdom of Spain grew temporarily wealthy, so too did the reputed Kingdom of God on earth. The Catholic Church began to amass riches especially during the course of the late sixteenth century. Although the church generally did not extract resources from the abusive encomienda system, it did benefit more readily from repartimiento. As Native Americans converted, they became subject to the church tax, while secular clergy (who did not take vows) also required a range of fees for various services and sacraments—most notably baptism, marriage, and burial. Many dying conquistadors bequeathed their estates to the church, while some silver barons financed the construction of ornate churches entirely on their own. In the seventeenth century the church acquired large tracts of land, again often via inheritance, and in turn it frequently rented out properties and effectively became a moneylender as well, typically earning around 7 percent per annum. Convents and monasteries also became rich, in part through possession of prime real estate in urban areas. In

Figure 6.2. Churrigueresque architecture is a three-dimensional feast for the eyes. Its flamboyance is obvious when compared with Baroque (as in figure 7.1 in the following chapter). Widely regarded as the best example in Mexico, Zacatecas's cathedral features a dizzying array of detail and depth. Silver-mining families funded construction of this gem, made of the city's distinctive pink-tinted stone. Though completed in 1752, it was elevated to cathedral status only in the nineteenth century.

1700 Mexico City had twenty-nine monasteries and twenty-two convents, most of them in the affluent core of the metropolis.

Catholicism's wealth was evident in its opulent mid-colonial churches. Earlier churches had been simple, albeit often bulky and fortress-like, with thick walls. Within decades, architectural motifs defined the famous Mexican Baroque. Stately and grand, these newer buildings featured a profusion of detail, including elaborate niches and curved lines, designed to strike at the senses (see figure 6.1). They rejected the Moorish influence still predominant in Spain. Construction on the biggest churches lasted for decades. A master architect often spent his entire career on a structure, supervising teams of masons and carpenters, who were organized in craftsmen's guilds. But the Baroque style itself gave way to the even more flamboyant Churrigueresque. With a wild depth of three-dimensional detail, Churrigueresque does not strike at the senses, it overwhelms them. Dominant in the seventeenth century, the "excesses" of Churriguersque inspired an eighteenth-century return to simplicity with the linear Neo-Classical. The rise of protestantism gave pause to extravagance too, though for Catholics vesting a church in riches was more noble than self-aggrandizement or an endless pursuit of greater business profits.

Within any given church were *retablos*, or freestanding altarpieces (the term evolved from the Latin words for "behind" and "board," or *retro* and *tabula*). Like churches, retablos were frequently elaborate and crafted with great care. Predictably, the best of all was built for the apse (center-front chapel) in Mexico City's cathedral: the Altarscreen of the Kings took seven years to construct and twelve years to paint and gild. Retablos were didactic, designed to instruct the faithful about saints and seminal events in the Bible. Mexico City's retablo pushed the envelope with its statuary of Iberian royals—though this was acceptable given the connection between church and crown via royal patronage. Carved of wood, a retablo is sheathed in very thin layers of silver and gold, and almost glows after polishing. But the discerning eye recognizes many other colors besides. Red clay, salt, ash, and other properties could produce various effects and hues; artisans mastered a technique (*encarnado*) for making realistic flesh tones. For its part, the Catholic Church, with its wealth and power, was a centerpiece of colonial order.

Trade and Pirates on the High Seas

With church and state in place, Spain's ability to maintain control of Mexico depended in large part on its merchant marine and navy. Shipping served as the umbilical cord between Mother Country and colony. In the wake of the conquest, the crown enlarged its fleets, and in the mid-sixteenth century had the most formidable navy and biggest boats on the planet. Galleons were the workhorses of the merchant marine, multi-deck vessels built in Andalucía beginning in the 1530s, stable even in rough seas and able to carry heavy loads. Though majestic, with an array of different sails and tall aftcastles, they offered few pleasantries for their crews. Packed into overcrowded quarters, seamen of diverse Mediterranean backgrounds (Italians, Portuguese, Moors, and others, along with Spaniards) endured long voyages of hard work and limited food, with terrible hygiene, mice, rats, and roaches besides.

As in so many other areas, momentum was soon beginning to shift to northwestern Europe, where the Dutch and English, in particular, were fast mastering the art of seafaring (and also cornering the trans-Atlantic slave trade). After the conquest, though, France was Spain's immediate nemesis. French pirates harried Spanish ships in the Caribbean; they even intercepted the first shipment of gold sent by Cortés to the king. Called *buccaneers*, for their fondness of smoked meat, these pirates manned sleek corsairs while maintaining clandestine bases among island inlets and along the remote peninsula of La Florida. Where the French buccaneers left off, English terrorists began. Starting out, Francis Drake had just seventy men and one ship at his service, but through daring raids he terrorized the Caribbean and reaped stellular profits. In a single year, he captured booty equal in value to England's government budget! It is no surprise that Queen Elizabeth knighted him.

The antics of Sir Francis enraged the Spanish king, Philip II, and helped inspire his decision to war on England. As a young man, Philip had traveled to England to wed his first wife, the devout Catholic Mary Tudor (known to Protestants as Bloody Mary). He had not been well received, nor did he much like the island nation, with its rabid Protestant underlings. When Mary died of natural causes a few years later, he lost his chance to master the realm through marriage. Hence, in 1588 he sent forth the great Spanish Armada. The fleet sailed with lofty goals: to rendezvous with an army in the Spanish Netherlands, subdue the English coastline, and strike a mighty blow for both Spain and Catholicism. Everything went wrong. Coordination was faulty, while smaller English and Dutch vessels ran roughshod among the warships in the English Channel. Taking heavy losses, the armada headed into the North Sea and then circumnavigated the British Isles, only to be caught in remnants of a hurricane off the Irish coast. Spain's already declining naval might suffered immeasurable loss.

As a result of the armada's defeat, the crown perfected an already operating Fleet System in order to ensure safe trade with New Spain and its other colonies. Twice each year, the remnants of the Spanish navy escorted nearly the entire merchant marine across the Atlantic Ocean. As this huge flotilla entered the Caribbean Sea, portions of it broke off, most notably to Cartagena and Panama. The largest contingent proceeded into Veracruz, where it was greeted with fanfare and a buzz of activity among excited merchants. This convoy system worked; pirates could not tangle with the full weight of the Spanish navy. But the twice-a-year visits proved problematic for merchants, creating inevitable cycles of shortage and glut. Prices for goods fluctuated wildly. Nor could Spaniards hold the sparsely populated islands of the Caribbean basin, many of which were eventually acquired by its rivals—Jamaica, for example, by the British, and Martinique by the French. Over the course of the seventeenth century, Protestant merchant ships audaciously visited illegal ports of entry, even in New Spain, and a black-market trade flourished.

To connect the audiencia district of the Philippines with New Spain and facilitate trade with the Far East, Spain financed magnificent ships known as the Manila galleons. Built by Filipino and Chinese laborers in the port of Manila, these enormous vessels, by far the largest ever built up to that time, traversed the vast Pacific Ocean for exactly 250 years. They sailed in solitude on a months-long journey that took them east to the mid-California coast, down to the modest port of Acapulco, then westward on a return, still north of the equator but on a latitude near that of the Marshall Islands. Their mammoth cargoes were of astounding value, with silk and spices from the Orient, and precious metals sent in return (mule trains biannually carried Asian goods overland to the Spanish fleet docked at Veracruz). Determined to keep the galleons safe, their very existence was a state secret, with only high-level officials and critical navigators privy to details about the operation.

In the late sixteenth century, Francis Drake circumnavigated the globe. When he captured a Spanish merchant ship off the coast of Peru, he found a confidential sailing chart for the galleons among its captain's papers. Years later, a Drake sidekick named Thomas Cavendish determined to lay in wait for one of the giant vessels. Holding a position near Cabo San Lucas, at the tip of the Baja California peninsula, one day he spotted the prize, quickly giving chase with his three small brigantines. Amazingly, since the galleons were never under threat, they were not issued cannon. The Spanish crew did not even have muskets! When the pirates came alongside and tried to scale up to the deck, they threw wood planks and empty barrels at them. After pulling away and bombarding the galleon for several hours, Cavendish finally forced its surrender. The pirates pillaged its cargo, executed a priest, then placed its 190-man crew ashore before setting it afire (among the Spanish sailors was a young man named Sebastián Vizcaino, who later gained fame by

Figure 6.3. The Manila galleons brought a distinctive art form to Mexico from the Far East. Biombos were first sent as gifts to the viceroy from Japanese shoguns. Featuring hinged panels that folded out, they became popular in the homes of the rich. Biombo paintings typically struck historical or mythological themes. But since the thin-wooded panels were frequently knocked over and easily damaged, few survive in as good condition as this beautiful one.
Source: Museo Soumaya, Mexico City.

exploring the coastline of California). Despite this setback, in a quarter of a millennium Spain lost only four Manila galleons. The British navy captured the *Santísima Trinidad* in 1762, the largest ship in the world at 167 feet in length, with a draft of thirty-three feet. English peasants walked for days from across southern England to gawk at the sight of it in Portsmouth.

CHAPTER SEVEN

Mid-Colonial Society

The colonials of New Spain loved parades and pageantry. They were quick to celebrate news from Spain of a royal ascension, marriage or birth, or a military victory. Religious holidays gave excuses to make merry, albeit with appropriate sobriety, and regional events, such as the arrival of a new viceroy or the biannual docking of the fleet in Veracruz, triggered carousing for several days. The *máscara*, a festive tradition in cities, presaged the modern-day carnival. Máscara parades stretched for blocks, with troupes of participants dazzling revelers with their masks and costumes. The rich astride steeds, adorned in silver and scarlet, rode alongside lower-class actors and acrobats. Colorful cloth hung from balconies, while torches lit up the night sky. Processions often had themes drawn from religion, history, mythology, or literature. These were reflected in floats and other parade components—a re-creation of the Conquest, for example, with Native Americans dancing with spears (acceptable by the 1600s), or a brief acting out of an episode in the life of the senile Don Quixote, performed to the amusement of the crowd. Máscaras incorporated the strange and risqué. Men and women wore each other's clothes; strutting ostriches were always popular, and observers howled their approval at displays of irreverence. In one máscara, a float featured a caricature of the viceroy himself being flogged. Political satire and reversed positions of class and status were acceptable in the context of public merrymaking.

Colonial Life and Womanhood

The widespread perception of a staid and somber colonial society is incorrect. While it is certainly true that the specter of death was omnipresent, colonials embraced life and lived it with vigor. Just surviving into adulthood was special: the infant mortality rate was over 50 percent. A successful birth elicited joy; a child living past the age of three was a sign of God's blessing. Gender considerations defined society, with males certainly enjoying far greater options than females. Women were valued for childbearing, the preservation of their premarital virginity of critical importance to both their family's and future husband's honor. If a woman was sexually active before or outside of marriage, her reputation could be tarnished for life. Males, on the other hand, were expected to demonstrate their virility as they came of age. They could have mistresses and cheat on their wives with little in the way of a societal reprimand. Of course, young couples predictably had premarital sex, and this was generally of little concern unless a pregnancy resulted. In such a case, a quick marriage usually solved the problem. If the male was reluctant to undertake nuptials, he could be obliged to do so by an economically powerful and irate father-in-law, anxious to preserve the honor of his daughter. Conversely, parents generally could not dictate choices or arrange marriages for their children. The Catholic Church, following the teachings of Thomas Aquinas, held that marriage was a willful act enveloped in consensual love. Once married, though, divorce or abandonment were not valid options. In the eyes of the church, a male who left his wife was in dire transgression before God, and if involved with another woman he could be tried and imprisoned for bigamy.

Gender relations were patriarchal. Under Spanish law, fathers had legal authority over children until adulthood. Those prerogatives over a daughter transferred to her husband upon marriage. Males had the right to discipline and control women. Physical abuse was common, especially among lower classes. Family ensured that abuse did not cross certain boundaries among the well-to-do, where reputation was more at play. Lighter-skinned and rich women were largely secluded from broader society, and they typically stayed at home, aside from outings to church services. Economic need drove lower-class women into the markets and streets, and put them in contact with other males besides their husbands. It is of course difficult to gauge the level of illicit sex in colonial society, but among the lower classes liaisons were common. Lewd, sensual dancing and romantic songs marked underclass nightlife in the cantinas.

Husbands and fathers handled all legal matters and dealt with authorities on behalf of their subservient women. Society saw no reason why a woman needed an education, though wealthier families ensured that their daughters could at least nominally read and write—the teaching done by mothers, elder sisters, or nuns. Widowhood was the exception that could result in legal, political, and economic power. When a woman outlived her husband, she inherited half of his estate, the remainder divided between children of either gender. Powerful widows arose over the course of the colonial era, some managing large factories and haciendas. Commerce remained the domain of males, and toward the end of the colonial era merchants attained great power. Their patriarchal control actually increased, with lucrative dowries on behalf of their daughters and economic interests constricting marital choice among their offspring.

The other option for women, besides marriage, was nunnery. Convents flourished in Mexico and had long waiting lists. Families had to pay a dowry-like admission fee in order to arrange the acceptance of their daughter, while religious obligations and living conditions varied greatly by order. In some, such as the Carmelites, sisters practiced an austere and disciplined life, sleeping on boards in dormitories and spending long days tending to the sick or serving the poor through acts of charity. Others were barely sacrificial at all, with comfortable apartment-like cells and small armies of servants and slaves handling all menial tasks. Nunnery provided women with a degree of independence otherwise unobtainable. In the convent they managed their own affairs while overseeing enterprises such as hospitals and orphanages. They also accessed education.

The most famous woman of the colonial era was a nun who chose the convent over marriage. Juana Inés de la Cruz was a complex and oft-troubled soul of incredible intellectual capacity. Born illegitimate, "Sor Juana" (Sister Juana), as she is popularly known, was charitably brought into the viceregal court, and in receiving a first-rate education soon proved herself a prodigy. Her appetite for knowledge was voracious. She read prolifically, could outthink most of the presumed intellectuals (all males) around her, and developed a subtle but nimble and at times sardonic wit. As a young woman she entered a Carmelite convent, finding its regimen of good works tedious and devoid of intellectual meaning. Switching to another order, she performed obligatory duties for part of the day, but otherwise retreated to her book-filled cell and immersed herself in study. She so longed to attend a university that at one point she contemplated sneaking in, dressed as a male.

Sor Juana is famous for her poetry. At times utterly brilliant, and nearly always sophisticated, it speaks of her longing for love . . . perhaps not for the body (via a man) but for the mind (via knowledge). Many poems are directed toward a mythical lover named Fabio, which is of course very similar to the Spanish word for wisdom (*sabio*). She also wrestles greatly with faith versus reason and freedom versus her subservient place under the wings of the patriarchal church—which in fact gave her access to learning, albeit of a limited degree, that she could not have otherwise obtained. Some see in her a precursor to modern feminism. She clearly ponders a woman's sad plight in verse innumerable times, noting vulnerability in the midst of false promises of love, and the snare of prostitution, in this stanza:

> Who has the greater guilt in a passion errant:
>   She, who listens to smooth words or he, the false declarant?
> Or who commits the greater sin, though both race to hell much faster:
>   She, who gives herself for pay or he, the sin paymaster?*

Just as the church provided a modicum of mobility for women like Sor Juana, it also opened some doors to the racially disadvantaged. Though restricted from the priesthood, natives could become parish assistants and serve as choirmasters—a highly visible and coveted position of status (the choirs, too, were all male, with soprano vocals provided by preadolescent boys). As musicians, natives mastered European instruments, including strings, harps, horns, and sometimes pipe organs. They could also join lay brotherhoods called *cofradías*. Cofradías organized civic celebrations for Holy Week and the veneration of saints, and they raised funds to decorate the local church. Women sometimes served on cofradías and, far more rarely, exercised some leadership in them. By the late seventeenth century female participation in church theatrical plays became acceptable, and in 1724 native women obtained the right to become nuns.

Medicine and Science

The Catholic Church famously looked askance at the scientific revolution in Europe, while the uneducated colonial masses persisted in rank superstition and frequently succumbed to hysterics. When an eclipse blackened the midday sun in Mexico City in 1691, panicked hordes rushed into churches to pray, convinced that the world was ending. In contrast, one of New Spain's gifted intellectuals, Carlos de Sigüenza y Góngora, positioned his telescope on a rooftop and tracked the solar movement with interest. As professor of mathematics at the royal university, Sigüenza y Góngora notoriously shirked

---

* I am taking considerable liberty in translation in order to create an English-language rhyme. The original Spanish, with a far more sophisticated A-B-B-A / C-D-D-C rhythmic pattern, is: *Cuál mayor culpa ha tenido / en una pasión errada: / la que cae de rogada, / o el que ruega de caído? O cuál es más de culpar / aunque cualquiera mal haga: / la que peca por la paga / o el que paga por pecar?*

his lectures and administrative duties, frequently taking leave to engage in research. Besides mathematics, he studied geography. He surveyed Pensacola Bay in La Florida, advising the crown of its attributes and the possibility of setting up a colony there. He collected archeological material and studied pre-conquest native society. Promoting nascent journalism, he published a newsletter that chronicled political affairs.

Sigüenza y Góngora was a contemporary of Sor Juana, and the two spent long hours discussing the latest scientific theories and world about them, always exchanging books from Europe. They both interacted with Eusebio Kino, an Italian-born Jesuit. Kino's worldly and inquisitive mind prompted him to do more than convert Native Americans in the Sonoran desert of extreme northwestern Mexico. He drew maps, documented plant and animal life, and maintained a thorough diary—the earliest written source on the American Southwest. To Sigüenza y Góngora, however, Father Kino was

Figure 7.1. The Catholic Church dominated intellectual life, as reflected in the experiences of Father Kino, Sor Juana, and Sigüenza y Góngora. Just before this noteworthy trio, in the mid-seventeenth century, Juan de Palafox epitomized the lofty intellectual in New Spain. He amassed a collection of thousands of books. As bishop of Puebla, he accelerated construction on the city's great cathedral. But just as the Baroque building looms over all, curious minds could not wander far from the arms of the paternal and often rigid church.

part brain, part blowhard. The two men sparred frequently. In rival booklets, they debated the nature of comets, Sigüenza y Góngora dismissing the idea that they were divine messengers or omens of future calamity. When a guilt-ridden Sor Juana renounced in blood her worldly possessions, mortified the flesh, and served the poor during a pestilence in which she herself died, a mournful Sigüenza y Góngora (who had studied theology and been ordained a priest in youth) conducted her funeral. He died years later, insisting that his body be dissected and studied for the cause of science.

Death was never far off in colonial Mexico, mature adults fortunate if they lived into their fifties. Funerary practices varied by race, with pre-contact rituals persistent among Native Americans well into the seventeenth century. Offerings of flowers, copal incense, and food honored the deceased, who in mid-colonial times was invariably buried in a shallow, unmarked grave in a church atrium. A fusion of All Saints Day (November 1) with All Souls Day (November 2) created a syncretic tradition that in time became Mexico's renowned Day of the Dead. For the lighter-skinned and wealthier, formal ceremonies paid tribute to the deceased, who was interred in the walls or under the stone floor of a sanctuary (larger churches had extensive burial vaults or crypts). Sometimes the seal was inadequate, and the wretched stench of a putrefying corpse permeated the building, nauseating worshippers attending services. Women generally did not attend funerals but dressed in black and stayed at home for several days of mourning. During epidemics, the sheer number of dead compelled mass burials in hastily acquired and consecrated fields.

The purpose of medical care was of course to preserve life, though if aliens from outer space watched colonial practices, they would be entirely rational to think otherwise. The nature of medicinal norms varied by race and location. Lighter-skinned townsfolk invariably abided by European convention, while villagers favored long-standing native remedies. There was some overlap. From the start, Spanish friars and physicians were curious about the medicinal properties of New World plants. Many accepted some of the perceived attributes as affirmed by Christianized natives, though anything akin to "devil worship" or rank superstition was rejected—and, since the line among natives between faith in certain deities and various healing rituals was blurred—this was frequently the case. Both traditions were awry in terms of healthy practices. Earlier Spanish diagnostics based on the four humors (blood, phlegm, yellow bile, and black bile), with the concomitant practice of bleeding the patient, were badly flawed, while the growing popularity of digesting mercury for a host of ailments was, of course, crazy (symptoms of severe salivation, itching, and vomiting might have been a clue to the clear-

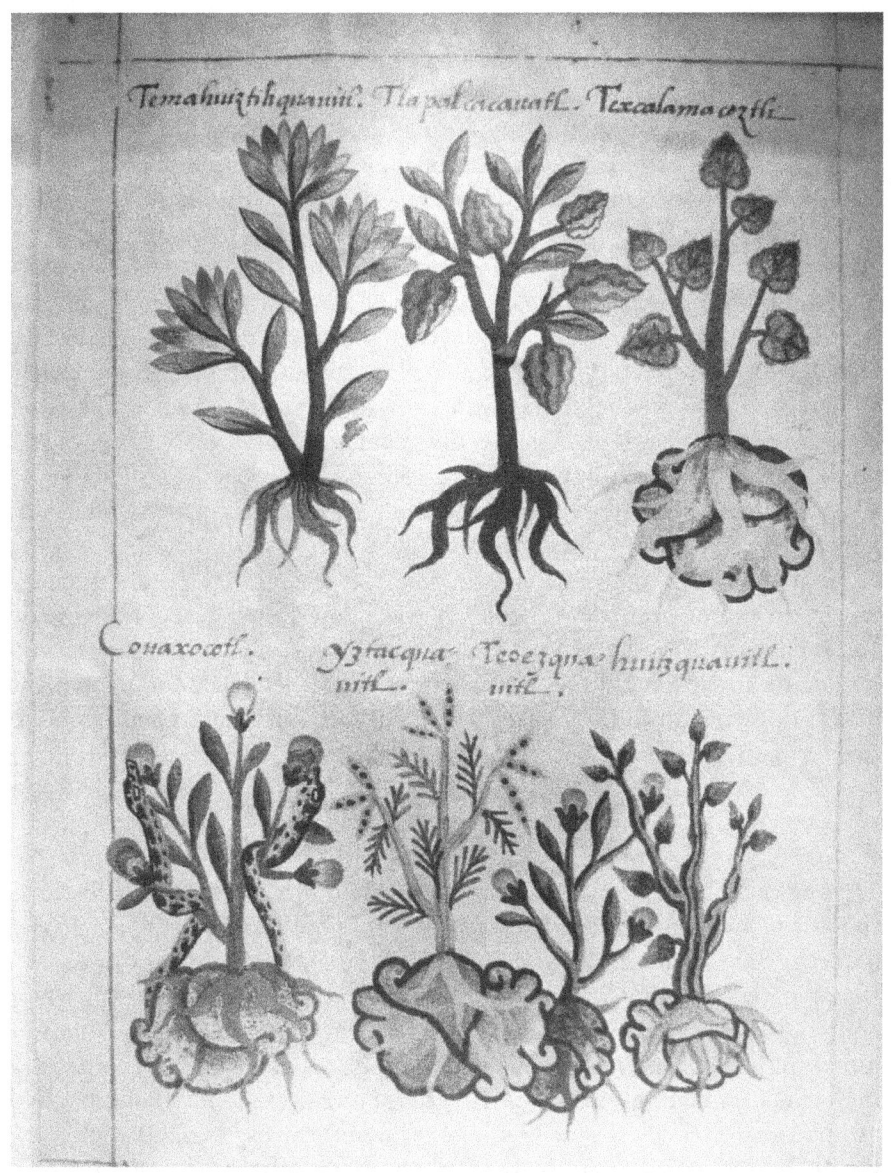

Figure 7.2. Early on, Spaniards were interested in the medicinal properties of New World flora. This page from a mid-sixteenth-century manuscript identifies healing herbs through a series of captioned drawings. Originally written in Nahuatl by a native convert, this small book was translated into Latin by Juan Badiano of the College of Santa Cruz. It is the first illustrated text of native botany in Mexico and documents a total of 250 herbs commonly used by the Aztecs.
Source: Cholula Regional Museum, Cholula.

headed that swallowing poison is a bad idea). While much has been written to celebrate the wisdom of native remedies—such as quinine from the bark of the cinchona tree to mitigate the effects of malaria—in truth, most indigenous practices were little more than superstition. Swallowing crushed rose flowers and seedlings for headaches might have had a placebo effect, but applying fresh human feces to scorpion bites is singularly ill-advised, and concocting a paste of ground earthworms and wine to treat a toothache brings little relief, unless the patient can get intoxicated. Waving a tapir's hoof in front of an epileptic is useless. Urine for eye infections might actually have sometimes worked because of the high sodium sulfide and acid content.

For mental and social well-being, black magic and witchcraft were widely employed. These practices empowered lower-class women who, with convincing demeanor and some luck, could develop robust clienteles. Spells and potions existed to control the actions of others—to woo a lover, manipulate a spouse, or torment an adversary. One remedy to cure a male's unfaithfulness involved slipping drops of menstrual blood into his drinks. Card reading supposedly allowed soothsayers, often female, to divine the future. Anticipating events through the stars (astrology) was widely deemed valid, even by the better educated. The church viewed women as inclined to irrationality, and its penalties for practicing witchcraft were typically lenient. More prominent males, however, were not to partake in the black arts and could be quite severely punished by the church for doing so.

Preserving Societal Order

The "enforcer" of Catholic and social orthodoxy was the Holy Office of the Inquisition, which arrived in Mexico in 1570. Inquisitional clergy sought out and checked social excesses via cases relating to either blasphemy or heresy. Blasphemous actions involved insulting the symbols of the Christian faith or church. Many of these types of cases might seem trivial to us today. One colonial got in trouble for using a cross as a drying rack for chilies. Another was prosecuted for stating in public that papal pronouncements should be used as toilet paper. Soldiers predictably often found themselves under scrutiny. One band of bored conscripts spent an afternoon lobbing rocks at a nearby cross—a "no-no" that aroused the disapproval of the Inquisitors. Much more serious was the charge of heresy, which could result in harsh sentences or capital punishment. Protestants were by definition guilty and were readily prosecuted, especially in the late sixteenth century. Jews were also in danger. Many Jews fled to Mexico and secretly practiced their faith after Spain banned Judaism under the devout monarchs Ferdinand and Isabella. Heretics were often compelled to confess their guilt through torture—such "proof" was admissible in inquisitorial courts. The Holy Office carried out punishments in public, through an Act of Faith (*auto de fe*) spectacle held in town squares like Mexico City's Alameda. The solemn parading of penitents drew large crowds of onlookers, with pomp and ceremony leading up to climactic acts of contrition, most commonly floggings but occasionally an execution by burning at the stake.

Most colonials found the Holy Office a benign and even positive institution. It defended social mores and a code of public decency of which most approved. For any victims, the slow grind of the bureaucracy was often more damning than actual punishment. Cases dragged on for months and even years, a time lapse that could become life-threatening for those stuck in unsanitary and darkened dungeons. Only a very small number of citizens faced investigation, as prosecutors and staff were limited in number and badly overstretched. Indigenous peoples were exempt, assumed by Spanish authorities to be at best child-like and inclined toward foolishness. In sum, few colonials had any reason to expect the Inquisition.

Despite the power of the church, the prestige of the viceroy, and the passing of the often out-of-control encomendero class, the middle period of the colonial era saw periodic unrest, some of which was dramatic. On the periphery, where settler numbers were low, native peoples occasionally challenged royal authority through rebellion. The most famous incident occurred in Nuevo Mexico, among the Pueblo first encountered by Vázquez de Coronado. Here, Franciscan friars had savagely punished "backsliding" natives who clung tenaciously to their pre-contact religious practices, flogging their former priests until flesh turned to bloody pulp. A shaman named Popé, himself brutally whipped, preached that if the whites were expelled, the former gods would return and bless the people. Frequent enslavement also alienated the Pueblo. D-Day in Nuevo Mexico was August 10, 1680. When Friar Juan Pío arrived in the village of Tesuque to perform mass, he found his parishioners waiting outside the church, wearing war paint. After reputedly asking, "Why my Children, have you gone mad?," he died in a flurry of arrows. Other priests suffered more gruesome fates; one was tied to the back of a pig and slowly beaten to death. Laying siege to Santa Fe, the Pueblo drove the entire white population away and ruled themselves for over a decade. Of course, a cruel retribution followed when the Spaniards returned.

Sometimes colonial unrest was nearly spontaneous. Such was the case in 1692, when grain shortages in Mexico City triggered what is known as the Great Corn Riot. Months of drought (which the poor blamed on a passing comet) fueled weeks of inflation; by early summer, with storage bins empty, crowds suddenly took to the streets. First appealing to the archbishop, who turned them away, they approached the palace, only to find that the viceroy was absent. Enraged, they set the building on fire, then began a looting spree downtown. Though lasting only two days, the incident alarmed authorities, who noted the speed with which civic order had collapsed. Weeks of investigations and trials followed, with ten citizens executed by the state, most of the rioters coming from the ranks of artisans and the low-skill employed, including porters.

Despite peripheral rebellions and periodic civil discord, much of the colonial era was in fact peaceful. Passing generations weakened the divisive distinction between conquered Native American and conquering Spaniard, though as demographic recovery took hold in the mid-seventeenth century racial cognizance actually increased. Whites became obsessed with blood purity as the mestizo population flourished. Many disdained mestizos as much as the indigenous, both commonly living in abject poverty. The rising importance of money also altered values, increasing social regard for the wealthy. Despite it all, by the end of the colonial period Mexico would still be overwhelmingly indigenous, poor, and rural. With six million inhabitants in 1810, roughly 60 percent were Native American, 20 percent mestizo, and 20 percent white. Critical new tensions, between Spaniards and the numerically superior creoles, would define the last century of imperial rule.

CHAPTER EIGHT

Late Colonial Reform and Revolt

Over time, colonies invariably develop their own identity. Traditional Spanish theater persisted in Mexico through the breadth of the colonial era, with accompanying orchestral music typically provided via a combination of violins, guitars, and a harp. In the late eighteenth century colonials in west-central Mexico adapted this model to facilitate folk music, creating small ensembles that performed lively tunes celebrating life in the countryside. Their collection of instruments came to include an oversized *guitarrón* (its deep shell providing a bass sound) and a high-pitched stringed instrument with a rounded back called a *vihuela*. Harps, expensive and awkward to transport, gave way to melodic trumpets, and soon the distinctively Mexican *mariachi* band took shape. Like in music, Mexico was politically finding its way and coming of age in the eighteenth century, too. Increasingly, a break with the Mother Country was just a matter of time.

The Bourbons Revive Their Empire

New ideas came to the fore in mid-eighteenth-century Europe that were destined to profoundly affect colonial life. Political and philosophical thinkers, especially in France, questioned monarchy and doubted the veracity of orthodox Christianity; economic theorists studied market economics and argued for changes in tax and trade policies. Though most of these thinkers hailed from northern Europe, their ideas—the basis of the Enlightenment—filtered into Spain. In 1713 a French noble acquired the Spanish throne through marriage and war, establishing the Bourbon dynasty. Hence, mid-century policy adjustments are termed the Bourbon Reforms.

In economic policies the crown's motives were simple: it sought to boost productivity and increase revenue. Though biased toward the Mother Country, many of the changes were practical and still positive for Mexico. Like the British with their North American colonies, the Spanish levied new duties and streamlined tax collection. Tariffs on trade had suffered for decades from a robust black market dominated by English merchant ships. The Bourbons cut tariffs, improved customs collection, and—after much colonial lobbying—opened new ports to legal trade. Revenues rose. Similarly, policymakers reduced taxes on mining while encouraging innovation and new technology. The establishment of a College of Mines in Mexico City led to advancements, particularly in drainage techniques, through the instruction of engineers from Prussia. Officials also restructured the royal monopoly on mercury, with production increasing even as prices declined. All this fueled a revival in the mines. A well-positioned and entrepreneurial Spanish noble, the Conde de Regla, used new methods to revive one of Mexico's longest-running mines, the Real del Monte near Pachuca. By late in life he might well have become the Western world's richest man. The great La Valenciana mine in Guanajuato also revived in the 1780s, employing nearly three thousand miners.

As with the British in North America, Spanish officials were anxious to exert more direct political control in their colonies. Over two and a half centuries, more and more creoles had obtained high political office. They were predictably tied to local interests, and with time their loyalty to Spain had diminished. The purchasing of political offices became widespread, with even the viceregal position eventually obtained by the highest bidder. Corruption flourished. The success of the American Revolution triggered further alarm in Spain. It was clearly vital to keep New Spain on an even tighter leash. Hence, the Bourbons consolidated lesser tiers of colonial offices and created a new system of districts called *intendencies* along the seventeenth-century French model. Mexico received twelve districts and intendants, the officeholders all Spaniards. Down the chain of the political pyramid that remained, the crown and the intendants saw to the appointment of hundreds of additional patriotic Spaniards.

Another avenue for enhancing oversight was the audit. Spain had a long political tradition of administrative "visits," where a Spanish official would arrive and "check the books," study legal decisions, question subordinates, and if necessary clean house. Backed by royal authority, a "visitor" could be quite intimidating and, if loyal and ambitious, very thorough. The frequency and intensity of administrative visits increased in the mid-eighteenth century. In 1765 José de Gálvez, a confidant of the king himself, arrived in Mexico City and stayed for six years as he micromanaged happenings at the viceregal level. To the chagrin of many creole officials, he sniffed out corruption and ensured that tax receipts were better documented.

In keeping with a rising anticlericalism in Enlightenment Europe, the Bourbon kings placed new restrictions on the church. They reduced the number and frequency of public religious ceremonies and festivals. They discouraged construction of new convents, and through multiple other means tried to reduce the overall number of mendicant clergy, though the mission-minded Franciscan Order continued to prosper. Most controversially, they ordered all Jesuit priests out of New Spain (and all of Latin America) in 1767. The Jesuit Order was troubling to Spanish officialdom, given its allegiance to the pope instead of the king. It had amassed wealth and influence, and had connections to Mexico's creole elite through its many prestigious schools, which educated the sons of the rich. The expulsion was unpopular with colonials, a few of whom had to say a lifelong "good-bye" to a departing relative who served in the order.

Popular religious devotion shifted in the mid-eighteenth century with the rise of the cult of the Virgin of Guadalupe, which has remained ubiquitous in Mexico ever since. Early in the century the church completed a new Baroque basilica to house the prized work of art, which encouraged more pilgrimage to the site. The Virgin's popularity also rose after parading the old portrait through the streets of Mexico City during a dreadful 1736–1738 yellow fever epidemic. Her presence seemed to help—the epidemic eventually subsided. As faith in the Virgin flourished, clerics successfully raised funds for the construction of a series of small chapels atop and astride the hillside of her fabled sixteenth-century visitation.

Finally, for the Bourbons, security concerns became preeminent in the mid-to-late eighteenth century. Officials took special care to strengthen coastal defenses, including improvements at the port of Veracruz. Like the British, Spain dispatched troops to its colonies, maintaining small contingents of trained soldiers under each intendant. Heavy cannons from the Mother Country arrived as well, most notably scores of fortress-enhancing "Tigers," manned by crews trained at a special artillery school. But improved forts and especially standing garrisons cost money; by the 1790s nearly half of the royal expenditures in New Spain were on defense.

Expansion on the Northern Frontier

Alarmed by the expansion of the break-away English colonies in North America, Spain took steps to survey and secure its northernmost boundaries.

Figure 8.1. The bulky Baroque Jesuit Church of Santo Domingo in Zacatecas sat empty for decades after the order's 1767 expulsion, one reason its marvelous Churrigueresque retablos are in such excellent condition. At the center of this gold leaf–covered masterpiece is a representation of the Virgin of Guadalupe, which reflects the rising popularity of the cult at the time of the retablo's construction in the 1750s.

It constructed forts, known as *presidios*, in the region called Tejas, and sent explorers into the mountains and deserts of the still largely unknown northwest. In California in 1776, a priest on such an expedition beheld white peaks in the distance and christened them in his diary the Sierra Nevada (Snowy Mountains). Another expedition brought the first Spaniards into what would become Utah, southwestern Colorado, and Arizona north of the Grand Canyon. This in turn led to the creation of the Old Spanish Trail in the early nineteenth century, a wagon road that ran from Santa Fe through present-day Utah and Nevada into California.

The northeasterly region of Tejas was the target of the most significant efforts along the frontier, a 1685 French attempt under Sieur de LaSalle to establish a settlement on its coast having generated anxiety. Here, church and state worked hand in hand. The Franciscan Order sent forth friars to convert semi-nomadic natives, establishing a couple dozen missions within proximity of several new presidios. The friars wooed the indigenous to their outposts by offering food, clothing, and protection, though they typically first pursued the strongest and most popular tribes with the hope that lesser groups would then follow. They were heartened when some natives told them a Woman in Blue had appeared, prophesying the arrival of holy men. With adequate converts, the Franciscans proceeded to construct stone churches, adorned with statues and paintings, some named after the recently canonized Franciscan St. John Capistrano. They often erected large wooden crosses atop ridges and near the mouths of rivers. But the Tejas missions still faced the danger of foreign incursions and the sometimes nefarious activities of French traders operating out of nearby Louisiana. The friars were also distraught by the presence of rowdy and undisciplined soldiers, covetous settlers (most from the Canary Islands) who sought free native labor, and unmarried males from among both groups who might take advantage of young women. Problems befuddled the Tejas missions, though the Spanish penetration into Tejas did deter Anglo-French expansion westward.

There has long been debate among historians about the effect of the Bourbon Reforms. There is no doubt that, both in New Spain and nearly all of Latin America, the economy came to life in the late eighteenth century, but why? Everywhere, there was a demographic revival, as birth rates recovered from the mid-seventeenth-century nadir. Population growth might well have fueled the economic surge as much as policy changes. It certainly drove up food prices. Drought in the early 1780s triggered serious malnutrition in much of Mexico for several years. Inflation in foodstuffs took hold, prices rising beyond wage growth for the next three decades. With more people competing for resources, too, competition and lawsuits increased over water rights and land. The rich were best poised to win these often-protracted battles.

The concentration of land into the hands of the wealthy continued in the eighteenth century, especially in the dry, often desert-like far north, where estates grew to astounding proportions. By the 1760s a family named Aguayo, in northeastern New Spain (in the present-day Mexican state of Coahuila), owned 14,700,000 acres—an area bigger than New Jersey. The hacienda had thousands of horses and mules and, at any given time, about a quarter million sheep. It employed a private cavalry to protect its animals from roving bands of Apaches. Twelve hundred souls lived in a town at the center of the estate, many working in a woolen-producing textile mill. Hundreds of others tended two hundred thousand grapevines that produced wine for consumption in central Mexico.

Near the Aguayo hacienda lived a trio of brothers named Sánchez Navarro, led by the eldest, a priest named José Miguel. Starting with a dry goods store, these ambitious young men built up a network of oxcart trade routes. José Miguel received a contract from the regional bishop to collect the church tax, earning 8 percent of it for his efforts, while also positioning himself to speculate in the livestock market as he possessed the tithe—most typically paid in the form of animals. In time, he and his brothers began to invest in land, while the youngest married into wealth and later inherited hundreds of thousands of acres. By the early nineteenth century, the Sánchez Navarro estate eclipsed that of the Aguayos in size, and eventually this family became the greatest landowners in the history of Latin America.

Though spectacularly large, the late colonial haciendas of the far north were more akin to giant ranches than farms. They often had to purchase grain from centrally located estates, as the arid region offered few options for crop cultivation. Water was of such value that grants of usage were often more valued than those for the land itself. Irrigation from a few shallow rivers was timed down to the hour, and seasonal droughts could spell disaster, especially for smaller estates that lacked cash reserves. Owners in the north networked through a cattleman's guild, which regulated irrigation and grazing rights, registered brands, and lobbied local and regional officials. Owners also coordinated their activities enough to discourage vagabonds and track down fugitive workers, their workforce held in debt peonage—as in the interior of Mexico. Shepherds of course had an easy time running away, but to where? Other owners would not hire them if their fugitive status was known, while in towns authorities were suspicious of lone newcomers, who otherwise might be forcibly drafted into the militia.

The constant danger of semi-nomadic natives in the far north also deterred a transient lifestyle. Indigenous people, often displaced from their lands, were a constant threat to herds—especially to horses and mules—

which they coveted both for possession and for their meat. Relentless and tenacious, in the province of Coahuila in the year 1790 alone, Apaches killed forty settlers and stole over eight hundred horses. Most Apaches cared very little for sheep, but coyotes and wolves constantly preyed on the flocks, while a badly timed freeze could kill tender lambs by the thousands. Cattle rustling was as often committed by poor settlers as by natives. If captured, rustlers were sometimes forced to work for the aggrieved hacendado, laboring to his satisfaction until he was certain that they would never steal again.

Father Hidalgo Leads a Revolt

If the American Revolution sent a chill through the Imperial Palace in Madrid, the French Revolution cast it into a deep freeze. A host of novel ideas about popular sovereignty, natural rights, and republican government rippled through the Western world. The internet of the age was the book, and a small literate segment of colonial society gravitated toward these outlawed publications, acquiring them with relative ease despite the best efforts of the Inquisition. The triumph of Napoleon Bonaparte, and his subsequent 1808 invasion of Spain and deposition of the king in favor of his brother, only added to the uncertainty and momentum for change. In the small town of Dolores, in the Bajío, a worldly minded creole priest named Miguel Hidalgo prolifically read the controversial literature emanating from Europe. He joined a literary club and discussed these new ideas with others, among them a creole cavalry officer named Ignacio Allende. Taking the next step, the group collected arms and prepared to unleash a revolt. When authorities got wind of their plans, Hidalgo threw all hesitancy aside. Ringing the bells of his church, he rallied his dark-skinned parishioners with an emotional speech and began marching them through the countryside in protest. A persistent famine in the region fed discontent, and when Father Hidalgo adopted the image of the Virgin of Guadalupe as his icon, hundreds, then thousands, flocked to his cause.

The natural target for the growing mob's ire was the intendancy town of Guanajuato. Here as officeholder, ironically, was Juan Antonio de Riaño, an unusually progressive Spaniard who had been reading the controversial new literature himself. Assigned to the region since 1792, Riaño had met Hidalgo on several occasions and even hosted him once in his house. In Guanajuato, Riaño was reasonably popular with the creole elite, overseeing a flood-control project and providing business incentives to mine owners. The hardworking intendant's latest undertaking was construction of a massive state-of-the-art granary in the center of town. Now, with the news of

Hidalgo's approaching horde, terrified Spaniards fled into the recently completed, thick-walled structure, along with Riaño himself.

Under Riaño's command was a modest garrison of two hundred troops. These faced the onslaught of some fifteen thousand dark-skinned rebels, most armed only with rocks and slings. Thousands were unemployed miners—disrupted mercury shipments from war-ravaged Europe having stifled the local economy. Racial and class tensions were at play. Atop nearby buildings, Hidalgo and Allende (along with his seventy-five light-skinned cavalrymen) directed the attack. Riaño's troops had a couple of artillery pieces, and at a critical juncture in the struggle the intendant himself emerged in an outer courtyard to supervise the repositioning of them. An entirely lucky shot from one of Allende's cavalrymen sank a ball into the intendant's left eye, killing him instantly.

Riaño's sudden death unnerved the granary's defenders. Indeed, the seemingly impenetrable structure had a couple of noteworthy flaws. Its walls were too thick for royalist troops to easily position their long muskets. When they leaned out over the edges to fire, they were inevitably struck by small slingshot-launched rocks—what locals called *matacanas* (literally "kill dogs"), small rounded stones used by local herdsmen to drive off coyotes. And though the granary's massive walls were made of stone, its giant doors were wooden. According to revolutionary folklore, a brave and unusually strong Native American named Pipila protected himself with a stone slab, reaching the doors and setting them on fire. Though Pipila's very existence is historically in doubt, there is no debate over what subsequently happened: when the giant doors burned and fell inward, thousands of rebels poured into the granary and massacred the mostly light-skinned inhabitants. A sacking of the town of Guanajuato soon followed.

The orgy of violence lasted for a couple of days, ending more through fatigue than a command decision. Indeed, neither Hidalgo nor Allende appeared to have much control over their "army," which in its frenzy had killed several of Guanajuato's creole citizens. We have no written record of what Hidalgo was thinking at this point, but subsequent events suggest that these happenings greatly troubled him. Word of the massacre spread to Mexico City, where its large creole population cast their support behind the governing authorities. The viceroy consolidated troops and mustered an army of several thousand. On the outskirts of the capital in late October, these faced tens of thousands of dark-skinned rebels, again poorly armed, in pitched battle. After the first day it was clear that the rebels would eventually overwhelm the royalists by sheer numbers, but at nightfall, as fighting temporarily subsided, Hidalgo inexplicably ordered a full retreat. Allende, operating independently, was appalled upon receiving word of the order and urged him to reverse course and pursue the attack promptly at dawn. The priest refused. The feverish coalescing of Hidalgo's forces was now matched by its rapid disintegration. Likely perceiving the whole ordeal as more of a righteous crusade than a long-term political project, the poor simply went home. Reviving the revolution's fortunes proved impossible. Hidalgo and Allende fled into the distant north with ever diminishing bands of followers. Hunted down, Allende was summarily shot. Hidalgo, as a priest, was turned over to the Inquisition. Tried and defrocked, he too faced the firing squad. His decapitated head was then stuck on a pike and hung atop Guanajuato's granary.

Pressed by the swift current of events, Hidalgo and Allende never issued a formal declaration, but both men clearly aspired to Mexican independence. In practical terms, their revolt was more or less an unnerving race war. Wealthy whites in Mexico City and elsewhere remained uneasy about the prospect of insurrection for years to come. Ardent royalists drew on these insecurities, while seeking to tighten control and buttress loyalty to Spain—especially in the wake of the defeat of Napoleon and restoration of the Bourbon monarchy in Spain. Royalists found their champion in Félix María Calleja del Rey. As the intendant of San Luis Potosí, Calleja del Rey

Figure 8.2. The site where Miguel Hidalgo was executed lies within the confines of today's Chihuahua (state) Palace of Government. It is memorialized with a small museum and this mural by Aarón Piña Mora. Shot in the back of the skull, Hidalgo's head was severed and shipped to Guanajuato, where it hung on a post as a warning to other would-be revolutionaries. His corpse was quietly interred in a Jesuit chapel across the street from the palace.
Source: Palacio del Gobierno, Chihuahua City.

had averted a further disaster during Hidalgo's revolt. His was geographically the largest and strategically one of the most important intendancies, encompassing the entire northeast, from the city of San Luis Potosí to the Tejas frontier with French Louisiana. He had astutely anticipated trouble and set up a web of spies throughout the intendancy. By monitoring book sales, infiltrating "literary" clubs, and gathering reports on literate citizens, he was in a position to squash insurrection when Hidalgo's revolt started. At his instructions, authorities summarily arrested presumed troublemakers and secured armories and treasuries. The intendancy stayed solidly royalist, and Hidalgo could neither draw on its resources nor later retreat into it in order to salvage his waning rebellion.

Recognized for his acumen, Calleja del Rey was appointed viceroy in 1813. He applied his aggressive model of surveillance to all of New Spain. The effort paid dividends: attempts to continue some type of insurrection were ultimately limited to the remote and mountainous south. Here, a former muleteer-turned-priest, José María Morelos, mustered only a modest following. He convened an assembly that formally declared Mexican independence, but militarily he could do little in the face of assertive royalist forces, the temporary capture of Oaxaca City his only real success. Calleja del Rey pressed his field commanders to hunt down the rebels without mercy, and in 1815 a captured Morelos was summarily tried and shot. Morelos's sidekick assumed rebel command. Adopting the *nom de guerre* of Guadalupe Victoria ("Guadalupe" appropriating the cult of the Virgin, combined with "victory"), he boldly attempted to transfer the rebel cause to the coastal region near Veracruz. These efforts faltered, and within a short time he was isolated and on the run. But Calleja del Rey had made many enemies among Mexico City's creole elite. His strong-arm tactics, coupled with a fondness for exiling persons of doubtful loyalty to the Philippines, inspired a petition to force his recall. The crown replaced him in 1816, yet the fires of rebellion were by then almost completely out. Mexico would have to gain its independence by other, unexpected means.

PART III

INDEPENDENCE AND MODERNITY

CHAPTER NINE

The Insurmountable Divide

It was a long and twisted road, from September 1810, when Miguel Hidalgo rang his church bells, to the sequence of events that ultimately delivered Mexican independence a decade later. After years of intermittent fighting, royalist troops were tired of garrisoning native towns and chasing rebels around the southern mountains. In 1820 news reached Mexico of a military coup in Spain that had forced a constitutional monarchy upon the king. Far more damning were the successful independence revolts throughout South America. Was Mexico really prepared to remain a royalist holdout? The Americas were coming of age, siblings were leaving home, and Mother Spain's radiant glory was clearly passing. An ambitious creole-royalist army officer, Agustín de Iturbide, led a large column into the field but secretly began to parley with the rebel leader, Vicente Guerrero. In a dramatic *volt face* he turned back on the capital, announcing that his command now constituted an Army of Three Guarantees. Though he rather muddled his pronouncement (conveniently, with regard to race), Iturbide assured Mexicans of their sudden and irreversible independence, the primacy of the Catholic religion, and the equality of all—but especially with regard to the political status and rights of all native-born creoles. The viceregal government collapsed as Iturbide's army approached Mexico City, and thus in a manner that Hidalgo could never have imagined, Mexico became independent.

Two Men of Ambition

If anything defined Iturbide, it was ambition. The sudden demise of royal authority left a power vacuum that hundreds of elated creoles scurried to fill. There was great excitement but also fierce competition for political control. A regency of five men, headed by Iturbide, took the reins of governance. A new constitutional assembly also convened. That assembly functioned like a congress, but there was almost no revenue and the bureaucracy sputtered haltingly. After months of turmoil, it appeared that the assembly-congress was about to convert Mexico into a republic, but troops loyal to Iturbide staged demonstrations and intimidated legislators into declaring an empire in the Napoleonic tradition. The degree to which Iturbide himself might have arranged for the military agitation has long been debated, but in his defense,

Figure 9.1. An artist's portrayal of Agustín de Iturbide's triumphant reentry into Mexico City. After more than a decade of turmoil, the opportunistic Iturbide ended the Wars of Independence with a bloodless coup, dislodging the royalists by returning his command to the capital unopposed. This fanciful rendition shows grand city gates (which did not exist) opened in welcome and rows of mounted soldiers following their triumphant champion and his cohort.
Source: Museo Nacional de las Intervenciones, Mexico City.

he was the man who almost single-handedly gave Mexico its independence and, if there was to be an empire, he was the most logical choice to lead it.

As in the young United States, and elsewhere in Latin America, the rich interpreted the *real* meaning of independence as freedom from paying taxes. During the 1810s revenue from the mines declined precipitously, in part due to tax evasion, though also because production was sagging—among other problems, rebels had frequently flooded the mines. Government coffers were empty, and Iturbide would not—and realistically could not—take the political risks necessary to assert taxing authority. The only reliable source of revenue was the customs duties at the major port of Veracruz. Unfortunately for Iturbide, a man of equal ambition named Antonio López de Santa Anna commanded troops and oversaw finances at Veracruz. When Iturbide tried to remove him from his post, Santa Anna issued a *plan*—a document announcing insubordination in a quest for political change. Shrewdly calling for the restoration of the since-disbanded congress, he appealed to republicans who resented Iturbide's usurpation of power. Luminaries of the independence struggle, Guadalupe Victoria and Vicente Guerrero, supported him. Iturbide's empire thus lasted only ten months, as the would-be Napoleon of Mexico took ship to Europe and sailed into exile.

Santa Anna was a dashing and charismatic figure, with striking good looks. By all accounts a charmer of women and suave host of lively parties, he made favorable impressions on people. Born to a middle-class family with six siblings in the town of Xalapa (famed for its xalapeño peppers), he had joined the army at age sixteen and, as an officer eleven years later, followed Iturbide in revolt. Now, he dislodged him. More politically astute than Iturbide, Santa Anna's dominating influence on Mexico would last for over three decades. The vain Iturbide, in contrast, was remarkably inept at reading the political tea leaves. In an Italian exile he grew restless and convinced himself that he was misunderstood and would be favorably received if he returned to his homeland. Within days after landing in Mexico, in 1824, he was taken out and shot on orders of the central government.

Liberals and Conservatives Endlessly Feud

It was fairly easy to oust someone from power, but governing was another matter. Deep cleavages within Mexican society persisted, most notably along lines of race and class. Santa Anna understood that he needed to bide his time in the turbulent decade of the 1820s, political winds constantly changing direction. In the wake of Iturbide's ouster, egotistical creole elites vied endlessly for control. No one seemed willing to give ground, and as two competing camps coalesced, few were prepared to try to understand the other side. The two groups were at least outwardly defined by ideology: one professed a classical liberalism in keeping with the values of the Enlightenment; the other clung to a Hispanic conservatism that leaned toward strong central government and preservation of the status of the Catholic Church.

Liberals believed that a new era of social progress was imminent with the triumph of liberty and through republican governance that would diminish the "negative" influence of the church. They heralded the political example of the United States and readily socialized with the U.S. ambassador to Mexico, Joel Poinsett, who unabashedly attempted to influence Mexican politics (even as a distinctive flower shipped back to the United States was named after him). Liberalism's intellectual icon was José María Luis Mora. Drawing on the writings of Frenchman Benjamin Constant, Mora advocated an elitist variation of republican rule that would ensure the status of powerful landholders. He rejected the notion of popular sovereignty (the idea that ultimate political power was vested in the people) and repudiated "democracy of the common man," as advocated at the time by Andrew Jackson. Less theoretical was another liberal thinker, Miguel Ramos Arizpe, who articulated the merits of a federalist system of decentralized states.

The counterpoint to liberalism was conservatism that, in its bias for Catholicism, was loath to celebrate the accomplishments of the protestant-dominated United States. Despite the recent schism with Spain, conservatives still valued their Hispanic heritage. They perceived that rupturing a three-century-long tradition of centralized power could not be easily or safely done, that tearing up age-old foundations could in fact be dangerous. Among their advocates was Servando Teresa de Mier, a creole cleric with impeccable independence credentials. Arrested in 1817 for distributing seditious literature, he rotted in a prison cell in Spanish Cuba at the time of Iturbide's coup, able to escape and return home soon thereafter. Mier argued, probably correctly, that only a strong centralized government could nurture a young Mexico and that the danger of anarchy was a greater threat than an aristocratic abuse of power. Some fellow conservatives went even farther, still insisting on monarchy, though the debacle under Iturbide discredited their position in the short term.

While his uprising triggered the collapse of the Iturbide regime, the astute Santa Anna quickly stepped aside from all of the debates in Mexico City. Liberals in the capital rallied and prepared to take control under a federalist constitution, ratified in 1824 and written almost exclusively by Ramos Arizpe. Following the American example, the document established nineteen states with governors and legislatures, the latter of which were to elect the president. It retained Catholicism as the sole religion, however, and said nothing to undermine special legal rights held by priests and army officers — among those, exemption from trial in civilian courts. As they adopted their constitution, liberals also drafted a law that created a civic militia comprised of nearly all adult males. Mindful that Iturbide had come to power—and been ousted—by troops, they hoped that the establishment of a militia could counter the rising nefarious influence of the army. Yet lacking sufficient arms and funds, the militia existed merely on paper.

With much fanfare, liberals disinterred Miguel Hidalgo's headless corpse from a small Jesuit chapel in Chihuahua City. Along with his head (which had been displayed in Guanajuato and later buried), the body was laid to rest at the base of the Altarscreen of the Kings in Mexico City's cathedral in a solemn ceremony. Such pageantry was perhaps helpful; shortly thereafter, the selection of a first constitutional president went well. State legislatures elected Guadalupe Victoria, the guerrilla fighter, who had come out of hiding when Iturbide betrayed the royalist cause in 1821, turning himself over to Santa Anna in Veracruz—who was startled to first encounter him buck naked. In a gesture of honor, Santa Anna had submitted his command to Victoria's authority. Now, Victoria became the first president of Mexico with the influential officer's blessing and the solid support of the liberal side of the political elite.

For his part, while president, Victoria tried his best to remain aloof from a widening liberal-conservative divide. This effort is undoubtedly what allowed him to serve out his entire four-year term—the only president to do so for the next forty-three years. As in the United States, the 1824 constitution allowed for a vice president of separate political affiliation. Victoria's was a conservative—a wealthy landowner named Nicolás Bravo. In 1827 Bravo had attempted to stage a coup, but when it failed, he was forced into exile. The proclivity of Mexico's creole elite to seek power instead of preserve order continued into the republican age.

In economic matters, Victoria's administration was weak and could do very little. The silver-mining industry, which accounted for the vast majority of colonial government revenue, failed to recover. Banks and commercial houses withheld capital since the start of independence unrest, and foreign investment was nonexistent. The money supply contracted, and Mexico entered a deflationary spiral. Trade, which could have generated revenue, continued to languish. While widespread destruction from the independence struggle is often overplayed (most fighting was in the marginal south, while Hidalgo's revolt was quickly over), brigands had flourished since the early 1810s and caused havoc. As a rebel fighter, Victoria himself had unwittingly helped destabilize the critical region between Veracruz and Puebla. Faced with few alternatives, his government ultimately turned to London banks, which extended loans at usurious rates. Most of the money went to paying bureaucratic salaries and, most ominously, the still numerous troops barracked in and around Mexico City.

Partisan animosities ever increasing, a new political crisis was perhaps unavoidable, but it was singularly unfortunate for Mexico that the 1828 election came down to just a few contested votes. Over several days of heated debate, liberals cajoled and bribed army officers in order to arrange the victory of Vicente Guerrero, who surely had more name recognition than his cheated conservative opponent. A mestizo of dark skin, tall in stature with penetrating eyes (along with a high-pitched and grating voice), Guerrero subsequently decreed the expulsion of all Spaniards in 1829. Popular reaction to the move was mixed. Spain took offense and dispatched a small army to Mexico, landing it at the minor Gulf port of Tampico in the sweltering heat of August. What, exactly, the Spanish government expected this modest force to do is uncertain, but its appearance stunned Mexico's political class. From his home base in Veracruz, Santa Anna rushed northward and took command of Mexican forces. In a pattern of field command that would repeat itself, the headstrong officer launched an audacious assault, instead of waiting the invaders out in a safely predictable siege. A tropical hurricane buffeted the coast at the very hour of battle. Bewildered and overcome, the Spaniards surrendered; Santa Anna's fame grew exponentially.

In contrast, President Guerrero faced rising opposition. With conservatives plotting against him and blocking policy initiatives, he temporarily disbanded congress. His treasury minister, an innovative and thoughtful Lorenzo de Zavala (whom Santa Anna disliked), implemented a progressive income tax. More controversially, Zavala sold off some church properties that the government had acquired during the course of the independence struggle. A conservative vice president, Anastasio Bustamante, soon plotted with the former vice president, Nicolás Bravo (who had returned from exile), and orchestrated a successful revolt. Santa Anna stayed clear of the affair, though rumors of his behind-the-scenes involvement circulated.

With partisanship at a fever pitch, Bustamante in turn practiced a distinctly dictatorial mode of governance. A creole medical doctor and military officer during the independence era who—like so many others—switched allegiance during Iturbide's revolt, he assumed all legislative powers and ruled by executive decree, even replacing liberal officials from posts in state governments. When the dark-skinned Guerrero attempted to launch a counter revolt from his base in southern Mexico, he was hunted down and executed.

Figure 9.2. Antonio López de Santa Anna dominated Mexican political life for over three decades. A nationalist before Mexican nationalism took hold, he passionately defended his vulnerable country. Conversely, his autocratic tendencies and penchant for military action made him a mediocre civil administrator. Tall and commanding, this famous portrait correctly captures his dapper looks and personal magnetism.
Source: Museo Nacional de las Intervenciones, Mexico City.

Rivalries were turning into feuds, political fights into vendettas. Guerrero's execution enraged liberals. An independence hero and former president, his stature surely warranted far more delicate handling. Liberals agitated for revenge. Opposition to Bustamante's dictatorship coalesced around Santa Anna, the "Hero of Tampico."

A short and nasty civil war erupted in the spring of 1832, Santa Anna's troops (ostensibly militiamen, but funded by expropriated customs duties at the port) charging into army parapets outside of Veracruz City. Triumphant, he subsequently won election to the presidency, but again—like a debutante refusing to take her first dance—withdrew to his stately Manga de Clavo hacienda while asking the new vice president, Valentín Gómez Farías, to govern on his behalf. For a year Gómez Farías obliged, himself pushed along by an assertive liberal congress bent on taking legislative initiative, especially with anti-clerical reforms. The mandatory church tax was abolished, mendicant clerics unbound from their oaths, and legal rights of priests reduced. The Jesuit Order was expelled for a second time, though relatively few had returned to Mexico in the interim. The government established a Ministry of Education and attempted to set up some public schools in the capital. Riskily, it cut the army's budget and reduced the number of standing troops. By mid-1934 a conservative backlash against these reforms gained momentum. Who stepped in to ride this rising tide of righteous indignation? None other than Antonio López de Santa Anna! The strongman, or *caudillo* in Latin parlance, returned to Mexico City and helped displace the very vice president he had empowered. He clearly felt that the legislature was out of control and that Gómez Farías had unbridled it too readily. Ultimately a military man who loved the trappings of army life and the exaltation of battle, he could not countenance the depreciation of the Mexican Army. Having long stood in the background of national politics, Santa Anna was now prepared to actively engage it. A period marked by his overt presence on the national stage began, as a long decade of divisive elite politics drew to a close.

And Life Goes On

It would be incorrect to assume that the political infighting of rich white men in Mexico City meant much to broader society. While it is a lasting tragedy that Mexico did not quickly stabilize in the wake of independence, for average folks throughout the vast country the political impasse meant little; daily life went on. At any given time in the 1820s and 1830s, a majority of people probably did not know who the president was, and most did not care.

In the early nineteenth century, Mexico was still overwhelmingly rural. Life was timeless. Most inhabitants hardly ever traveled during the course of their lives—save the daily walk to tend cornfields on the edge of a thousand ramshackle villages. Women rose early to grind tortillas on stone *metates* so that their husbands could carry a modest lunch in a knapsack and remain in the fields all day, albeit halting their work in the oppressive afternoon heat with the renowned *siesta*. In most native cultures, couples mated early, in their mid-teens, with the aspiration of many healthy children and ample grandchildren in old age. In the Bajío and north, the rural poor labored either permanently or temporarily on large haciendas. Conditions varied widely, with skilled workers, such as cowboys, able to make decent wages; sharecropping poor who rented seed and tools were perpetually in debt. Little had changed from the late colonial era. Wages tended to follow population density—the more people in a given area, the lower the wage. Planting and especially harvest seasons saw a flurry of activity, with hacienda workforces easily doubling or tripling.

All of Mexico was home to about seven million people in 1830, its population growing at less than 1 percent annually. Some areas lost people. Veracruz, due to disruptions from Guadalupe Victoria's rebels in the mid-1810s, experienced a sharp decline in economic activity (namely trade) and went from sixteen thousand residents in 1803 to just seven thousand in 1830. Mexico City had about 160,000 inhabitants. For centuries the largest metropolis in the Western Hemisphere, it had recently been overtaken by New York, thanks to an influx of mostly Irish immigrants into the North American seaport. Mexico City suffered terribly from poor drainage and sandy subsoil. During the late summer rainy season most of its streets turned to muck. Some flooded so badly that locals took to canoes as a mode of transport. Flooding moved raw sewage into homes and trash into neighborhoods. Cholera outbreaks followed. In 1833 some twenty thousand died—swept away by the same worldwide strain that had incubated in southern Russia. Some clerics complained that sin was the cause; others were not so sure. Child mortality rates in the first half of the nineteenth century improved, but still hovered at nearly 30 percent. Many poor could not afford the funerary blessing of a priest, hence small bodies were dumped in consecrated church atriums with little fanfare.

Foreign visitors were consistently appalled at Mexico City's filth. The poor especially bathed rarely, the markets filled with a collective human stench, Indians walking by in ragged clothes, with scabs, lice, and matted hair. But streets and markets were lively. Few residents had cooking facilities, so most purchased basic foodstuffs from vendors. Many of those were women, hawking tortillas and corn tamales. Melodic shouts and calls filled the air. While mules were used as beasts of burden, and carts rumbled over the stone-paved streets in the city's center, most transport was provided on the backs of hunched-over natives. Indians carried everything, from baskets laden heavy with fruit to large crates and slabs of wood, furnishings, and enormous flasks of potable water.

The rich of Mexico City lived in the center in mansions, much as they did in the colonial era. Several thousand residents had sufficient wealth so as to hire multiple servants. Women were most typically domestics, many as young as ten or twelve. These were predictably vulnerable to physical and more rarely sexual abuse, though conditions varied greatly by employer. The city's population was unusually skewed, with 58 percent female. Besides domestic service and street vending, women had some limited access to employment in artisans' shops. Underemployment and poverty were rampant. Wealthy women were sequestered in elite homes and avoided the congested and dirty streets, though they still ventured out frequently to church.

During Holy Week the entire city changed in tone, a great solemnity filling the air. On Palm Sunday throngs of people flocked into the metropolitan cathedral, so much so that trampling and injuries were not uncommon. One contemporary observer noted that the nave resembled a palm forest, seven-foot-high branches swaying by the thousands, wagonloads of palms having been brought up from the tropics for the celebration. On Good Friday, enormous crowds packed the churches. In the cathedral, dark-skinned masses pressed against one other in feverish anticipation of the procession of the cross and the arrival of the priests and archbishop. Communicants wept, profusely kissed the feet of Christ statues, and beheld in adoration images of the Virgin. Parish churches vied with one another in rich displays of candlelit, black shrouded altars. Services culminated with Easter Sunday, with each mass and every church and chapel overflowing, the rich seated prominently and dressed in their finest. Religious life brought a sense of deeper meaning and interrupted the tiresome grind of the poor for daily food and survival. It provided a transcendent hope that, clearly, Mexicans in the 1830s could not find in the political realm.

CHAPTER TEN

Showdown with the Americans

In the 1830s Mexico had a problem. Unwanted illegal immigrants were flooding across its borders from the United States. No matter what it did to stem the tide, the illegals kept coming. Despite the presence of the Sabine River, the border along the Louisiana territory was porous, and migrants from the American South coveted land in Tejas, much of which was ideal for growing cotton. This influx of immigrants eventually led to rebellion and war, and was just one of several existential threats facing Mexico in the mid-nineteenth century. Economically weak, and unable to put its political house in order, the young country had to fight for its very survival. Like a little boy bullied on the playground, it was targeted for abuse by the more powerful. The United States, years older and eager to flex its muscles, posed the greatest danger. During the Wars of Independence, sugar planters in Mississippi had underwritten filibustering expeditions to break parts of Tejas off from Mexico. Though provincial authorities were able to prevent this, American encroachment continued.

What would eventually become the U.S. state of Texas was part of the vast San Luis Potosí intendency in the late colonial period, administered from the regional town of Saltillo. Under liberal federalism, it became part of the state, Coahuila y Tejas. An enterprising Moses Austin—as every Texas school child learned over subsequent generations—obtained permission from Mexican authorities to bring migrants into sparsely populated Tejas, a project his son Stephen brought to fruition after his death. Mexico wanted to develop its northeastern region, and the migrants' promise to abide by certain rules and accept Catholicism seemed to suggest their trustworthiness. Unfortunately for Mexico, the migration initiated by the Austins spun out of control. By 1835, twenty-five thousand Americans were living among just thirty-five hundred Mexicans. The vast majority of these English-speaking migrants were protestant and continued to regard themselves as Americans. The political dominance of more populated Coahuila in the state government annoyed them, just as they disliked various rules and laws promulgated by national authorities. Their estrangement only grew when centralists under Bustamante came to power. As the San Jacinto battle monument states today, "Following a series of revolutions begun in 1829, unscrupulous rulers successively seized power in Mexico. Their unjust acts and despotic decrees led to the revolution in Texas." One of their "despotic decrees" was the abolition of slavery. Since slavery was only practiced in Texas by Americans (the vast majority of whom were southerners, though only a minority of them owned slaves), this constitutional change clearly targeted them. As Santa Anna consolidated power after the ouster of Gómez Farías in 1834, he very soon had to deal with the presence of a gun-toting, potentially violent immigrant community along the U.S. frontier.

In office, Santa Anna promulgated a new and simplified constitution known simply as the Seven Laws, which repudiated federalism. Despite his many years of supporting various liberals and federalists, as an army officer and regional caudillo Santa Anna's proclivities leaned toward strong-armed centralism. Perhaps his earlier support for liberalism was authentic; there is a case to be made that by the mid-1930s he and others were concluding that only a centralist state could hold Mexico together. Whatever the rationale, this shift was predictably decried by the Ameritexans. In 1835 they held representative meetings in which they plotted for U.S. statehood. When Mexican authorities declared their activities illegal (as any nation would naturally do), the "Texans" rebelled. In truth, nothing would have appeased them—they were inevitably going to attempt to break Tejas away from Mexico, because they were Americans who wanted to live in, and expand, the United States.

The Texas Filibuster

Santa Anna was not a man who enjoyed sitting at a desk and filing paperwork (likely one reason why he kept evading the presidential chair); what he did enjoy was army life and field command. Always headstrong, he gathered an army and rushed northward to suppress the revolt. But his army was actually not comprised of many trained or standing units—the Mexico City barracks needed to be manned for reasons of political security. Thus, Santa

Anna collected conscripts from the countryside, including vagabonds and criminals, and marched them across expansive deserts on their way to San Antonio de Béxar.

The small town of San Antonio (de Béxar) was the focal point of western Tejas, the Nueces River long demarcating the border with Coahuila. On its northeast side was the San Antonio de Valero mission, which had closed in 1793 and for a few years had been turned into a garrison for two hundred cavalry lancers assigned to combat marauding Apaches. These Mexican lancers hailed from the Coahuilan town of Álamo de Parras; hence, locals came to refer to the old mission as simply the *Alamo*. During the hot summer of 1835, as insubordination festered, an officer named Martín Perfecto de Cos arrived with five hundred reinforcements (the garrison having dropped to one hundred fifty). He dispatched a small detachment to retrieve a cannon in the town of Gonzales, to the east, which had been loaned to townsfolk to scare off Apaches. Now, the Ameritexan townsfolk refused to return it, and instead hoisted a flag with the words "Come and Get It." The Gonzales

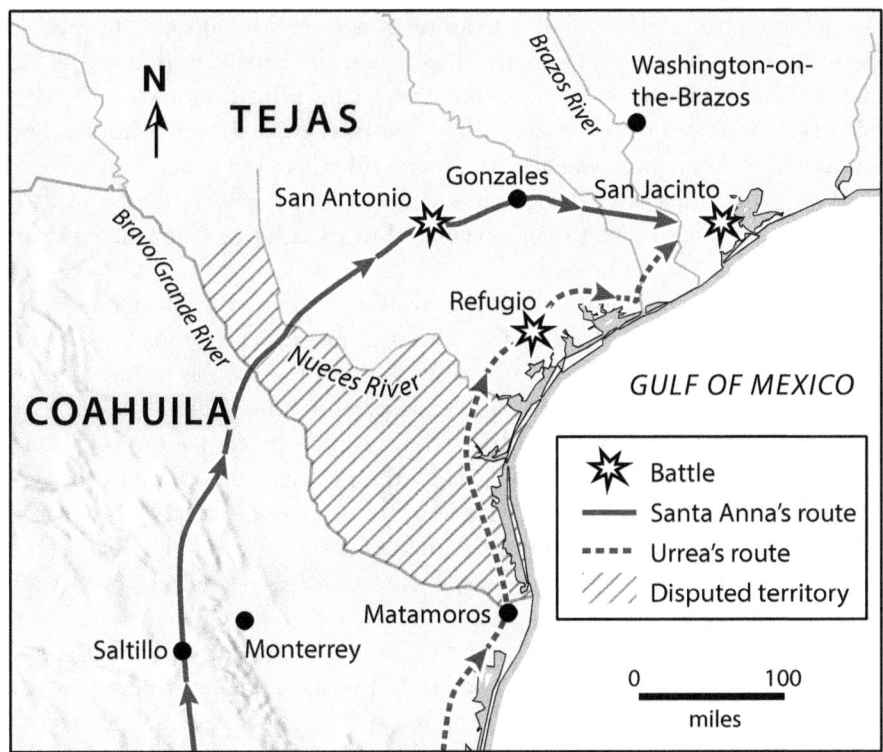

Map 10.1. Texas Filibuster

incident fanned the flames, stirring passions on both sides. Months later, two thousand Ameritexans surrounded Cos's command and besieged the Alamo compound. The Mexicans held out, despite dwindling supplies and the vociferous threats of their besiegers. As winter approached, many Ameritexans went home. As Cos and his men emerged, fighting ensued with the remainder, at close quarters, house to house, on the north side of town. Cos and his men were obligated to withdraw, but first blood had been drawn, and now the Ameritexans possessed the enhanced defenses of the old mission.

Santa Anna approached San Antonio in February 1836. A smaller force, numbering fifteen hundred men under the competent José de Urrea, advanced up roughly parallel roads to the east. As the Mexican armies closed in, Ameritexans met in a settlement called Washington-on-the-Brazos (named after the U.S. capital) and declared their independence. Urrea encountered stiff resistance at the town of Refugio, where a small number of Ameritexans had seized another thick-walled mission and used its natural defenses to good effect. Would the Ameritexans never come out and fight in the open? Mexicans incurred heavy losses as they took Refugio and were in no mood to parley when they encountered a second rebel force at another presidio a few days later. Urrea's officers executed many prisoners, as did Santa Anna's troops as they overran the Alamo. But theirs was a pyrrhic victory. The Ameritexans had artillery nearly as good as Santa Anna's, and hundreds of Mexicans perished as they assailed the outer and inner stone walls. To Mexicans, the Ameritexans were not fighting fair; they used Mexican-built presidios as defensive bulwarks while desecrating Catholic missions via their chosen sites for battle.

In the mid-nineteenth century a prevailing maxim of military command was to arrive on a battlefield first with the most men. Unfortunately for Mexico, Santa Anna was adept at only the first half of the proposition. It was perhaps in his disposition—almost hyperactive in personality—to rush forward. He frequently reached battlefields early but often showed up with almost no functional forces. Enraged by the Ameritexan affront to his beloved Mexico, after taking heavy losses at the Alamo, he raced to catch Sam Houston's remaining insurrectionists in the swamplands around Galveston Bay. His men were exhausted. They lacked supplies—some had not eaten for days—and yet Santa Anna pressed them onward. He called up reinforcements by a forced march as well, and on April 21 the entire command was languid with fatigue. An officer failed to follow instructions to post sentries, and just hours later thousands of Ameritexans, generously supplied with arms and ammunition from across the Louisiana border, smashed into the Mexican army's camp.

The humiliation of capture and the subsequent forced withdrawal of all Mexican forces from Tejas was a bitter pill for the nationalist Santa Anna to swallow. The Ameritexans immediately petitioned for Tejas to be folded into the United States, but to Sam Houston's shock, his old friend Andrew Jackson, in the waning days of his presidency, rebuffed him. The idea of admitting Texas as a slave state triggered vigorous opposition in the North and threatened to aggravate already heightened sectional tensions. Texas would have to wait. The Ameritexans temporarily coopted Mexicans to their cause, including Lorenzo de Zavala, the former treasury minister. His acceptance of the vice presidency of a now-independent Texas must have galled Santa Anna, the two men being longtime rivals. But as Texas entered an unanticipated period of self-governance, Ameritexans designated the very American settlement of Austin as its capital, and few Anglos seemed saddened by Zavala's accidental death in a canoeing accident on the Buffalo Bayou, near the little town of Houston. Today, a marker to the founders of Texas stands just west of the state capitol in Austin, and neither Zavala nor a single Mexican collaborator is listed. Texans celebrate the 1835–1836 fighting as an independence struggle, but their ancestors' design was, all along,

Figure 10.1. Today, the San Jacinto battlefield sits in a bend of the Houston Ship Channel, marked by a large concrete obelisk. How could Santa Anna and the Mexican army get trapped here? The topography of the area has changed greatly since 1836, with the early-twentieth-century dredging of the channel. A confusing network of swamps and bayous created a maze of roads, paths, and easy disorientation.

that of a filibuster. How can we be certain of this? When the United States absorbed Texas in 1845, not a single proud settler raised his musket to fight for a free and independent homeland.

Santa Anna's humiliation and absence (he was kept in the United States for over a year) facilitated the return of Mexico City's creole political class. But soon they were feuding, as ever, the nation mired in chaos and still weak. It was now France that harried Mexico. A French army landed at Veracruz intent on taking control of its customs house, claiming that French citizens in Mexico had been exploited. On one occasion in particular, it seems, Mexican troops were passing a Frenchman's pastry shop and helped themselves to scores of his freshly baked cookies. Just returned to his homeland, Santa Anna was in the port at the time and mobilized its garrison and citizenry to fight in what was soon dubbed the "Pastry War." As with the Spanish at Tampico, warring in his home base with inspired supporters, his aggressive tactics worked: he drove the French troops out, though a cannonball from a frigate instantly killed his majestic stallion and ripped off his lower leg. Yet again, Santa Anna became a national hero. When Gómez Farías engaged in a violent coup attempt against a Bustamante-led government in 1840, he intervened and returned as president.

Santa Anna ruled in the early 1840s for nearly four years, albeit nonconsecutively, in effect matching the office-holding record of Guadalupe Victoria. His regime was marked by excessive, almost imperial trappings. While certainly a man of healthy ego, perhaps this kind of decorum was needed as a means to elevate the presidency and establish a semblance of order. While in office he waged new fights with the Ameritexans, who themselves were filibustering in search of more Mexican land. In 1841 Ameritexans attempted to trigger a revolt in Nuevo Mexico, dispatching a small army ladened with wagons of valued merchants' goods. The convoy lost its way, ran out of supplies, and eventually surrendered to unwavering Mexican authorities. In response, Santa Anna's government sponsored a punitive expedition under French-born general Adrián Woll. Woll briefly occupied San Antonio and engaged in a modest firefight with Ameritexans on its outskirts before successfully retiring.

War with the United States

These smoldering embers of conflict helped bring about an even bigger showdown with the Americans, as the United States coveted an enormous swath of Mexican land. Americans wanted California, in fulfillment of a supposed manifest destiny that would expand their country from sea to sea.

Tensions increased as the United States annexed Tejas, and in a quest for war the southern-born U.S. president, James K. Polk, positioned an army on the disputed Texas-Mexico border, below the Nueces River, along the Río Bravo (known to Americans as the Río Grande). The Nueces had long been the recognized divide between Coahuila and Tejas, and given the fact that Americans had once tried to purchase the land their army now occupied, claims of U.S. sovereignty here were rather ludicrous. The oft-quoted statement of U.S. Army Colonel Ethan Hitchcock, that "we do not have a particle of right to be here," of course came from the lips of a northerner. Sectional partisanship was at play; southerners wanted a westward movement to facilitate new land for soil-depleting cotton and the territorial expansion of slavery.

When the predictable first clash occurred in April 1846, Polk roused public indignation with his statement that "American blood has been shed on American soil." An obscure, taunting congressman from Illinois subsequently introduced so-called Spot Resolutions, insisting that the president show Congress the exact spot. Despite Abraham Lincoln's legislative antics, and Henry David Thoreau's civil disobedience, a war hysteria gripped the United States. It took a while to field large armies, but by spring 1847 the invasion of Mexico was underway. Yet even in its greatest moment of crisis, Mexico's politicians kept feuding. Many were unaffected by the war and refused to sacrifice anything for a cause greater than themselves. Some anticipated the arrival of the Americans and prepared to collaborate with their occupation. Millions of ordinary Mexicans were ambivalent. Untouched by nationalism, they saw the war as just another hardship they must endure. Santa Anna, who had spent time in Cuban exile just before the war, had met various American contacts and officials there. But he was no traitor; he plotted his return and was the one major figure who passionately prepared for his country's defense.

The United States unleashed three armies upon Mexico. A small force, taking shape in Missouri, rushed west and successfully captured Nuevo Mexico and California with nearly no resistance. A much larger army advanced overland from Texas, while a second major force took sail to Veracruz. Zachary Taylor's Texas-based column advanced into the northeast, capturing Monterrey after a tenacious Mexican stand there. Back in charge, Santa Anna rushed northward from Mexico City with many professional soldiers. At San Luis Potosí he levied obligatory loans upon the church and gathered thousands of additional conscripts. He marched his poorly supplied army over two hundred miles of harsh desert, promising his hungry followers that they would eat heartily upon the ample provisions of the Americans.

108   Chapter Ten

Unfortunately, an unusual freeze gripped the region, the Mexicans suffering terribly, toes and fingers turning blue with frostbite. Women, who followed their men and carried knapsacks of woefully insufficient food and supplies, also endured the dreadful conditions. When the Mexicans encountered Taylor's army near a mountain pass southwest of Saltillo, they were physically weak, yet through leadership and coercion Santa Anna still inspired them to fight.

At the battle of Buena Vista, Santa Anna ordered a large portion of the Mexican army to shift rightward to strike the American left flank. It was a bold plan, but also one fraught with peril—if the flanking movement failed, withdrawing to the west and onto the main southbound road could be dif-

Map 10.2. U.S. Invasion of Mexico

ficult. In fact, despite abysmal shooting (nearly all U.S. officers' diaries noted the inadequacy of the Mexican infantrymen's training), the attack made some headway. At a critical juncture, eight hundred Mexican cavalrymen attempted to extend the flank and encircle Taylor's army. Two American regiments, one from Indiana and another from Mississippi, stood in their way. Under a southern officer named Jefferson Davis, these troops skillfully held their fire until a distance of about seventy yards, then unleashed a withering barrage. Mexican men and horses fell in heaps, casualties writhing in agony on the hard desert ground. Survivors retreated hastily, just as the infantry advance also began to falter. As Santa Anna continued to feed reinforcements eastward, U.S. artillery began to find its mark. Clusters of Mexicans laid down or hid, as best they could, in several shallow ravines, taking heavy losses. Morale began to break. A late afternoon struggle to the west, near the road, also failed to dislodge the Americans. While often criticized for retreating after a single day's fight, in truth Santa Anna had a difficult call to make. Though he had a robust numerical advantage, his ranks were positioned terribly while facing a vastly better command in supplies and training. Army morale is a fickle thing. Another bitterly cold night and one more day of hunger raised the specter of wholesale surrender.

Aware that another American army was landing at Veracruz, Santa Anna rushed back to defend the Mexican capital. Once again, he raced forward with great vigor, determined to hold an advanced position rather than exercise prudent caution. He established his line at a place known as Cerro Gordo, outside of his hometown of Xalapa. Having to improvise in the face of uneven support from Mexico City's liberal-dominated political class, one

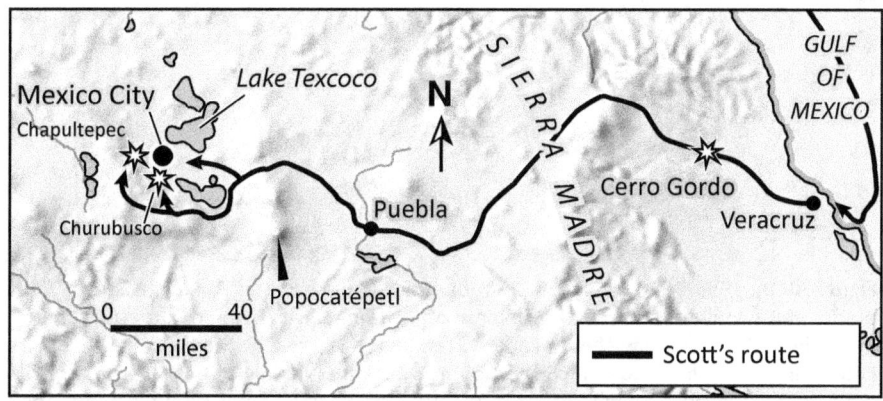

Map 10.3. Scott's Army

110   Chapter Ten

advantage here was that he could use his own nearby hacienda workers to dig trenches. Conversely, a much better choice would have been any number of narrow mountain passes closer to Mexico City, which would have also afforded more time for battle preparation. A couple of steep hills made Cerro Gordo appear formidable, but in fact the Mexican army was exposed. A young engineer from Louisiana, named P. G. T. de Beauregard, discovered a natural flanking route, and after a day's fight Santa Anna was dislodged.

Now in wholesale retreat, the Mexican leader scurried to protect the capital itself. As the Americans descended into the Valley of Mexico and approached from the south, they grew disdainful of their adversaries and heady with confidence. But at an old stone convent, one wing of Winfield Scott's army was stiff-armed by a Mexican force and took heavy losses. The determined defenders at Churubusco surrendered only when compelled to do so by lack of supplies. When the American commander bruskly ordered his

Figure 10.2. The 1848 battle at Churubusco was payback, as Mexicans successfully used a stone-walled convent as a defensive position—just as Americans had done repeatedly in Tejas. Among the defenders was a band of Irish Catholics called the Saint Patrick Brigade. They had defected from the U.S. Army, mainly out of religious conviction, their captured leaders later tortured on the order of General Winfield Scott. Their story is dramatized in the 1998 film *One Man's Hero*.

counterpart to turn over his remaining ammunition, the Mexican retorted, "Sir, if we had ammunition, you would not be here."

In the city itself, a climactic battle came atop an unusual limestone outcropping at a place called Chapultepec. Here six hundred Mexicans, including teenage boys from the military academy, attempted to stave off thousands of veteran American soldiers. Again low on supplies and understaffed, the Mexicans faced improbable odds. As Americans ascended the cliffsides and overran the position, according to popular folklore, six despairing cadets cast themselves to their deaths rather than surrender. Though historical facts belie the famous sacrifice of the *Niños Héroes* (Boy Heroes), it is a powerful nationalist yarn that has served to inspire the Mexican people. Watching the American flag rise over Chapultepec through his field glasses two miles away, Santa Anna turned to his staff and muttered, "God is a Yankee."

The loss of Mexico City effectively ended the war, though Santa Anna returned to the vicinity of Puebla, to the east, and attempted to launch hit-and-run attacks on the Americans. When these efforts failed, he fled to the remote mountains of Oaxaca and prepared to undertake guerrilla warfare. But the governor of that state, a full-blooded Native American named Benito Juárez, opposed his feisty plans and turned the state's own resources against him. Santa Anna was forced into exile. He left his beloved Mexico for Colombia, where he took great pleasure in restoring a hacienda outside of Cartagena once owned by the South American liberator Simón Bolívar.

The treaty that ended the war was signed in a dusty village on the outskirts of Mexico City called Guadalupe Hidalgo. For Mexico it was a bitter peace: the nation lost over 40 percent of its territory. Recompensed $15 million, it ceded a vast region that included (Upper) California, where, adding angst to injury, gold was discovered just one year later—by a Mexican. Mexicans who remained in the forfeited lands were guaranteed all the "rights of citizens of the United States," including the freedom to practice Catholicism. This notwithstanding, thousands packed their belongings and migrated southward. The aggression and land-grabbing of its northern neighbor dispirited Mexico and aggravated internal tensions, yet provided no immediate respite from the internecine political strife that plagued the country.

CHAPTER ELEVEN

Juárez, War, and the French

The Treaty of Guadalupe Hidalgo ended the war with the United States, but it hardly brought Mexico peace. On the contrary, fighting in the north and east was followed by an exponential rise in brigandage. Some armed actors had political motives. In the Sierra Gorda mountains on the eastern edge of the Bajío (see map 6.1), an uprising occurred in 1848–1849 under Eleuterio Quiroz, an army deserter. Joined by hundreds of other disillusioned survivors of the Buena Vista campaign, Quiroz pronounced against the hated draft. But as he and his rebels networked with local villages, they expanded their agenda to include land reform. Increasingly, Quiroz also appealed to grievances of racial injustice against Native Americans. Mexico's government was so weak that it had to parley with him for nearly two years—until his final capture and execution. Just months later, from his base in Monterrey, an opportunistic liberal politician named Santiago Vidaurri declared the creation of the Republic of the Sierra Madre, as he attempted to sever the entire northeast from the Mexican nation. These rebellions show how feeble the central government had become, unquenched fires burning elsewhere in a shattered and fractured land.

Despite the best efforts of Antonio López de Santa Anna, Mexico reached its lowest point as a nation in the 1840s. Not only was Texas filibustered and taken, followed by a cataclysmic defeat at the hands of the United States, but distant Yucatán fell out of Mexico City's orbit, too. Peripheral regions splintered off; the center could not hold. Guatemala, once part of Iturbide's empire, was permanently lost long ago. With formidable geographic obstacles, and a weak sense of national identity and purpose, Mexico was in danger of breaking apart.

Race War in Yucatán

For most of the 1840s the Yucatán peninsula was on its own. In the 1830s an export industry arose in its northwestern quadrant. Henequen, a cactus fiber that made for excellent rope, was milled (its strands separated) in the state capital of Mérida and shipped from a nearby port named Sisal. Some sugar plantations also catered to foreign markets, and water rights—so critical in the river-lacking peninsula—were increasingly privatized. The beneficiaries of these changes were lighter-skinned inhabitants called *ladinos*, mestizo descendants of conquering Spaniards who lived primarily in the towns of Mérida, Valladolid, and Campeche, and who spoke Spanish. Roughly one-third of the populace, they counterbalanced a majority native population that lived in backwoods villages and continued to practice subsistence agriculture, still eating much corn.

Wealthy ladinos, comprising a political class, embraced liberalism and predictably championed federalism for their state, which was so distant from the rest of Mexico. In 1841 they drew up a new state constitution, to the vexation of the centralist-minded Santa Anna, then president. One of Santa Anna's bastard sons led a landing party at Sisal and attempted to occupy Mérida. With battlefield proclivities not unlike that of his father, he overextended himself, ran out of supplies, and was obligated to surrender his entire command. For the next two years, Mexico closed its ports to Yucatan's commerce, while authorities in Mérida hired three vessels of the Texas navy to defend their coastline. In 1843, an agreement of reincorporation was reached, though Mexico City was forced to grant great autonomy to Yucatán.

Friction between the ladino minority and the Mayan majority, however, continued to increase, in part due to ongoing economic changes. When a rebellion erupted in 1847 south of the interior ladino town of Valladolid, panicked authorities overreacted. Racial tensions spun out of control as state authorities reintroduced the traditional punishment of mass floggings of Maya, having previously outlawed it in the 1841 constitution. The rebellion spread and soon degenerated into a wholesale race war. Different native factions laid siege to various ladino towns, most notably at a place called Sotuta, where a vicious struggle ensued with the warrior-proud indigenous Cocomes people. Valladolid itself came under siege, and when columns of soldiers attempted to seize the nearby Mayan base at Dzitnup, with its spectacular natural water pool, they were ambushed. By summer 1848 Mérida itself was threatened, its forty-eight thousand inhabitants, especially ladinos, consumed with fear.

With little help available from a newly defeated Mexico, Yucatán's ladinos mustered their own resources. They drafted all healthy adult males, seized church valuables and sold them for arms, and enlisted the help of a thousand American mercenaries, who arrived from New Orleans. Most importantly, they retained the services of Maya living in western Yucatán, tens of thousands of whom served in labor crews and transported ammunition and supplies. In contrast, the cogency of the rebellion was limited. As in the mid-sixteenth century, the Maya were divided by tribal and geographic loyalties, and rarely coordinated their resistance. In summer 1848, as the Maya returned to their villages to plant corn, they became vulnerable to counterattack. Taking the offensive, ladino columns practiced war without quarter, destroying crops, executing prisoners, and torching villages—the elderly frequently burning to death inside their huts. Both sides mutilated the dead, severing heads and gouging out eyes. Though American mercenaries left quickly—recognizing their dream of filibustering Yucatán as unrealistic—superior foreign weaponry helped drive the Maya back into the southeastern jungles. A grinding war of attrition ensued, over decades, with disparate Mayan villages and divided groups eventually subdued. In the late nineteenth century, the most recalcitrant natives were enslaved and sold to hacendados as chattel in distant parts of Mexico and to Spanish sugar plantations in Cuba. Intermittent fighting persisted until 1901, though historians have exceedingly limited sources and knowledge about this, the entire process more or less a decades-long genocide.

Liberal Reforms and Civil War

In the early 1850s, as the Mayan revolt in Yucatán festered and Mexico absorbed the shock of losing its vast northern territories, Santa Anna made an unlikely final comeback and returned from exile in Colombia. Ensconced in the presidential chair, he accepted lofty accolades befitting a monarch from sycophants and conservatives who found solace in glorifying a fellow Mexican at a time of such low national self-esteem. When he replenished an empty treasury by selling the Mesilla Desert (southern Arizona) to the United States for a generous sum, political opponents cried "treason." Americans made the Gadsden Purchase primarily because it provided favorable terrain for a transcontinental railroad. Santa Anna, for his part, surely had every reason to believe that if he did not accept this "kind" offer, they might well seize the land outright; still, it was an inopportune decision. A liberal opposition, ostensibly in the cause of nationalism, coalesced and ousted him from power.

Many of the liberals who ascended in the mid-1850s held deep ideological convictions, as the second generation of a political class that had long feuded with conservatives. One hallmark of Enlightenment liberalism was of anticlericalism—the desire to constrain the historically potent Roman Catholic Church. A clique of what were called "Purist" liberals determined to genuinely weaken the church, which in much of Mexico was still more influential than the state. Among these was Melchor Ocampo, who became minister of the treasury after serving as governor in the west-central state of Michoacán. Ocampo had long crusaded against clerical fees charged for the sacraments of marriage, baptism, and burial, which burdened the rural poor and helped keep them trapped in debt. Exiled during Santa Anna's final stint in office, he befriended Oaxacan Benito Juárez in New Orleans. As minister of justice, Juárez concurred in Ocampo's anticlerical sentiments, as did Mexico City politician Miguel Lerdo de Tejada, who as a city councilman had collaborated closely with occupying American military forces.

In the 1855–1857 period, these three Purist liberals orchestrated passage of a series of laws that significantly weakened the Catholic Church. They limited sacramental fees, eliminated clerical rights known as *fueros*, and, most significantly, obligated the church to sell properties not directly used in religious ministry. Monasteries and convents were subject to the latter measure, and this was significant: in Mexico City and other cities these institutions possessed prime real estate. When the Purists confiscated properties in the famously devout city of Puebla, east of Mexico City, it triggered rebellion. As the Purists incorporated their legislation into a new constitution in 1857, making it clear that they would not back down, the insurrection spread through much of the countryside—for opaque wording in the constitution made not only select church properties subject to state seizure but also legally threatened the status of communal village lands.

In late 1857 garrison troops in Mexico City joined the insurrectionists, easily taking control of the capital and disbanding the liberal-dominated legislature. But Juárez and other prominent Purists fled, determined to press their cause in sympathetic parts of the nation. Their ideological intensity, unlike in previous coups, ensured a lengthy fight; it cast Mexico into its first authentic civil war—known as the War of the Reform. Some of the lines in this struggle, which lasted until 1861, were at first glance improbable. Many wealthy hacendados, traditionally predisposed toward conservatism, embraced the Purist emphasis on private property and welcomed the opportunity to acquire both church and native communal lands. Conversely, many indigenous people responded to the fiery homilies of angry priests and rallied in favor of the conservative cause. One localized insurrection, in the western state of Jalisco, generated thousands of Native-Americans-turned-fighters with a distinctively impassioned religious zeal.

Unfortunately for the Purists, almost all of the army aligned with the conservatives, which by this time had within its ranks several seasoned commanders. Most notable of these was the disciplined and astute Miguel Miramón. In contrast, like the Maya rebellion in Yucatán, the Purist cause was diffused and dependent on multiple factions of often questionable loyalty, many of which frequently failed to coordinate with one other. At Ahualulco, a town in the northeastern Bajío region, Miramón won a decisive victory over a split liberal command that included a faction badly led by the one-time separatist Santiago Vidaurri. Marching his forces in a driving rainstorm, the conservative general seized high ground, positioned his troops between those of his opponents, and beat them piecemeal, inflicting seven hundred liberal casualties.

In time, however, Purist forces strengthened, in large part because of the audacious political seizure and selling of church lands. Clerical estates were sold to eager hacendados for under-market prices. The consequence of this policy was twofold: the Purists acquired money with which to hire soldiers and buy arms, even as they secured the loyalty of the landed elite. Many Purists themselves also became rich. Guerrilla tactics, employed by a Purist commander named Jesús González Ortega, harried and fatigued the garrisoning troops of Miramón. Juárez's government also had the good fortune of controlling Veracruz, with its important port revenue. Despite his best efforts, Miramón was unable to penetrate this coastal enclave, and the tide of battle slowly turned against him.

By the fall of 1860 the Purists held the upper hand. Mexico City fell at the outset of 1861, and presidential authority descended upon Juárez after the untimely natural death of Lerdo and the execution of Ocampo by a band of conservative guerrillas. In much of Mexico, however, Purist control was far less convincing. Zealous religionists stayed independently in the field in Jalisco, while petty infighting among liberals elsewhere weakened the cause. In Guanajuato and two adjoining states, a frustrated Juárez disbanded all state authority and implemented a military occupation—in the name of liberalism the Purist president was practicing centralism. When priests spoke out against his government, he used a heavy hand, fining and arresting them. But before Juárez could fully consolidate his rule, a new external predator tried to devour Mexico.

The French Intervention

The great loser in the War of the Reform was the church. Both sides in the conflict milked it to finance war: the Purists most directly, by seizing and selling properties, but the conservatives as well, through obligatory "contributions" and loans. Unfortunately, overseas creditors came to believe that Juárez's government was awash in cash as the civil strife wound down. Parisian banks in particular had bankrolled the conservative cause and now demanded that their loans be honored. A half brother of French emperor Napoleon III held Mexican debt through a Geneva banking house. In truth, as had nearly always been the case since obtaining its independence, Mexico was broke. The costs of war greatly exceeded revenues. Nor were the rich paying taxes. A steady cash flow came in via port duties, but Mexico City had little else in its favor. When Juárez suspended all foreign debt payments in July 1861, European powers convened a meeting and determined to act. Britain, Spain, and France sent naval vessels to enforce a blockade, then landed troops unopposed at Veracruz. It was soon apparent that the French had more ambitious plans, as they augmented their landing force and took control of the port with its tariff revenues. As Spanish and British units withdrew, a French army took shape and began to advance on Mexico City.

Haughty French officers, egged on by the pompous Napoleon III—who sought Mexico as a new imperial colony—anticipated little effective opposition. The Vatican supported the invasion, too, priests blessing the French troops, who anticipated friendly crowds in Puebla. Yet when the French arrived on the outskirts of Mexico's second-largest city, to their amazement, they found thousands of Mexican infantrymen positioned in small forts and ready to fight. Multiple infantry charges up a steep grade failed to dislodge them, the stunned French taking heavy losses. After several weeks of a failed siege, they retired to Veracruz. For the first time, Mexicans had beaten a large and professional foreign army—ensuring that the culminating date of the struggle, *Cinco de Mayo*, would eventually become a celebratory day.

Embarrassed and appalled, Napoleon III sent ample reinforcements and dispatched a new commander. Juárez declined the offered services of Miguel Miramón and placed the veteran González Ortega in charge. But in spring 1863, with thirty thousand French infantry at Puebla, little could be done except to defend the city via an even more extensive system earthworks. Besieged, placed under heavy and constant mortar fire, and brought to the brink of starvation, the Mexican army surrendered. Juárez fled Mexico City in what would become a potent symbol—an austere black carriage—while

Figure 11.1. A general named Ignacio Zaragoza commanded the Mexicans at Puebla in spring 1862, when they defeated the French. Zaragoza was an unlikely military hero. Born in remote Tejas, bookish and erudite, he had little in the way of formal military training. After visiting ill soldiers in a hospital in mid-1862, he too succumbed to a fever and died. His body is interred beneath a walkway on the north side of this elaborate monument to his memory in Puebla.

clerics and conservatives welcomed the arrival of the French with a celebratory mass in the city's great cathedral.

Opposition to French rule began almost immediately, encouraged by the elusive Juárez. Rival European powers condemned the colonial acquisition. Seeking a means of appeasing Mexicans and silencing his critics, Napoleon III embraced the idea of giving Mexico its own sovereign. With the approval of a few prominent Mexican conservatives living in European exile, he selected Archduke Maximilian of Austria. Maximilian had been denied the Austrian throne by his eldest brother, Franz Joseph (a famous monarch who would rule into World War I); Mexico was his consolation prize. Yet at age thirty-four he possessed a remarkable naiveté about the world. Well read and even somewhat idealistic, he and his younger wife, Carlota, took ship and prepared to embark on their new adventure together.

When the royal couple arrived in Mexico City, they enjoyed the support of most conservatives. This was payback: recalling how so many liberals had welcomed the Americans, it was their turn to taunt their opponents and embrace the French. A visit by the royal couple to the shrine of the Virgin of Guadalupe went particularly well. A royal palace was soon under construction atop the limestone outcropping in Chapultepec, where the legendary Boy Heroes had supposedly fallen. Determined to provide Mexico with good governance, Maximilian settled into a regimen of daily work. He set up a constitutional monarchy, convened a competent cabinet of ministers, and read their reports with earnest. He and Carlota ventured to towns in the vicinity of the capital, greeting curious onlookers while donning local garb and eating native foods.

To nearly everyone's surprise, and to the great dismay of conservatives, Maximilian appointed several moderate liberals to cabinet positions and gave others important regional posts. He postured in favor of several liberal tenets, even advocating a modicum of land reform. On a few public occasions he criticized the clergy. To the chagrin of Rome, exceedingly few properties were returned to the church; some were appropriated for charities and civic causes. While the government did assume its debt obligations to French banks (in exchange for the continued service of French troops), it distanced itself from the patronizing French state. And when liberal rebellion spread, especially in the far north, it shunned the services of the talented Miramón, dispatching him instead on an assignment overseas. Though probably a sincere reformist at heart, Maximilian's appeal to liberals was a political disaster. He had arrived in a polarized nation with nearly half of its inhabitants receptive to his rule. By alienating conservatives, he lost their support, while in exchange he gained nothing—Juárez and the Purists were implacable. His political strategy doomed the imperial enterprise to failure. He could have easily gained the goodwill of half the population; instead, within two years, nearly everyone opposed him.

In the northern provinces, French troops alienated the populace by waging a ruthless war of counterinsurgency. Thousands of Franco-Algerian troops arrived to help: the infamous French Foreign Legion fought their most renowned battle in Mexico, at (in French) *Camerone*, where sixty Legionnaires staved off attackers for nine hours, with only five surviving. Despite this, Mexico became a mid-century quagmire for France. When French troops began to summarily execute prisoners by hanging or firing squad, Juárez ordered Mexican troops to retaliate in kind. More French generals arrived and took high posts in an increasingly militarized imperial government. Maximilian criticized their tactics; they criticized him. Divisions were rife. As the

Figure 11.2. The imperialists fostered a cult of personality around Maximilian and Carlota, as reflected in these statuettes, which stand about a foot tall and are polychromatic with gold leaf, made of molded plaster. The imperial cape donned here by Maximilian is a figment of the artist's imagination. The emperor in fact often dressed unpretentiously, even for public appearances.
Source: Museo del Fuerte de Loreto, Puebla.

French argued, Mexican conservatives openly broke with the regime. Even Maximilian and Carlota had a falling out. As he chased Mexican mistresses, she refused to sleep with him. When his advisors suggested he build a royal arch to Carlota, he dedicated it to Mexican independence instead. Pressures only worsened as Juárez shifted operations southward. Once driven all the way to the U.S. border (to El Paso del Norte, which was later rechristened as a city in his name), he gained arms and political support from the United States, the Union having emerged victorious in its civil war. Napoleon III, who had anticipated a Confederate victory, now faced an assertive United States, with fifty thousand troops amassing along the Texas-Mexico border.

As Washington pressured the French to withdraw, Maximilian welcomed a small number of ex-Confederates into his kingdom. Southerners distraught in defeat proposed to carve a "New Virginia" out of land in northeastern Mexico. Maximilian granted them permission to come with black slaves, though they would be legally designated "indentured servants." Very few ex-rebels ultimately undertook migration—among other factors, Union troops and logistics standing in their way—while Robert E. Lee and other prominent Confederates remained cold to the idea. Those who did arrive, such as Tennessee governor Isham Harris and Virginia general Jubal Early, remained only for a few weeks or months. When it was apparent that no harsh retribution awaited them, most returned home.

In contrast, as liberal guerrillas received ample arms and ammunition from the Americans, Napoleon III decided it was time to pull the rug from under a rather incompliant Maximilian. The emerging unification of Germany weighed heavily on him, and instead of bringing in money Mexico increasingly bled funds from his treasury. When a pleading Carlota arrived in Paris for an audience, he quickly dismissed her. Determined to hold on, even as French troops withdrew, Maximilian recalled General Miramón. But the talented officer could do little. He ably defended the royal in the sympathetic city of Querétaro for weeks, seven thousand troops (with a handful of American Confederates) besieged on all sides. Battle lines ran along a small riverbed on the city's northern edge, where artillery eventually breached a critical wall in May 1867. Captured, Maximilian spent his final night in a small cell at a convent. On instructions from Juárez he was taken out and shot on a hill just west of Querétaro, along with Miramón and other "traitors to the nation." His body was embalmed and photographed before shipment to Vienna, the Austrian government later funding a modest chapel at the execution site. For Mexicans, nearly twelve years of relentless fighting subsided. It was time to re-create their still ill-defined and war-weary nation.

CHAPTER TWELVE

Age of the Railroad

After the demise of the French imperium, Mexico entered a much-needed era of recovery under Benito Juárez known as the Restoration. Liberalism was at last fully triumphant, conservatives first defeated in civil war, then further discredited by having collaborated (at least early on) with the French. The army was also in disrepute, since most of its officers had aligned with either the conservatives, the French, or both. Juárez dramatically cut the military's budget, dismissing hundreds of officers and tens of thousands of poorly paid enlisted soldiers from service. Some of these turned to transient lives of plunder, the countryside rife with gangs and thieves. Crime on the Mexico-City-to-Veracruz stagecoach was so common that bandits actually posted a sign at one transit stop: "Carry at least twelve pesos for robbery or be beaten."

Juárez and his supporters advocated, in principle, an egalitarian model of republicanism—like that which they saw prospering in the United States. In practice, they collaborated closely with an allied rural elite, which had amassed land during the War of the Reform and aspired to even greater wealth. Many rich who had sided with conservatives or the French now lost their lands to their liberal rivals, among them the Sánchez Navarro clan in the northeast, which held ranching tracts in sum bigger than the state of Indiana—but who had made the fateful error of supporting Maximilian's regime. The church lost many of its few remaining properties. With their belief in laissez-faire economics and development, liberals also attacked indigenous communal lands, laying the legal groundwork for future divestment.

Like their contemporary, the renowned Argentine Domingo F. Sarmiento, Juárez and most of his associates held native culture in disdain—despite the fact that Juárez was himself a full-blooded Zapotec. The liberal government believed that Mexico's fastest route to civilization lay with an influx of white Protestant immigrants, and as a consequence, large swaths of public lands were held in reserve, especially in the far north, for a wave of homesteaders who never came. On paper, Maximilian—like Czar Alexander II in Russia—had abolished debt peonage, but Juárez's government neither honored nor enforced this; liberals failed to pass legislation that would have eliminated hacendados' authority to set up jails, dispense (often arbitrary) justice, and hold the poor in perpetual debt. In sum, there was a great gap between stated liberal ideas and political measures taken. Yet Juárez's administration did have some modest successes. Like Sarmiento in Argentina, he sharply increased the education budget and built the nation's first substantial numbers of secular and free primary schools. The completion of a first railroad, from Mexico City down to Veracruz (designed and partly built under Maximilian), dramatically cut travel time to the port and was a source of national pride. One thousand five hundred miles of telegraph lines linked most of the interior state capitals with Mexico City by 1875. A number of lesser initiatives wooed the small middle class (of lawyers, shopkeepers, skilled artisans, and the like) to the liberal cause, especially in Mexico City.

In politics, Juárez showed himself something of a dictatorial centralist in practice, though early in his career he had denounced Santa Anna for exhibiting the very same traits. In multiple states, internal feuding among liberals bred chaos. San Luis Potosí, so often an excellent microcosm of national trends, had four different governors in a period of ten months. When two governors tried to rule simultaneously, Juárez engineered a legislative bill allowing the national administration to suspend the payment of tax revenues to any given state, allowing the president to—in effect—impose his political will. Juárez violated his own constitution by running for a third term by way of a special election. He did so again, for an even more brazenly illegal fourth term. His death by a massive heart attack a year later ended this charade and helped ensure his celebrated place in history. A lackluster successor ruled until 1876 and then himself maneuvered for reelection. He was ousted in a revolt led by one Porfirio Díaz, who expressed disgust for continual reelection. Díaz was subsequently reelected seven times, ruling Mexico until his overthrow in 1910.

Porfirians Seek Order and Progress

Following Santa Anna and Juárez, Porfirio Díaz is the third luminary of nineteenth-century Mexican history. Typically portrayed as a devilish

Figure 12.1. A young Porfirio Díaz, photographed in 1867. Five years earlier, at the First Battle of Puebla, Díaz distinguished himself in secondary command while fighting the French. While certainly ambitious, he had a seemingly innate ability to read people and anticipate political currents. His ascension to the presidency by force of arms was widely accepted and was even popular in many sectors of Mexican society though history would ultimately vilify him.
Source: Museo Francisco Villa, Durango.

dictator, the truth is much more complex. His thirty-four years of political dominance, known as the *Porfiriato*, saw great technological and structural change. Worldwide, business capital penetrated peripheral regions, creating tensions nearly everywhere. His task of negotiating these changes was not an easy one. The stability he brought to Mexico—thirty-four men had tried to govern it over the previous fifty-five years—is by any account remarkable. An astute reader of character and a savvy politician, he endlessly played individual and institutional challengers off one another.

The army posed a conundrum for Díaz, given its long-standing record of interfering in political affairs. Conversely, an army was needed—if not for defense from foreign adversaries, as a tool for imposing internal order. Reduced in size by Juárez, it now underwent a modest degree of professionalization, with the standardizing of regulations, ranks, insignia, uniforms, military conduct, and the like. But its loyalty was frequently on Díaz's mind. The troops also had a pattern of singularly unprofessional behavior, which even the crafty Díaz had difficulty handling. Discontented enlisted draftees drank and brawled in public streets. Marijuana, while rarely used in Mexico's villages, was easily obtained by troops, who called it "toasted tortilla." Soldiers also deflowered young women and routinely hired prostitutes (they suffered from sexual diseases at a much higher rate than the general populace; as the medical corps treated syphilis by cauterizing genital sores, soldiers tended to avoid seeing the doctor).

Díaz created a new force to keep order alongside the army. The Rurales, or rural police, had a mandate to patrol the countryside. Often wearing tight leather *charro* (cowboy) pants and short jackets, with boots and sombreros, they quickly gained a fearsome reputation. In fact, some were former cutthroat bandits, wooed into government service by money and prestige. Rumors of their sadism flourished. One tale alleged that a group of Rurales once buried hapless peasants up to their necks, then proceeded to play a game of polo among them. Popular myths stoked fear, which was exactly what Díaz wanted. In truth, the Rurales were often ill-equipped, having to supply their own weapons and accessories. Nor were they particularly numerous, while most were kept near the capital, at least early in the Porfiriato, as a counterbalance to the unreliable army.

The push for stability came in conjunction with an unprecedented influx of foreign capital. By the late 1870s the Second Industrial Revolution was underway in the United States and Britain, while New York and London banks had amassed tens of millions of U.S. dollars' worth of bullion. With just a tiny drop of their treasure, foreign bankers could erase Mexico's debt and amend its long-disreputable finances. They were willing to do so in exchange for access to the nation's industrial commodities. The appearance of foreign capital had a salutary effect on Mexico's body politic. Ideological divides quickly healed, as the prospect of newfound wealth drew the elite toward an alliance with foreign entrepreneurs. As Hernán Cortés had discovered on the beaches of Veracruz (when facing potentially hostile, newly arriving troops), the promise of gold makes men forget their petty differences—at least until the riches are acquired.

The Porfirian government modified Mexico's mining code to the benefit of foreign investors. Landownership now included mineral rights (as opposed to traditional Hispanic law, which separated the two). All state taxes and tariffs were abolished, and national taxes on mines reduced to a pittance. By 1900, thirty-one major operations extracted metallurgy from Mexico, which in the worldwide lottery of resources had industrial wealth similar to its unprecedented colonial-era endowment in silver. Lead and copper especially poured forth, enabling U.S. and British factories to dominate the incipient production of industrial goods (twenty-seven of the thirty-one big operations were American- or British-owned). New techniques of cyanide-based processing also revived gold and silver mines, again almost all owned by foreigners.

In order to remove Mexico's great mineral wealth, a modern transportation system was needed. Foreign investors demanded and received excellent

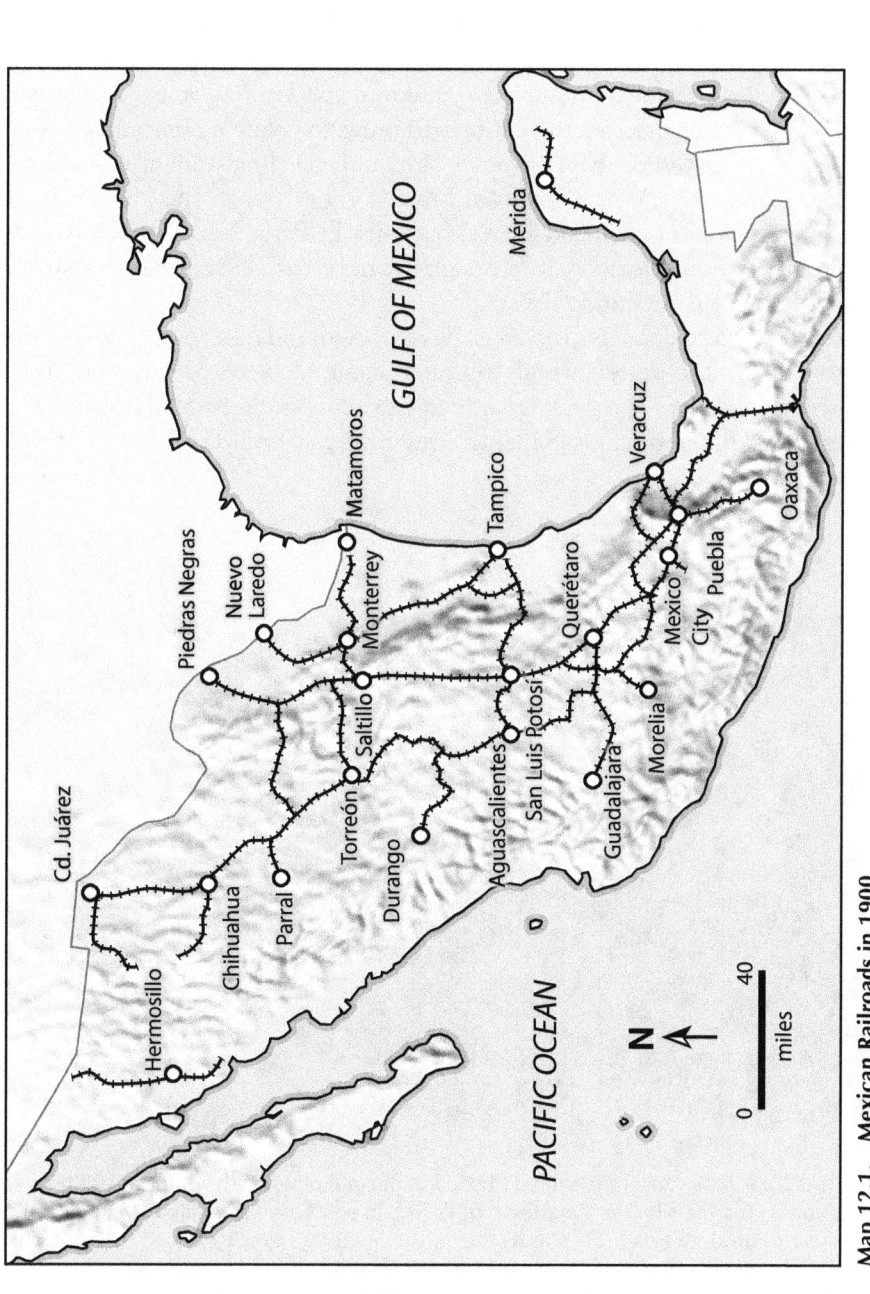

Map 12.1. Mexican Railroads in 1900

concessions from the Porfirian government, which gave them enormous swaths of land in exchange for constructing major lines (the land was not generally astride railroad tracks; much of it was in the north—that held in reserve by Juárez's administration). Unlike in the United States or Europe, railroads did not crisscross the country in order to create a domestic market. Instead, they were linear for purposes of export, heading straight to the border. The Mexican Central ran from Mexico City through the Bajío and up the broad plateau to Ciudad Juárez, opposite El Paso, Texas; the Mexican National ran from Mexico City through the northeast, terminating in Nuevo Laredo, on the Río Grande River.

A modicum of domestic capitalist development did take root in the northeastern city of Monterrey, which in time became Mexico's premier industrial center. Geography played a large role in this process. Positioned on the edge of relatively flat and accessible lands stretching northward to Texas, just 140

Figure 12.2. Railroads transformed Mexico in the late nineteenth century. A sixty-mile spur connected the silver-mining town of Parral, in southern Chihuahua state, with the Mexican Central Railroad (despite its name, the line was never extended to Durango). Here, a train crew poses with one of the U.S.-manufactured steam locomotives that worked the line. Note the variety of clothing and hats worn by the men, all of whom are in the prime of life.
Source: Casa Griensen, Museo de Historia Regional de Parral, Parral.

miles away, the city was almost guaranteed to become an entrepôt with the United States. While mountains directly to the south were a formidable barrier, passes southwest via Saltillo opened onto the central plateau. Monterrey benefited greatly from the completion of the Mexican National Railroad and by an 1881 spur northeast to Matamoros, near the mouth of the Río Grande. Historically, its citizens were long inclined to look north. Occupied during the 1840s war, its artisans and merchants learned some English and sold provisions to American troops. During the U.S. Civil War, they dealt similarly with Confederate authorities in Texas. In the 1880s, with German assistants, entrepreneurial Mexicans crafted a beer called *Carta Blanca* and established the Cervecería Cuauhtémoc, a brewery that would eventually gain worldwide acclaim; Cuauhtémoc's owners and managers included Garzas and Sadas, important surnames among Mexico's super-rich up to the present day. A Protestant local, Benjamín Salinas Westrup, made cotton saddle blankets in the 1880s, then expanded into household items with his brother-in-law Joel Rocha. Mexico's famous Salinas & Rocha Department Stores emerged from this partnership. Local officials suspended all taxes on upstart industries and granted twenty-year exemptions to foreign firms. Industrial equipment was imported duty-free. By 1895, three large smelters operated in Monterrey, and its population reached forty thousand.

Though Monterrey's industrialization proved an exception, the benefits of modernity were thin for most Mexicans. Theirs became an "export nation," as it is in the present day. Mexico's astounding mineral wealth was shipped off without significant remuneration. In the mines and railroads, foreigners held managerial and high-skill positions; Mexicans worked low-skill jobs. Since the Porfirian government hardly taxed foreign businesses, it acquired very little revenue. It was able to jointly fund a system of drainage canals to halt Mexico City's incessant seasonal flooding. And conversely, not all foreign enterprises were successful, as they faced uncertainties and market risks. A British firm built a railroad across the isthmus of Tehuantepec, in southern Mexico, in order to facilitate trans-oceanic trade. Its ports were too small, and its rolling stock too limited, while problems with drainage repeatedly damaged tracks in mountain passes. Just as the firm gained its footing and began to turn a profit, the Panama Canal opened, bankrupting it.

One way some Mexicans did benefit from development was through insider information. A political elite made enormous sums of money speculating in land related to railroad construction. Government officials got wind of where railroads would be built and acquired nearby property, which of course skyrocketed in value. This money in turn "greased the wheels" of local political machines, with networks of officeholders beholden to powerful

Figure 12.3. A textile industry in Mexico began in the mid-nineteenth century but greatly expanded during the Porfiriato. Large mills, like this one in the capital, employed hundreds of workers. Noisy and dangerous machinery made the workplace unpleasant—yet it was notably better than conditions on most haciendas. Like the haciendas, some factories paid workers in tokens, redeemable in company stores. Malcontents were quickly fired. But though conditions were harsh, they were bearable enough to steadily draw the unemployed.
Source: Fototeca, Instituto Nacional de Antropología e Historia, Pachuca.

and constantly reelected bosses. In San Luis Potosí, which had dozens of governors over the five previous decades, a single man, Carlos Díez Gutiérrez, held the state's highest office for twenty-one straight years. His vested power in railroads and land was transparent; the train repair shops sat alongside his hacienda in the middle of the state.

Poor Mexicans lost ground during the Porfiriato—literally. In 1882 the government passed a law entrusting private companies to survey land and determine ownership. Surveyors could purchase up to a third of unclaimed land at favorable prices. Since they paid the government for any such "public" land, authorities had reason to collaborate with them rather than defend the rural poor, who rarely had legal papers proving title. A significant transfer of property ensued in areas useful for commercial agriculture, as large haciendas hired lawyers to obtain surrounding properties and expand their holdings.

Railroads made exporting cotton, sugar, coffee, rubber, henequen, and other agricultural commodities profitable. Middle-class farmers also lost out, as they could not compete with the biggest producers, who often received preferential treatment from railroads during harvest time.

Lifestyles of the Poor and Rich

During the Porfiriato the rich grew much richer, and the rural poor languished. The quality of life generally improved for all in the cities, though the gap between the haves and have-nots was stark. The rural poor on haciendas worked relentlessly, while the lower classes in towns and cities had limited leisure time. They socialized in taverns and consumed traditional agave cactus-based alcoholic drinks—pulque and mescal now joined by a Guadalajara-produced concoction called *tequila*. Along the coast and nearer to ports, cheap sugarcane-based rum (*aguardiente*) predominated. The poor sang simple songs of love and life (*corridos*), frequently accompanied by guitar, and continued the colonial practice of suggestive and lewd dancing. Games of chance were popular. Rolling dice, made of animal bone, facilitated gambling. Playing cards came in the form of the Spanish deck, comprised of forty cards (the numbers 1 through 7, a knave, a horse, and a king) in four suits. The most popular game was called *Rentoy*, a rather tumultuous diversion for two to eight players, openly involving all the things bad bridge players aspire to do—gesture, grunt, and pass signals—by etiquette all done somewhat discreetly, losers typically buying drinks for the winners (and optionally observers) after each hand. Badly played Rentoy, coupled with eventual drunkenness, led to arguments and occasional fights.

Public spectacle in the Porfiriato was tightly regulated. Gone were the colonial era máscaras, and any trace of political criticism was quickly suppressed. The government even abolished bull fighting in Mexico City, Veracruz, and other areas frequented by foreigners, who generally disapproved of the practice. In contrast, American workers introduced the new game of baseball, which Mexicans readily embraced. By the end of the Porfiriato, a semi-professional league was in place, and when the Chicago White Sox played exhibition games in 1907, they were received by enthusiastic crowds. Foreigners also brought bicycles. Bicycling clubs and racing began among the well-to-do; women were even able to nominally participate. Horse-racing still caught the fancy of the super-rich, however, with two large tracks on the outskirts of Mexico City. Men and women showed off their finest clothes at the races and impressed one another with their large wagers—and displays of nonchalance when gambling went badly.

The rich continued to live in city centers (absenteeism on haciendas common), in expansive cut-stone houses of two or three stories, typically with an inner courtyard. In furnishings and dress, everything French was the rage. By the turn of the century, telephones had arrived, with a basic network in place among the rich and select businesses in each substantial city. Gas and electrical lighting transformed especially the capital, which expanded westward with the construction of a wide, paved boulevard named La Reforma. The elite sent their sons to the National Preparatory School, an institution founded by an Auguste Comte disciple named Gabino Barreda. Following the lead of his French mentor, Barreda emphasized a "scientific" curriculum of hyper-rationality, steeped in a heady humanism that repudiated Christianity and celebrated a budding age of unbridled progress. Graduating "Positivists" saw themselves as protagonists of this new age. Similarly, in many elite parlors, weekend sessions engaged humanist thought through mental reflection, despite continuing professions of Catholicism.

Figure 12.4. Porfirian elite pressed city fathers to build state-of-the-art theaters and opera houses. These became social venues for the wealthy but also reflected their desire to embrace European "high culture." The elite saw their nation as finally coming of age as it acquired the sophistication of France and Britain. Zacatecas opened the stately Caldrón Theater in 1891, at a time when Italianate architecture was all the rage.

A professional class under the super-rich emerged. For the technicians of business and society, mining engineers, factory managers, architects, and the like, there was economic mobility without political rights or access to the highest echelons of society. Professionals readily interacted with foreigners, especially Americans; some became Protestants. Women gained ground in certain fields, including medicine and teaching, with law and journalism also slowly opening up. As in Europe and the United States, anesthetics and surgery arrived in Mexico, with state-of-the-art care available for those with money. Asylums opened for the mentally ill. Urban police forces began, and prison construction followed—including a massive panopticon on the east side of Mexico City that would, decades later, become home to the national archives.

Even with improving health care and hygiene, for Mexicans the specter of death was ever present. If calculated with child mortality rates, the average life expectancy in the Porfiriato was twenty-eight years. Nearly half of all deaths were of children under the age of ten. Smallpox, yellow fever, typhus, and tuberculosis swept away tens of thousands annually. Cholera, communicated by dirty drinking water, continued as a major problem in Mexico City. Funerals were frequent. Though the societal gap between rich and poor was wide, in death rites there was a modicum of democracy. Traditional Catholic beliefs compelled tolerance for the poor and respect for all of the deceased. A sad cortege of lowly peasants carrying a wooden coffin to the cemetery could expect even well-to-do passersby to remove their hats and stand still.

For every Mexican, the color associated with death was black. Mourners wore black clothing, a black shroud over the front door symbolized the passing of a loved one, and coffins of both the rich and poor were painted black. The wake, not uncommonly held for three days until the body began to reek its wretched odor, drew extended family, friends, associates, and neighbors. Poor spent their limited savings to ensure the proper burial of long-living adults, though newborns were often still interred quickly and with little fanfare. Unlike in colonial times, it was now common for women to attend burials. In Mexico City, mourners who could afford to do so hired horse-drawn trams, the trek to the sprawling northside Dolores Cemetery far from the city center. Positioned on a hillside, both trams and mourners sometimes had difficulty reaching the cemetery in the mud of the rainy season, accidents and the toppling of a coffin occasionally disrupting the solemnity of the proceedings. Within the confines of Dolores and other premier resting places, the democracy of death rites gave way yet again to economic class. Burial plots of the rich were separate from those of the poor and featured small vaults resembling miniature churches, bequeathed with statuary of mourning women, Mother Mary, or graceful cherubs. Italianate and Gothic-style architecture predominated. In contrast, the poorest in Mexico were buried in modest cemeteries with the site marked by a simple wooden cross.

PART IV

THE AGE OF REBELLION

CHAPTER THIRTEEN

Twilight of the Porfirians

"Poor Mexico," Porfirio Díaz once reputedly quipped, "so far from God, so close to the United States." The remark was filled with irony, coming from a man who proactively engaged the Colossus of the North by welcoming American investment. For average Mexicans, this influx of capital was a mixed blessing. Foreign (mostly American) property ownership was so extensive by the early twentieth century that it was very nearly possible to walk from one end of Mexico to the other without ever stepping foot on Mexican-owned land! In industry, Americans with superior capital and technological know-how created larger and more efficient enterprises. They took advantage of poverty, however, often employing unskilled workers with little regard for their long-term betterment.

Such was the case with William Greene's Cananea Copper Company, located in northern Sonora just miles from the Arizona border. Greene, who fancied himself a "colonel" though he had no military rank or service, managed his mining operation with business savvy. When his Mexican miners agitated for safer working conditions and better pay, he shunned their appeals and refused to negotiate. A strike erupted and spun out of control, frustrating workers, who congregated and damaged some company property. Greene and his American supervisors shut themselves in their comfortable houses and telegraphed the authorities for help. Since there were no Rurales available in the vicinity of Cananea at the time, the Porfirian governor of Sonora approved the use of Arizona Rangers. A posse of Americans crossed the border, rounded up the strike leaders, and hung them. As their limp bodies swayed from nearby trees, terrified miners sullenly returned to work.

Still More Investment and Industry

History books invariably focus on commercial enterprises and rising urbanization during the Porfiriato, making it easy to forget that, even by 1910, about 75 percent of Mexico's population still lived in small towns and villages of less than 2,500 persons. Most rural areas were now penetrated by large commercial haciendas, however, and on multiple levels (unlike their colonial predecessors) these giant estates interfaced with the new capitalist economy. First, they produced overwhelmingly for export, shipping agricultural products out by rail. Second, many developed their own light industries. At a hacienda named Gogorrón in southern San Luis Potosí, for example, the owner constructed a textile mill for making cashmere coats from wool, almost all exported overseas. A cluster of nearby workshops made brushes out of wild plant fibers. The owner himself built a mansion in the state capital and lived there most of the time. He invested in regional mines and factories, and regularly interacted with a business elite that dominated the economic and political life of the state. Nearly everywhere in Mexico, the later years of the Porfiriato saw a sharp increase in landless peasants, while homeless persons shuffled endlessly on the streets of big cities. The commercial nature of even the rural economy made it increasingly essential to have money in order to survive.

Many poor migrated to cities in search of work. In Monterrey, industrialization accelerated. The Cuauhtémoc brewery began a process of vertical integration, establishing a cardboard plant for packaging and a glass company to make bottles. Mexico's first steel mill was built here in 1901, underwritten through a combination of domestic and foreign capital. The Salinas family, already invested in household goods and department stores, built a factory to make brass beds, then expanded into furniture sales, which in turn prompted a move into the financial sector with the creation of Banco Azteca, in order to provide credit to potential customers. Prosperous and confident, the city's roughly two hundred entrepreneurial rich gathered in a pretentious club, socializing and intermarrying their children. They appreciated the cooperative spirit of the regional government under longtime governor Bernardo Reyes. An honest man of modest tastes, Reyes served Monterrey's upper class but also remained discreet, staying out of their way. He was confident that their ultimate success would be his, that political recognition on a national scale could come as his city and state prospered.

A new industry took root in northeast Mexico. American railroad workers reported spotting bubbling tar pits in the environs of the port of Tampico as they laid a spur to the Gulf Coast. An Irish-born oil entrepreneur in Los

Angeles, Edward L. Doheny, was intrigued and came to investigate. Paying locals five pesos for each tar pit they showed him, Doheny quickly realized his good fortune—that he was atop giant pools of "black gold." Arranging to meet Díaz through the U.S. ambassador, he secured a series of leases and the right to import equipment duty-free. It 1901 his work crews hit gushers at just five hundred feet. These deposits yielded heavy crude oil, excellent for railroad fuel and asphalt. Subsequent strikes tapped large quantities of light crude, and in 1906 Doheny's Mexican Petroleum Company began building a 125-mile, eight-inch pipeline to Tampico. The first tanker left the port in 1911, a year in which Mexico provided 1 percent of the U.S. market for oil. By 1919 it reached 14 percent, and only five years later, Mexico produced one hundred million barrels of oil.

The Díaz administration was concerned about the disproportionate influence of Americans and their businesses in Mexico, and attempted to diversify among foreign interests while exerting more direct economic control. It began to slowly purchase major railroads in 1902, eventually acquiring most of them, though incurring debt via London banks in the process. British

Figure 13.1. President Díaz's train arrives in Ciudad Juárez as dignitaries and a formal honor guard (and a dog) await. Díaz traveled sparingly during his decades in office, but in 1909 he took a train up the Mexican Central Railroad to the border town, where he greeted U.S. president William Taft on the International Bridge. It was the first meeting between presidents of the two countries.
Source: Museo de la Revolución en la Frontera, Ciudad Juárez.

interests received contracts to modernize Mexico City's trolleys, with electrification speeding up the cars but resulting in scores of deaths through careless accidents each year. In the oil bonanza, Díaz encouraged Sir Weetman Pearson, who had worked on the capital's drainage system, to enter the fray. Unfortunately, Pearson had terrible luck in his search for crude. Wells in Tabasco, near his failing Tehuantepec railroad, spewed more mud than oil. When he received a generous fifty-year concession for all fields in the state of Veracruz, he moved his operations north to within range of Doheny's easy finds. Alas, ironically on the American July 4th holiday in 1908, his engineers struck something at a depth of over 1,800 feet. A thunderous explosion blew boilers and sent equipment flying 1,300 feet in all directions. For two months crews and even part of the Mexican army tried to cap a dangerous wellhead that in fact was primarily burning natural gas. The blow out killed many, left a crater one thousand feet in diameter, and yielded almost no oil. The July 4th "find" was rather a bad joke for the temporarily luckless British entrepreneur. It took several more years before Pearson had his El Águila (Eagle) Oil Company turning a profit.

Díaz and Mexican Liberalism

Porfirio Díaz and his government recognized that developing Mexico at the behest of foreign investment posed dangers to the weak nation. A distrust of Americans in particular lingered in the national psyche, given the events of the mid-nineteenth century. Despite this concern, the Porfirians plunged head-on into capitalist development, embracing monopolistic market economics. But in political ideology the Porfiriato was a paradox: were the Porfirians liberals or conservatives? Díaz and others claimed the liberal mantle of Juárez. In practice, the regime was a conservative dictatorship, based largely on an exploitive capitalism, with the threat of brute force exercised over a marginalized and culturally disparaged peasantry. Yet the structures of power under Díaz were diffused, and he was obligated to play different forces and factions against each other. His own marriage, to a much younger Carmen Romero Rubio (she was eighteen, he was fifty-one) was a strategic alliance with a conservative family historically close to the Catholic Church.

In order to enhance its nationalist and liberal credentials, the Díaz dictatorship used history. In particular, it resuscitated Miguel Hidalgo. The Hidalgo revolt of 1810, with its overt racial dimensions, had previously been taboo—ignored by liberals and maligned by conservatives. Beginning in the 1880s, however, Díaz and Mexican officialdom created a national cult around Hidalgo. Now dubbed the Father of Independence, the priest-turned-rebel became the male counterpart to Mexico's Mother, the Virgin of Guadalupe (whose banner he had opportunistically employed in his insurrection). The regime tracked down his descendants and gave them generous pensions and recognition (especially a granddaughter—the "Good Father" having produced many other, less convenient heirs through extracurricular liaisons). July 30 was designated a national holiday in memory of his execution. Porfirian officials joined the Hidalgo Patriotic Council, while carefully edited schoolbooks gloried in the now-deemed-courageous events of 1810.

Public memorialization of Hidalgo swept across the country. In 1885 Díaz traveled to the town of Dolores (soon thereafter renamed Dolores-Hidalgo), setting the cornerstone of a large monument. Nearly every state capital followed this lead, each establishing a Hidalgo Plaza with a corresponding statue as its centerpiece. Hidalgo's body was disinterred from Mexico City's cathedral—Porfirian liberals appalled that it had laid so long among Catholic clerics and in proximity to Iturbide's tomb. After being studied by forensics specialists, it was displayed with fanfare in 1895, thousands flocking to view the sacred urn in the zócalo. A few years later construction began on an Independence Column, today one of Mexico's most renowned symbols. Popularly called *The Angel*, in 1910 Hidalgo's bullet-pierced skull was placed on a pillow, under glass for public viewing in perpetuity. By celebrating Hidalgo, and creating a national myth around him, Díaz crafted a historical narrative in which he himself could then fit. Hidalgo was a convenient hero, since he loved and led the dark masses (the same masses who were not doing particularly well under Díaz). If Díaz honored Hidalgo, should not the masses honor Díaz? Sometimes the link was explicit: in Chihuahua City a stately new opera house was named the Theater of National Heroes, with busts of Hidalgo, Juárez, and Díaz gracing its foyer. The annual celebration of Hidalgo's bell-ringing conveniently landed on September 16, one day after Díaz's birthday.

Despite its best efforts, many thoughtful middle-class liberals grew frustrated with the Porfirian regime on ideological grounds, seeing through its façade. The hallmark of mid-century liberalism had been attempts to curtail the authority of the Catholic Church. But in Díaz's Mexico, the church and its clergy seemed to again enjoy privilege and status. Such was certainly the case for Ignacio Montes de Oca, Mexico's most renowned bishop. Born of an aristocratic silver-mining family, he studied in Britain and at Rome's Gregorian University, mastering several languages before assuming clerical duties in San Luis Potosí. A man apparently not predisposed to Jesus's teachings about the merits of humility, he accumulated religious honors and accolades while maintaining a steady correspondence with the pope. He once praised Díaz while officiating at a funeral in Mexico City, and at a church conference in Paris he

Figure 13.2. Though the pigeon atop his head might not be exuding much respect, Hidalgo gets his due in the city of Durango. This unusual bronze casting, by Italian sculptor T. Garandete Tartaglio of Mexico City, is otherwise typical of the veneration apportioned the "Father of Independence" in the late Porfiriato. The statue itself dates from 1895 but stands in a square rechristened Hidalgo Plaza during the centennial celebrations of 1910, just a few blocks north of the state's capitol.

assured his coreligionists that the Mexican flock was prospering and at peace, enjoying "harmonious relations" with the Porfirian state. Montes de Oca had established a seminary in San Luis Potosí that flourished, training scores of priests and even drawing numerous foreign theologians and students.

Observing all of this, while put off by the bishop's pretentious style, a small number of locals formed a Liberal Club. The most influential of its members was one Camilo Arriaga, whose father had accompanied Juárez as he fled north from the French. Having studied technology at Barreda's prep school, he worked as a mining engineer. Most club members were singularly middle class: lawyers, teachers, doctors, and the like. Professionals did well enough in a modernizing Mexico; now they sought to exercise their supposed political rights. Their upstart club inspired similar groups in other regional cities, and a lively correspondence soon ensued. Despite mail tampering and some police harassment, in 1901 this network of clubs dispatched delegates to a conference in San Luis Potosí.

As the liberals met in the city's theater, curious crowds gathered outside. Fifty delegates and hundreds of observers heard criticism of the government from the podium, at one point a firebrand named Ricardo Flores Magón stunning all by calling Díaz and his cronies a "den of thieves." When Arriaga and others later met in a hotel across the street, police officers and a Porfirian congressman sat among them. Rising at the end of Arriaga's speech, the congressman shouted that the nation's president had been dishonored. As he fired his pistol into the air, more policemen rushed inside, arresting Liberal Club members en masse. Scores were hauled off to jail, many serving sentences for defamation and other trumped-up charges for years to come.

The fiery Flores Magón also ended up in jail. When released, he and a determined group of followers fled to San Antonio, Texas, where they began printing an anti-Díaz newsletter called *Regeneración* (*Regeneration*). The Díaz government sent a knife-wielding assassin their way. Breaking into Flores Magón's house by crawling through a window, he nearly succeeded in his mission. Dutifully alarmed, the cohort accepted the invitation of sympathetic American socialists and moved their operations into the interior city of St. Louis. From there, they continued to publish *Regeneration* and decry the abuses of the

Figure 13.3. Late in his career, lithographer José Guadalupe Posada mocked Porfirian society by portraying the powerful as skeletons. Long after he died in poverty, his prints became immensely popular; they became associated with Mexico's Day of the Dead. Here, a close-up shows journalists racing to death on bicycles (the captions are names of Mexico City's weekly newspapers—one, which went out of print, is on the ground being run over). The original image was an etching made in zinc.
Source: Metro, Zapata Station, Mexico City.

dictatorship. Eugene Debs, the perennial American socialist presidential candidate, highlighted Flores Magón's cause and harshly critiqued Mexico's unbridled capitalism on the 1908 campaign trail. A supportive American socialist named John Kenneth Turner visited henequen plantations on Yucatán, where he watched the flogging of a Mayan at the whim of a hacendado. His muckraking book, *Barbarous Mexico*, also removed some of the glimmer from the perceived transformation of Mexico north of the border. In Mexico itself, a sociologist named Andrés Molina Enríquez penned a 1908 work titled *The Great National Problems*, which many middle-class citizens read. In short, all these activities were the first rumblings of discontent, and should a pathway to change appear, a politicized segment of the small middle class was receptive to walking through it.

The End of the Porfirian Regime

Liberal Club agitation posed only a modest threat to the Porfirian regime. The real danger to the dictatorship was an emerging division among Mexico's elite. A rift had developed in the 1890s between Mexico City's Positivist rich and a more traditional elite residing especially in the secondary cities of the northern states. The tightly knit Positivists were allied more directly to foreign interests, while the northern rich were more independent of foreign influence, some tracing their wealth back several generations to large landholdings in the late colonial era. Many of these anti-Positivists rallied to the governorship of Bernardo Reyes in Monterrey, a city whose industrial elite was not particularly close to Díaz and his inner circle. For years Díaz had astutely balanced various powerful groups and interests. In 1900 he brought Reyes into his cabinet as minister of war, an important portfolio. But four years later he tossed Reyes out, replacing him with a Positivist, while selecting another Positivist as his vice president. This apparent triumph of the pushy Positivists triggered a backlash of resentment from the northerners.

Among the anti-Positivists was a powerful family in Coahuila. The Maderos had amassed great wealth, first through land and subsequently through diversified industries. They owned a smelter. Proud Mexicans, they had relatively weak connections to foreign banks and investors; indeed, in a series of lawsuits they had battled American firms over irrigation rights and had gained a reputation as hostile to foreign business. As if the Positivist–northern elite divide were not enough, in subsequent years a second divide surfaced among the rich relating to preferences for American versus European (mostly British) investors. An increasingly combative rivalry began to emerge among European and U.S. interests in and beyond Mexico. When a New York stock market crash occurred in 1907, tensions arose on all fronts. Multiple factions of various shades and degree had emerged among Mexico's rich, who were divided as the 1910 presidential election approached. When an elderly Díaz carelessly hinted that he might not run for reelection, some of the rich in Monterrey began to promote the candidacy of Reyes. Like a failing dam leaking water, the elite divide was now bleeding dangerously into the political system.

After too long a pause, Díaz finally announced his 1910 candidacy. Reyes dutifully withdrew his tentative election bid, but a movement among the anti-Positivist northern rich, along with some popular grassroots activism, had already gained traction. At this juncture, one of the Madero sons stepped forward, publishing a short book titled *The Presidential Succession of 1910* and announcing that he would run for president. Francisco Jr. was a quirky man. At five feet two inches tall and weighing 140 pounds, with a squeaky voice and childless marriage, he did not fit the bill of a Mexican *macho*. A follower of the teachings of French spiritualist Allan Kardec, he was a practicing mystic who believed that he could summon the spirits of the dead via séances. Educated at the Sorbonne in Paris and the University of California at Berkeley, he was also an enlightened hacendado who had schools and pharmacies constructed on his estates. And he was rich—heir to wealth that made him in all likelihood one of the twenty richest men in the country. With resources and connections, coupled with the momentum of the defunct Reyes movement, his anti-reelectionist campaign took fire.

A befuddled Díaz watched Madero (whom he had met on various past occasions) tour by rail and draw enthusiastic crowds in northern cities. In San Luis Potosí, two thousand supporters braved the ire of local authorities, dismissing an announcement by the police chief that Madero was not coming as the disinformation that it was. When his late-arriving train pulled into the station, Madero received their wild adulation. For Díaz, this was too much. He wired instructions to have Madero arrested. Confined to the opulent house of a hacendado supporter, Madero was idled until election day, when authorities announced that Díaz had in fact won reelection. Had Madero accepted the result, insurrection would likely have been avoided; but instead, in disgust, he left Mexico upon his release, and from San Antonio issued his Plan of San Luis Potosí, in which he audaciously called upon Mexicans to revolt on November 20.

Every year, Mexico celebrates November 20 as Revolution Day, all government and many private offices closing. But in reality, on the designated day in 1910 nothing happened. Madero, surrounded by aides, crossed into Mexico from Texas, only to scurry back across the border to evade Rurales. Only weeks later did some pro-Madero revolutionaries begin to attack the Rurales in the mountains of northern Chihuahua. The rather inept Rurales melted in the face of these cocky insurrectionists. When Díaz dispatched a column of Federal troops, the rebels successfully ambushed and killed them.

146 Chapter Thirteen

Figure 13.4. Liberal revolutionaries pose for a photographer in 1911. Most of the early Maderista fighters were peasants, but some more genteel advocates of change joined them. In the center (holding his hat) is Antonio Villarreal, a schoolteacher who worked on the *Regeneración* tabloid with Ricardo Flores Magón. Villarreal felt it his duty to fight with arms after condemning the Díaz regime in words. He regarded Flores Magón as a coward for not joining him.
Source: Museo de la Revolución en la Frontera, Ciudad Juárez.

They sent their bloodied uniforms to the National Palace, taunting the president with the message "Here are the wrappers. Send us more tamales."

The mountains of Chihuahua were ideal for guerrilla tactics. Close enough to the U.S. border, the rebels received smuggled arms and ammunition. Supply coordination came from a well-connected anti-reelectionist leader in Chihuahua named Abraham González. Madero was underwriting costs for the insurrection on his behalf. After a few months of small skirmishes and solid success, he came to Chihuahua in order to take direct command. The rebels were positioned nicely to strike at one of the most important cities in Mexico. Ciudad Juárez, the northern terminus of the Mexican Central Railroad, was an entrepôt every bit as important as Veracruz, where so many nineteenth-century rebellions had started. It fell in May 1911, in a battle along the border watched by hundreds of Americans perched atop their El Paso houses. Seeing that his time was up, Díaz resigned, took a train down to Veracruz, and went off to exile in Paris. As he boarded his ship, he turned to the press and ominously prophesied, "Madero has unleashed a tiger. Let's see if he can control it."

CHAPTER FOURTEEN

The Season of Rebellions

Porfirio Díaz, who left Mexico in May 1911, was smarter and much more politically adept than his usurper, Francisco Madero. Had Madero spent more time studying history and less time reading Kardec, he would have understood the improbability of managing a revolution. Almost all revolutions fail. Most, like those of France and Russia, descend into civil war. Strongmen like Napoleon and Stalin emerge from internecine strife and establish dictatorships every bit as abusive as those they replaced. Violence begets violence, and blood feuds of hatred and revenge are not easily quenched. That there were gross injustices in Porfirian Mexico is beyond dispute, but the ousting of the aged dictator held little promise of rectifying those abuses, much less of creating an idyllic new society. The tiger that Madero unleashed in fact soon turned around and tore him to pieces.

Mexico's divided elite reacted to the demise of the dictatorship, some rallying to Madero's cause, others to a counterrevolutionary agenda, and many more to the necessities of their own self-interests. Nearly all evaded laws and taxes, and took the ensuing confusion as an opportunity to acquire and exploit. For the lower classes, including urban workers and landless peasants, pent-up frustrations burst to the surface—a volcano of passion and resolve that could not easily be channeled. Typical were the events in the state of San Luis Potosí, where a Maderista governor spent the next two years putting out fires. Miners in the north seized dynamite and arms, and rebelled in demand of higher wages. Ultimately, the governor had to rely on army troops, which savagely repressed the strike and hung its ringleaders. Factories also experienced strikes and unrest—property destroyed in the process—as the governor and his aides negotiated and cajoled endlessly in a quest for civil accord. Some owners began to pack their bags and leave. Peasants on the large estates took over idle and sometimes even cultivated lands, generating great tension in the countryside. When Madero dispatched Pedro de los Santos, a close personal aide to San Luis Potosí, he engaged in a power struggle with the governor, only adding to the general confusion. Throughout Mexico, restless lower classes demanded land and change. Indigenous rural poor in the south insisted that communal lands, lost to commercial haciendas during the Porfiriato, be immediately restored. Madero, who won the presidency easily in an electoral landslide, was slow to act and reluctant to answer the rising demands of the underclasses.

Counterrevolution and Another Rebellion

By early 1913 the hapless Madero oversaw a national government that was increasingly dysfunctional. Even many of his supporters found fault with him, and when a would-be assassin missed shooting the president on a busy Mexico City thoroughfare, some citizens were likely disappointed. A few of Madero's most erstwhile adversaries were in the capital city's prisons. Among these was Bernardo Reyes, who had plotted an early revolt, and Félix Díaz, an ambitious and conniving nephew of the former dictator-president. In February, working with sympathetic jailers and army units, these two men were suddenly released. Reyes, mounting a white stallion, led a column of troops across the plaza toward the National Palace. Madero's loyal presidential guard gunned him down. Díaz went into hiding, his partisans holding various positions around the city.

What happened next is known to Mexicans as the Tragic Ten Days. The majority of the army, ostensibly loyal to President Madero, began to fire indiscriminately with artillery in the heart of the great city. Most of its generals were Porfirians, Madero never having replaced them. One of these, Victoriano Huerta, took command; the carnage and chaos only grew worse. When Madero urged him to bring the fighting to an end and take more care in protecting civilian lives, Huerta assured him that the finale was imminent and that he had matters under control. On the ninth day, Huerta met with Díaz at the U.S. embassy, and with the blessing of the ambassador, the two made peace and agreed to orchestrate a coup against Madero. The next day, artillery fell silent and fighting suddenly stopped. Troops approached the palace and successfully disarmed the presidential guard. A colonel entered, brusquely telling Madero, "You are my prisoner." Madero responded, "You are a traitor!"

In the 1960s, when most of Latin America was under military rule, Mexicans occasionally told a political joke: "Why is there never a military coup in Washington, D.C.?" The answer: "There is no U.S. embassy." The favorable conditions of the Porfirian regime for American investments made a turning back of the clock, if possible, the best economic option for the United States. Admittedly, as is so often the case in human history, greed trumped principle. The American commitment to democracy proved only skin-deep. General Huerta, backed by the army, made himself president. His government soon announced that Madero had unfortunately been shot while trying to escape his guards at the city's federal prison.

Throughout Mexico, over subsequent days and weeks, Madero's faithful fell. In San Luis Potosí, the Maderista governor was arrested. Pedro de los Santos fled to the hills and tried to launch a rebellion, but he was betrayed and gunned down. In Chihuahua Abraham González, the rebel-supporting anti-reelectionist, had become governor of the state. He was abducted and put on a train to Mexico City. At a country depot, he was dragged off and shot. But when the Huerta government dispatched a peace delegation to rebellious peasants south of the capital, their leader, Emiliano Zapata, summarily executed them. And when González's corpse was recovered, thousands turned out for his funeral in Chihuahua's grand Theater of National Heroes. An early Maderista rebel mounted the podium and gave a moving eulogy, vowing revenge against Huerta for both his and Madero's murders. His name was Francisco "Pancho" Villa (*Pancho* a common synonym for the name *Francisco*), a physically imposing and charismatic gunslinger destined for revolutionary fame.

Little is known about Villa's background. Born on a Durango hacienda to sharecroppers under the name Doroteo Arango, he had little hope of living anything but an obscure life of hard physical labor, especially after his father died when he was young. But as a teenager he took the unusual step of fleeing this existence—perhaps, as Villa later claimed, because of an altercation with the hacendado—and roamed Mexico's sparsely populated northwest as an outlaw. There was little romantic about the unsettled lives of rogue vagabonds, who survived off seasonal work and petty crime. Arango changed his name to Villa in early adulthood to confuse authorities, but he does not appear under either name in police records, suggesting that his life was mundane and his criminal activity limited. His excellent horsemanship indicates long days in the saddle; most definitely a cowboy, he might have been a horse thief. In 1910, just as the political storms began, he shot a man emerging from a bar in Chihuahua City, a cold-blooded act of murder apparently tied to a dispute over money. He was not arrested.

Figure 14.1. Destined for revolutionary fame, Francisco "Pancho" Villa (mounted, to the right rear) was of humble origin. It is said that Villa's two loves in life were women and horses, but not necessarily in that order. His favorite wartime mount was a mare named Seven Leagues. Here, he surveys preparations for the siege of Ojinaja, on the Texas border, in 1914. From the start of the rebellion he astutely welcomed photographers and journalists, understanding the benefits of favorable media.
Source: Museo Francisco Villa, Parral.

After González's funeral, popular forces against Huerta arose under a now imminently political Villa in the rebellious northwest. Weeks later, reasonably certain that a storm was brewing, the governor of Madero's home state of Coahuila also declared himself against Huerta. Military authorities had not been able to arrest Victoriano Carranza, who, at first, seemed dutifully compliant anyhow. But in the northeast a messy divide among both elites and lower classes made for unstable politics; in a short time, Carranza drew enough support, including from some military officers, to hold his own and field an ill-defined regional army. In the hills immediately south of Mexico City, Huerta's troops continued to fight mostly Native American peasants under the tenacious Zapata—frightful dark-skinned hordes in the eyes of the capital's mostly light-skinned middle class, who dubbed this unbending chieftain the Attila of the South.

Facing a three-pronged insurrection—under Villa, Carranza, and Zapata—General Huerta militarized Mexico and increased the size of the

Figure 14.2. Victoriano Huerta militarized Mexico in 1913–1914, drafting tens of thousands of men and flooding the nation with arms—most imported from Europe. The consequences of this policy were profound; civil war enveloped Mexico, with factions turning upon one another and the bloodshed lasting intermittently for the next decade. Here, Federal troops learn how to position, sight, and fire a tripod-supported, air-cooled machine gun.
Source: Museo Toma de Zacatecas, Zacatecas.

army sevenfold. He did so by greatly expanding the draft, which invariably targeted the poor. Men on the streets, in taverns, and from prisons suddenly found themselves in the army. Equipped with shiploads of weapons from Europe and placed under often abusive Porfirian officers, they were marched out to confront this second wave of rural rebellion. While Carranza's northeastern forces advanced unevenly, and Zapata's Indians constantly nipped at Huerta's heels, the real threat was from Villa. Now known as the "Centaur of the North," he led a ragtag army that, like a snowball rolling downhill, multiplied into the tens of thousands and gained momentum as it moved along the route of the Mexican Central Railroad toward Mexico City.

The climactic battle came in the environs of the old colonial mining town of Zacatecas, where Huerta's Federals made their stand. Roughly fourteen thousand troops positioned on surrounding ridges faced an oncoming force of nearly twenty thousand. While the army had more professionally trained officers and better equipment, Villa's men (with women and supplies in tow) had considerably higher morale. Flanking movements and heavy fighting left thousands of casualties as the rebels invested and then broke the army's ring around the city. Huerta, who spent long hours drinking heavily, often in his parked car in Chapultepec Park, realized after the fall of Zacatecas that his bid for power had failed.

Nearly Class Warfare

As General Huerta fled Mexico in July 1914, the web of rebellion only spread. Carranza had tried to control the military operation against Zacatecas but found an uncooperative ally in Villa, who called his own shots. Though multiple "revolutionary" factions emerged, at its most basic divide was the centuries-old issue of race in Mexico, with the related element of economic class. Villa's mestizo cowboys and peasants from the rural northwest, Zapata's dark-skinned indigenous fighters, and Carranza's mix of units led by mostly lighter-skinned professionals and middle-class officers all coveted political power. Carranza called himself the First Chief of the Revolution and found the prospect of working with the uncultured likes of Villa and Zapata quite galling. A wealthy hacendado and earlier associate of Madero, light-skinned and refined, he was certain that the nation's future rested upon him. At a meeting of delegations from these three large factions, the Carrancistas thanked Villistas and Zapatistas for their services, but effectively attempted to dismiss them as they prepared for the First Chief's ascension to the presidency.

The darker-skinned masses, however, were disinclined to just go home. It was true that neither Villa nor Zapata personally coveted the presidency, but their followers were demanding deep economic and social change. Both men came to strongly dislike and distrust the arrogant Carranza, which in turn fueled their will to fight. After a brief reunion in the capital, Villa and Zapata jointly imposed their own interim president, to the outrage of the First Chief. Wholesale fighting resumed in short order. This phase of what would eventually be called the Mexican Revolution was merciless. Heartfelt hatred drove men to commit horrendous acts. Throughout much of Mexico, small groups of rebels and former Huertista army troops also turned to brigandage. Order dissolved. The nation descended into near anarchy.

Carranza, realizing his limitations as a military commander, entrusted his forces to a professional army officer named Álvaro Obregón. Reading about tactics being used in the unfolding Great War in Europe, Obregón sought out new military hardware, including additional machine guns and better artillery. Fortunately for the Carrancistas, in the twilight of Huerta's governance the United States' navy had taken possession of Veracruz. Now, Americans willingly supplied Carranza's army, which for recruits relied primarily upon city dwellers who feared the dark-skinned rural masses. Carranza also ha-

Figure 14.3. Felipe Ángeles (on the far right, with his staff aboard a train) was a senior officer under Pancho Villa. A military academy graduate and skilled artillery engineer, Ángeles was a far better tactician than Villa. He exercised field command at Zacatecas, and in 1915 he urged Villa to quickly assault the Carrancista forces around Veracruz. Villa failed to do so and took personal command at Celaya—with terrible results.
Source: Museo Toma de Zacatecas, Zacatecas.

rangued factory workers with speeches promising labor reform, drawing thousands of industrial workers into his army's ranks. By spring 1915 Obregón was ready for battle. He encountered Villa northwest of Mexico City, at a town called Celaya. The passion-driven Villa, unappreciative of what machine guns could do, drove waves of his beloved cavalrymen into the teeth of guns and steel. The carnage was awful. Villa lost thousands, Obregón, hundreds. Like Hidalgo's hordes over a century earlier, as Villa retired from the environs of the capital, his forces disintegrated. A few months later, the United States recognized Carranza as the legitimate ruler of Mexico.

An angry Villa struck out at the United States, raiding the small town of Columbus, New Mexico, where the 11th Regiment of U.S. Cavalry was stationed. The U.S. Army sent thousands of troops into Chihuahua to hunt down and kill him, but Villa eluded them with relative ease. He thus became the only "terrorist" to ever attack the United States and survive. But his lower-class movement could not endure. The Americans coordinated actions against it with Carranza, while the First Chief created the First Section, an intelligence-gathering office within his bureaucracy that monitored political activities and spied on political adversaries. In this, he seeded Mexico with the beginnings of what would, by the late twentieth century, become its complex security apparatuses. His spies and informants arranged to ambush the hated Zapata. They filmed his corpse and showed it to Native American villagers in order to break their resistance. There was also no quarter as Villa's movement petered out in the northwest. Carrancista officers occupying Chihuahua City took Villista prisoners out by the hundreds, summarily hanging them from trees.

As the fighting subsided, Carranza and his supporters promulgated a new constitution, drawn up by teachers and lawyers from the urban middle class. The lofty document promised all kinds of reforms. It was anti-clerical in the nineteenth-century liberal tradition, making marriage a civil ceremony and restricting religious worship to church buildings; in Article 3, it promised secular education and free public schools; in Article 27, it made landownership the exclusive right of Mexicans, while Article 123 promised a generous range of labor reforms. Carranza himself was not happy with all the constitutional promises that a wing of "Jacobins" (a term harkening back to the French Revolution) had made, but he also realized that enforcement depended on the executive. A particularly bitter pill was soon swallowed by the industrial working class. The First Chief reneged on the constitution's and his own personal assurances of labor reform and—after helping defeat their dark-skinned rural counterparts—the lowly urban masses got back to work. Factories ran more or less as they had before the great series of rebellions and arbitrary and often abusive managerial practices resumed.

As the designated election year of 1920 approached, the assumption was that, in accordance with the new Constitution of 1917, no presidential re-election would be possible. The entire fracas began, of course, with Madero's insistence that Porfirio Díaz could not endlessly serve as president. And was not Carranza, at first, an outspoken Maderista? Obregón, among others, prepared to launch a bid for the presidency. Then, on Carranza's orders, his and other campaigns were suppressed by the First Section. Carranza prepared for reelection. Obregón declared himself in revolt, easily retaining the loyalty of officers and troops who had served under him. Within weeks he was marching fairly bloodlessly on Mexico City, forcing Carranza's hasty departure. On the train ride down to Veracruz, some holdover Zapatistas scored a partial revenge for the death of their own leader. Sabotaging the tracks, they forced Carranza to abandon the gold bullion he had taken from Mexico City banks and flee on horseback, then on foot. In a dusty village in the remote mountains of the eastern Sierra Madre, one of Carranza's own guards dispatched the First Chief, shooting him as he slept. His last nemesis dead, Pancho Villa agreed to retire from politics, while Obregón secured the presidency.

Consequences

In the 1910s nearly one million (of sixteen million) Mexicans died in a political convulsion soon denoted as *The Revolution*. But what had changed? For the Porfirian elite, the upheaval was traumatic, yet most survived it, their wealth intact. Some of the Positivist elite had fled with Díaz in 1911, but most remained in the relatively safe cities, especially Mexico City (where nearly all had mansions) and waited out the storm. Many sent sons and daughters into safety overseas; the brewery-owning Garza Sada family in Monterrey sent one of their sons, Eugenio, to the Massachusetts Institute of Technology for extended study. Northern rich backed various factions, sometimes shifting their allegiances, and contributions, as needed. Even in Villa's domains, there were wealthy men who parleyed with the warlord successfully. A few, most notably a silver baron named Pedro Alvarado, maintained cordial relations with Villa—until his military fortunes declined.

The true winners of the turmoil were select, politically astute middle-class families, especially those who anticipated Carranza's eventual victory in mid-decade. These rose with him and took control of the government bureaucracy. They received plum positions and accessed avenues for enrichment, the long-standing practice of corruption continuing unabated. As they gained power, in the 1920s they intermingled and intermarried with the surviving Porfirian elite. The wealthy did tend to make and perpetuate their wealth after the rebellions in different ways—landownership and commercial agriculture absolutely declined—but all in all, they adjusted and survived, while the poor for the most part remained impoverished.

The rebellions of the 1910s affected the United States. Hundreds of thousands of poor fled the violence by crossing the border—the beginnings of a migratory pattern that has lasted to the present day. Though many returned home in the 1920s, others did not. Within Mexico, some badly positioned individual Americans lost property, and a couple within Villa's territory lost their lives. The *gringos* were not particularly popular with the would-be revolutionaries, and many Americans dutifully fled. But large commercial interests laid low, cut back operations, and then recovered fairly quickly in the 1920s. The Constitution of 1917 complicated matters, but only on paper. Article 33 allowed for foreigners to be expelled without trial or appeal, but in fact this rarely happened. Technically, under the constitution, all subsoil rights were the sovereign domain of the Mexican state. This provision was evaded as well. Carranza's administration simply ignored it, while Obregón's looked for a long-term fix. In the early 1920s, the statute annoyed U.S. oil companies, whose operations in Mexico were rapidly expanding. Obregón's Supreme Court subsequently held that properties could not be tampered with or seized if foreign investors had committed "positive acts," such as the installation of drilling equipment. The wonders of legal semantics had saved the day for corporate America; business continued as usual. After a decade of unprecedented carnage, with little to ultimately show for it, Mexicans began to reconstruct their country and reconstitute its economic and political fabric, a task that in time did yield some surprising results.

CHAPTER FIFTEEN

Return of the Strong Arm

In 1923, during the presidency of Alvaro Obregón, rumors flourished that Francisco "Pancho" Villa would return to the political arena. Though Obregón (on behalf of Carranza) had decisively defeated Villa in battle years earlier, the bandit-turned-revolutionary remained popular, especially with portions of Mexico's underclass. Having settled down on a government-provided hacienda since 1920, an apparently sedate Villa sent few signals regarding his intentions. But on a hot summer's day in July, as his Dodge automobile rolled into the nearby town of Parral, in southern Chihuahua, all speculation was put to an end. Assassins waylaid his vehicle at a sharp turn in the road, plastering its occupants with heavy gunfire. Yet even in death, Villa had no peace. Vandals raided his tomb, decapitating the corpse. Did Villa's skull end up among the wealthy brotherhood of Yale University's grave-desecrating Skull and Bones Society?

Creating the Mexican Revolution

In the 1920s, a state-supported narrative emerged that defined the sequence of rebellions in the previous decade as a singular revolution. Anyone who had lived through the 1910s would never have perceived it as such; its political twists, myriad orgies of retributive violence, and the near disintegration of a badly fractured society belie such an interpretation. Yet as part of a state-building project, the new storyline had great merit. It could unite a divided people and convert all their suffering into a national rite of passage that placed Mexico metaphorically on the road to something better. The argument that the bloodletting brought positive change is highly suspect; in the mid-twentieth century academics found that Latin American nations devoid of revolutions developed just as quickly, if not faster than Mexico. In the 1950s and 1960s, a cadre of mostly American historians arose, also narrating the Revolution (typically spelled with a capital "R") with enthusiasm and detail. The idea of the Mexican Revolution has persisted, producing such comical episodes as the annual pilgrimage of presidents to the grave of Emiliano Zapata. Here, the chief executive honors and eulogizes the great Mexican *revolutionary*—a guerrilla leader that of course the state had in fact ruthlessly eliminated.

The creation of the Mexican Revolution began in earnest under Obregón and his eclectic minister of education, José Vasconcelos. A middle-class lawyer involved in the politics of the Villa-led rebellion, Vasconcelos sought to instill hope and aspiration in a war-weary people. He called Mexicans part of a Cosmic Race, an *avant-garde* of humanity that would one day usher in a panacea of dignity and freedom. Instead of the dark Social Darwinism prevalent at the turn of the century, Vasconcelos contended that the best of miscegenating races would coalesce in a "natural selection of love," and that this metaphysical triumph was in fact underway in Mexican society. His ideas were a little quirky—and his politics an unlikely ideological mix of far left and far right—but his writings inspired at least a portion of the intelligentsia.

In practical terms, when given an augmented education budget, Vasconcelos built schools and proactively supported the arts. He funded artists, among them a group of innovators who painted bold nationalist murals. These muralists eventually garnered international acclaim. Their canvas was the stairwells, hallways, and courtyards of stately public buildings. Among them was José Clemente Orozco and Diego Rivera. Both men gave little insight into their backgrounds, and many Mexicans to this day believe that they were lower-class heroes born of a revolutionary struggle that they narrated so forcefully in their artworks. In fact, both were from well-to-do families and neither fought in, nor experienced, rebellion firsthand. Both studied at Mexico's premier art school and spent considerable time in Europe. Rivera emblazoned his ideas of economic and racial warfare on the walls of the National Palace, celebrating Native Americans while denigrating the Spaniards. The oppressors, from Hernán Cortés to the Porfirian elite, are finally swallowed up by the just and courageous masses—noble workers, peasants, and indigenous armies led by Villa and Zapata. The more abstract Orozco frequently imbues an optimism similar to that of Vasconcelos in his art—a faith that, in the face of dehumanizing machines and insidious,

Figure 15.1. The first building selected by Vasconcelos for murals was the National Preparatory School. The installation of revolutionary art here symbolized the displacement of European-infused Positivist ideology with a new Mexican nationalism. Orozco spearheaded this work. Here, his 1924 ceiling painting titled *Youth* reflects the abundant energy and determination of the nation's children, poised through learning to accomplish great tasks in a revolutionary society.
Source: Antiguo Colegio de San Ildefonso, Mexico City.

fascistic ideas, the noble spirit of humankind is destined to finally create a lasting utopia.

While the muralists conveyed a positive assessment of the supposedly coherent revolutionary turmoil, at the behest of the government, a more pessimistic accounting came through literature. Remembrance of the violence spawned two of Mexico's greatest literary works. Mariano Azuela's *The Underdogs* (1920) reconstructs the decade of bloodshed through the eyes of a fictional peasant named Demetrio. Visited by soldiers who kill his beloved dog, Demetrio takes to the hills, bonds with other rebels, and sputters through years of violence that become a blur. Over time, it is unclear why anyone is even fighting or dying. Demetrio loses his friends, his sensitivity, and at the end of a dark yarn finds himself alone and in peril, fighting against impossible odds. More grounded in historical reality, Martín Luis Guzmán's *The Eagle and the Serpent* is a partially fictionalized account of the author's experiences as a Villista, with candid admission of his own inability to do much except save his own skin. In this and other writings, Guzmán dwells on the great men of history (though over time Villa becomes less "great"), while Azuela shows us the raw brutality of the revolution from below.

For much of the rest of the world, the works of B. Traven define early twentieth-century Mexico at the time of its rebellions. The actual author behind this pen name is still not known with absolute certainty—a great literary mystery. Definitely a German, Traven published a series of adventure stories with lowly workers and peasants as the main characters, the most famous being *The Treasure of the Sierra Madre* (1927), in which three American oil workers head into the mountains in search of a secret gold cache. The cultural and societal nuances in his writings demonstrate that the author spent years in Mexico and knew the country well. B. Traven's books are the best selling, with regard to Mexico, ever written: several million copies sold in Europe alone, with translation ultimately into over two dozen languages.

The New Boss and the Cristeros

The rebellions of the 1910s did not engulf all of Mexico. Geographically, they tended to arise in regions transformed by Porfirian-era railroads and commercial agriculture, along with nearly the entire north, with its disaffected anti-Positivist elite. Other portions of the country, most notably the remote, only partially developed south (except for Zapata's rebels in Morelos, nearer to Mexico City), Yucatán, and the west-central highlands, remained relatively tranquil. The west-central region, anchored in Jalisco state with its large capital city of Guadalajara, was the cultural heart of Mexican Catholicism. A part of the country that had long seemed almost apolitical, it began to awaken in 1924, when Obregón, astute enough not to reelect himself, pushed for a staunchly anti-clerical sidekick to become his presidential successor.

Plutarco Elías Calles had gained a reputation as a fiercely dogmatic opponent of religious faith, openly dismissing traditional Christianity as nothing more than rank superstition. Many Catholics wrongly believed, given his middle name, that he was Jewish. He drew around him a cadre of comparably irreligious men, one of his favorite governors even naming his newborn son Satan; soon after obtaining the presidential chair he made it clear that he would vigorously enforce the anti-clerical provisions of the 1917 constitution. A dramatic rupture between the Mexican state and the church began soon enough, when compliant, pro-government priests attempted to take over a Mexico City parish popular with militants. The early 1925 incident, probably set up by the Calles government, triggered a firestorm of reaction. Middle-class Catholics flocked to a new organization called the National Defense League for Religious Liberty; within three months it had tens of thousands of members, and by 1926 it had hundreds of thousands.

Catholic lay militancy stiffened the resolve of the church's bishops, even as Calles himself implemented a constitutional statute requiring all priests to register with the government. Tit-for-tat measures followed: lay Catholics orchestrated a boycott of state-connected products; Calles expelled foreign-born priests; Catholics engaged in a campaign of tax resistance; Calles closed most remaining convents and church schools. Finally, in a stunning move urged by lay militants, the bishops suspended all masses throughout the country. A sacrament believed by millions as essential to eternal salvation, curtailment of communion sent shock waves through devout rural communities. In the west-central highlands it spawned a rebellion, thousands of faithful *Cristeros*, who took up arms under the slogan "Long Live Christ the King!"

Calles, for his part, would not bend. He dispatched tens of thousands of Federal troops to the region, and by early 1927 the army was engaged in firefights and occasional pitched battles. Perhaps as many as fifty thousand Cristeros were under arms, but many also fought part-time, remaining in their villages while drifting in and out of service. With superior numbers and far better equipment, the army held the upper hand. As it consolidated control of railroads and cities, the struggle degenerated into hit-and-run guerrilla warfare. For the Cristeros, women played an important supporting role as spies and smugglers. While a few priests stayed with the common people, most fled to the safety of the cities; several bishops headed overseas. The lay militants who had pushed the church into a confrontation now found themselves managing the insurrection. Yet despite their efforts, the Cristeros were always woefully short of ammunition. Predictably, in desperation, many turned to more audacious tactics, sabotaging infrastructure, dynamiting trains, and murdering government officials. The army, in turn, raped female rebel operatives, desecrated churches, and shot prisoners. The viciousness of the Cristero conflict equaled that of the bitter fighting in the mid-1910s.

After three years of bloodletting, the church hierarchy and the Calles government looked for a way out. American Catholics, too distant to be of much help to their beleaguered brethren, pressed for a resolution as well. In June 1929 an arrangement was negotiated, in part through the assistance of an astute U.S. ambassador, in which the government stated that it did not intend to "destroy the identity of the Catholic Church." The bishops authorized the resumption of mass. The crisis subsided slowly, with about fourteen thousand Cristero fighters eventually accepting amnesty. Hundreds were assassinated over the next several years after having laid down their arms. An echo of fighting revived in the early 1930s, making the comparatively understudied Cristero revolt as long-enduring as the 1910s civil war.

Calles in Control

Calles's feud with the Catholic Church reflected a stubborn irreligiosity, but the seminal feature of the man was a domineering urge to control. He neither delegated authority nor yielded power readily. Yet the political culture prevented him from reelection. So as 1928 approached, he and Obregón amended the 1917 constitution in order to allow for six-year terms and nonsequential reelection. Obregón announced his candidacy; Calles backed him. It was clear to all that the two strong-willed men from Sonora intended to rotate the presidency. But after snuffing out an incipient anti-reelectionist rebellion and winning a manipulated electoral contest, Obregón fell to an assassin. At a luncheon in an upscale restaurant outside of Mexico City, an embittered Cristero calmly approached the president-elect and fired several bullets into his head at point-blank range. With this act, the last major figure of the 1910s rebellions died violently, giving credence to the age-old maxim "He who lives by the sword, dies by the sword."

Ironically, the Cristero's action effectively returned the fiercely anticlerical Calles to power. Overt retention of the presidency was still not possible, so Calles installed an interim officeholder who was wholly under his control. Now styling himself the *Maximum Chief* of an "institutionalized revolution," Calles pulled political strings and arranged for a special election in 1929. Going into the contest, he launched the National Revolutionary Party, which at its first convention committed itself to "the perfecting of Mexican democracy." Yet, in reality, opposite dynamics were at work. All government employees had party dues automatically deducted from their paychecks, while Calles governed from behind the scenes and undercut the authority of the ballot box. He also strengthened Mexico's intelligence services (begun under Carranza), which began using nefarious tactics such as mail tampering and telephone wiretapping to monitor and intimidate political opponents. Mexico was skirting with dictatorship again.

Yet the installation process of a second puppet president via the special election did not go smoothly. Calles's man, an obscure diplomat named Pascual Ortiz Rubio, faced a robust challenge from Obregón's renowned first-term education minister. José Vasconcelos ran an energized campaign, trekking across Mexico and drawing enthusiastic crowds not unlike those of Madero in 1910. The nature of his support defies the facile boundaries of political right and left. Devout Catholics, angered by the Cristero war, rallied to his cause, as did agrarians frustrated by the effective end of land reform (which Calles had termed a failure). Independent-minded labor activists looked to Vasconcelos for hope, while better-educated Mexicans endorsed his call for women's suffrage. Yet at times the education minister sounded almost fascistic: his speeches had an anti-Semitic pulse, as he called Calles a Jew (which he was not) and the Judas of the Mexican Revolution (which in some ways he was). At the end of the day, all the popular enthusiasm for Vasconcelos meant nothing: the unknown Ortiz Rubio garnered 1.8 million votes to the well-known challenger's unbelievable 106,000.

With the election, Mexico entered a six-year period of domination under Calles known as the Maximato. The circumstance of governance was captured in a popular ditty:

The man who lives in this house is the president,
but it's from the opposite house that his orders are sent.*

Ortiz Rubio was completely a puppet. When he tried to exert some degree of independence, he discovered that he had resigned—by reading the front page of the morning newspaper. His successor, an opportunistic Sonoran named Abelardo Rodríguez, survived until 1934 by proving himself a completely obedient lackey.

Calles ensured his control in part by tight censorship of the printed press. Mexico's first daily newspapers had begun under Carranza in the late 1910s, when El Universal and Excélsior began competing for readers among the tens of thousands of literate middle-class residents in the capital. Larger secondary cities saw dailies begin in the 1920s, circulation often numbering only in the low thousands. Radio was slow to arrive in Mexico, though the technology was available from the United States in the early twenties. The first station was owned by the Good Tone Tobacco Company, which interspersed cigarette ads among mariachi music, some of which was recorded live in Mexico City's Garibaldi Square. In 1930 Emilio Azcárraga launched station XEB in Monterrey, the modest beginnings of what would one day become a giant media empire. Azcárraga had married into the Monterrey elite and, with ample funding (and the assistance of RCA technicians from the United States),

---

* I am translating liberally to create an English-language rhyme. In Spanish the poem is El que vive en esta casa es el Señor Presidente, pero el señor que aquí manda vive en la casa de enfrente.

Figure 15.2. Prohibition in the United States from 1920 to 1933 proved a boon to northern border towns, as free-spending, alcohol-seeking tourists arrived. Here, on Tijuana's Avenida Olvera (today Revolution Avenue), well-dressed but fun-loving Americans pose for a photographer. Abelardo Rodríguez, Calles's loyal pseudo-president from Sonora, made big money in borderlands casinos, gambling, and drinking establishments.
Source: Museo de Historia de Tijuana, Tijuana.

his pioneering station prospered. Calles, though, saw radio as insignificant, and even in the early thirties failed to appreciate its political potential.

One of the most important Callista mechanisms of control—one that would persist into the twenty-first century—was with regard to organized labor. Industrial workers are naturally regimented and generally can thus be bureaucratically manipulated with relative ease, Marxist theories notwithstanding. A typical lack of education also makes this social contingent highly malleable. An umbrella labor organization known as the Regional Confederation of Mexican Workers, or CROM, was promoted by the government. Led by a loyal Calles sidekick, Luis Morones, the principle was simple: in exchange for peanuts, the CROM would perform service for the state by abiding by contracts while vigorously suppressing all internal labor opponents. Upstart independent and communist-led unions were quickly and often savagely suppressed. With great public fanfare, the government bequeathed on the CROM exceedingly modest benefits, while Morones and his cronies atop the labor pyramid got quite rich. The CROM was more or less a state-sponsored, closed-shop mafia.

Calles's CROM, of course, had an uneasy relationship with the industrial elite of Monterrey, a tight-knit cadre of arch-capitalists ideologically stuck in the Gilded Age. By the Calles years, this powerful group was in its second generation, numbering several hundred and socializing not just in their elite club but through the Rotary, Chamber of Commerce, and Knights of Columbus. Among the previously noteworthy Garzas, Sadas, Salinases, and Rochas were families like the Zambranos, who established a cement company named after Hidalgo, and through acquisitions and mergers now created the soon-to-be-massive CEMEX Corporation. To all these businessmen even a compliant body of organized labor was somewhat disturbing. Still, they tolerated the CROM and appreciated its suppression of far more dangerous grassroots elements. When Calles visited their bustling city, its population nearing

Figure 15.3. In the 1920s and 1930s, Mexico made significant advances in the treatment of the mentally disabled. The ill were taken off the streets and out of jails and housed in public institutions. Physical abuse, while not uncommon, declined with the professionalization of health-care staff. Here, middle-aged women in an asylum calmly do needlework together.
Source: Museo Regional de Cholula, Cholula.

one hundred thousand, they welcomed him with deference and tempered appreciation. During the Maximato, the government's codification of the constitution's Article 123 (on labor reforms) also made Monterrey's business elite uneasy. They answered this perceived threat by creating an Owners' Confederation, which sought to build a nationwide business lobby while employing lawyers to find ways to evade new labor laws. To their pleasure, though, it was soon apparent that the Calles government had no intention of seriously enforcing pro-worker statutes.

The Maximato, of course, coincided with a noteworthy global economic downturn, with exports to the United States in sharp decline and Europe shaken by the election of the Nazi Party in Germany. Mindful of external pressures, the Calles government tread carefully with the business elite, whose repertoire with the government was still strong enough to elicit low-interest bridge loans and temporary tax relief. The Cuauhtémoc brewery actually had more favorable market conditions in the 1930s, as U.S. prohibition ended and beer flowed freely across the U.S. border. Migrants moved across the border readily, too, with hundreds of thousands of Mexicans entering the United States in search of work. U.S. authorities eventually forcibly deported many of these as a public backlash against foreign immigrants matured. Hopes of a better life within Mexico were soon raised with political change, as ten years of rule under Plutarco Calles was about to come to an unexpected end.

CHAPTER SIXTEEN

The Limits of Idealism

In 1934 Plutarco Calles was the master of Mexico. For ten years he had pulled the strings and dominated the political life of the country. But as he approached the 1934 election cycle, he badly misgauged the reliability of the man he designated as the National Revolutionary Party's next presidential candidate. Lázaro Cárdenas was a mild-mannered and long-compliant regional politician, seemingly a perfect fit to become the Maximum Chief's next servile footman. But Cárdenas had backbone, and he was an idealist besides. By the mid-1930s his vision of what Mexico should become was greatly at odds with that of his mentor. Unfortunately for Cárdenas, however, it was also at odds with that of many Mexicans.

Dangerous Power Moves

After being designated the official party's candidate, Lázaro Cárdenas began trekking across Mexico on an extensive campaign tour—something Calles must have found either perplexing or humorous as, after all, he was guaranteed to win the election. But as he traversed the nation, Cárdenas had opportunities to meet local political bosses, gauge political forces, and weigh possibilities for real change. In order to free himself from the Maximum Chief's control, he prepared to unleash limited but potent popular forces that wanted to alter Mexico in keeping with the government's own rhetoric about the supposed Revolution. Agrarians sought land distribution to the poor; some industrial workers longed to break free of the control of Calles's CROM union (Regional Confederation of Mexican Workers) in a quest to secure wage concessions and better working conditions. To both camps, shortly after his election, Cárdenas gave the "green light."

In the realm of organized labor, unleashed militancy triggered strikes in cities throughout the country. It also spawned a dangerous power struggle with Monterrey's business elite. The champion of "new labor" was one Vicente Lombardo Toledano, an articulate intellectual and professed Marxist who led an upstart organization called the Mexican Workers' Confederation (CTM). With its help, rank-and-file activists wrested control from the CROM at the Vidriera glass company and subsequently undertook a strike in Monterrey. But Cárdenas and Lombardo Toledano appear to have underestimated the strength and political acumen of the city's tightly organized capitalists. They countered with a full-throttle assault on the new administration. In newspapers and on radio stations owned by Emilio Azcárraga, commentators warned of rising communism in Mexico. The preexisting Owners' Confederation funded and launched Civic Action, a network of activists who waged a relentless local campaign against both the CTM and the strikers. The Owners' Confederation itself hired provocateurs and agitators, bought off lukewarm strikers with bribes, and utilized street thugs in the form of a fascistic organization called the Gold Shirts. It was not easy to create an entirely new union movement from scratch; Lombardo Toledano had long been in the CROM, and some militants distrusted him. Rumors and internal divisions did much damage to the nascent CTM's cause.

In February 1936 Cárdenas himself entered the fray. His arrival in Monterrey triggered an anti-government general strike throughout the city. The industrial elite shut their factories down and encouraged participation in "anti-communist" marches, some of which drew tens of thousands of participants. In Monterrey public opinion was decidedly against Cárdenas and the CTM. Even the city's workers were at best divided, a majority preferring to maintain peace and willing to collaborate with management. The president had tense meetings with the industrialists, who were busily networking with factory owners and sympathizers throughout the country. He had to wonder if they might all link up and then unite with Calles's loyalists—a grand alliance that could perhaps topple his government. Shortly after Cárdenas returned to Mexico City, his appointed governor made friendly overtures to the rich, while the CTM settled its strike with limited gains. Spies within the CTM kept management well informed in the months that followed, anti-CTM agitation continued unabated until the compliant CROM regained control at Vidriera, and political allies of the business elite retook control of strike-overseeing arbitration boards. The attempt to exert political control through workers in Monterrey had failed.

The tumultuous labor unrest in Mexico's cities enraged the rich and unnerved the middle class, but it also threw Calles and his cronies off balance. The Maximum Chief was particularly incensed when the CTM successfully organized a strike at Mexican Telephone and Telegraph, a company in which he was a major shareholder. In June 1935, through his compliant newspapers, Calles issued so-called Patriotic Declarations in which he warned of the specter of communism in Mexico. Then, in a second major blunder, he left the country, heading to the United States for several months, apparently anticipating that loyal elements in the army would take action against Cárdenas (of which he could wash his hands by being absent). Instead, just the opposite happened. Cárdenas was able to take the initiative, replace army commanders, win over many Callista governors, oust Callistas from his cabinet, and greatly curtail the power of his now out-of-touch former mentor. When Calles returned, he soon realized his mistake. Within weeks, Cárdenas had him arrested and deported. He was flown back to the United States, where a sympathetic press aired his concerns about "reds" running rampant in his homeland. His family then won a free house in San Diego as part of a promotional scheme relating to the International Exposition in Balboa Park, either an improbable streak of luck or a nice American gesture, though he had amassed more than enough illicit money to live comfortably in retirement.

With Calles gone, Cárdenas dramatically reduced labor activism. Had he used the CTM more as a political weapon than a genuine mechanism for reform? Perhaps. Maybe he feared taking on both urban and rural powerbrokers simultaneously, for by 1937, his attention shifted decidedly to the countryside, where he launched a great agrarian initiative. Within just three years, his administration distributed nearly forty million acres of land to about one million recipients. It was an unprecedented transfer of resources, though many of the properties had been dormant or neglected since the 1910s rebellions, or were still undeveloped public lands. In Yucatán, Indians received title to henequen plantations; in the north-central plateau, several large haciendas were broken up. Almost all the land was distributed communally (as *ejidos*), which in the mestizo north was not terribly popular.

Of course, Cárdenas's sweeping agrarian reform won the hearts of most recipients, but millions of other Mexicans missed out on the distribution, and many disagreed in principle with the entire process. The bureaucratized system of acquiring land upset some participants, with competition and envy surfacing among various communities. Compared to other regions, very little land was apportioned in the west-central part of the country where the Cristero rebellion had raged and where devout Catholics and other conservative forces balked at such a "communistic" endeavor. A secondary reform in the countryside, that of socialist education, sparked widespread opposition. Sexual education was also a lightning rod, drawing the ire especially of the Catholic Church. In myriad villages, the authority and prestige of the priest was now challenged by that of the schoolteacher. Scores of teachers were murdered, and hundreds were driven away by villagers who found their activities unacceptable. The intrusion of the state, and its brazen and more direct control of local schools, also angered many.

Even in states where land reform was undertaken, sentiment toward the government often remained uneven. Part of this was a legacy from the past: there was widespread distrust of the supposed revolutionary and overtly anti-clerical state under Carranza, Obregón, and Calles. In San Luis Potosí, the breakup of large estates in the eastern region was popular, but there was never enough land for all, and entire villages that received nothing were predictably distraught. Preexisting smaller land holders found the process disruptive, the availability of seasonal employees now less certain, while urbanites had no vested interest and cared little either way. An influential surviving Callista governor, Saturnino Cedillo, became a focus of nationwide opposition to Cárdenas. But the power of the modern nation-state was ir-

Figure 16.1. Saturnino Cedillo's tomb today. The popular and powerful governor of San Luis Potosí attempted the penultimate major insurrection in Mexico (only followed by the Zapatista rebellion in Chiapas in 1994). It faltered rapidly. An intelligence services agent shot him upon capture. Thousands of citizens braved the ire of the Cárdenas government by attending his funeral.

resistible. When Cedillo rebelled in early 1938, the army and intelligence services easily snuffed out the insurgency, hunting him down in the hills near his hometown and summarily executing him.

The timing of Cedillo's revolt was awful. He broke with the president just weeks after the government seized the holdings of foreign oil companies—a bold and exceedingly popular move. The oil expropriation of March 1938 was the high tide of Cárdenas's reforms. U.S. oil companies in particular had long ignored regulations and had arrogantly flaunted Mexican laws. Cárdenas had learned to distrust the companies back in the 1920s, when he was assigned as a military commander to the Tampico region (Standard Oil sent him a new Packard sedan as an out-of-the-blue gift—a bribe which Cárdenas refused to accept). The subsequent creation of a national oil monopoly, called PEMEX, ultimately transferred tens of billions of dollars into the hands of Mexicans—oil would become the centerpiece of the nation's economy by the 1970s. But predictably, in the short term, tensions spiked with the United States, even in the era of Franklin Roosevelt's Good Neighbor policy. The rising threat of Nazi Germany distracted the United States, however, and created space in which Mexico could pull off this audacious move.

A Powerful Governor in Puebla

The brief popularity of Cárdenas's government in spring 1938 steadily evaporated thereafter. The nationalization of oil triggered capital flight and frightened away further U.S. investment. The economy slowed markedly within months. Domestically, too, Mexicans were increasingly caught up in the left-right ideological debate of the 1930s, with fears of atheism and communism gripping segments of the rural poor and the urban middle class. Long alienated from their government, many (especially devout Catholics) were still not about to make peace with it. When Cárdenas extended a visa to the Russian Bolshevik Leon Trotsky, and to refugees from the civil war in Spain, many saw their deepest fears being brought to fruition. There was a red plot to undermine family and faith in godly Mexico! Though modern polling data is not available, there is little doubt that Cárdenas was a polarizing figure, evincing strong likes and dislikes as his term in office wound down.

The principled Cárdenas's hold on power was tenuous enough that he had to deal with at least some unscrupulous political bosses, whether he wanted to or not. A generation of ambitious men had clawed their way upward under his three predecessors. Fierce rivalries and a cutthroat culture were transferred from war into politics, where generally the least-principled men fared best. Such was the case for an opportunistic easterner named Maximino

Figure 16.2. Leon Trotsky in the garden of his Mexico City home. Driven out of Russia by the Stalinist purges, Trotsky was welcomed into Mexico by a sympathetic Cárdenas in 1937. A Stalinist assassin later accessed his bunker-like abode by posing as a journalist. When Trotsky turned his back to him, the assassin lodged an ice pick seven inches into his skull. Trotsky's presence in Mexico was deeply unpopular, many seeing it as a harbinger of a "red" invasion.
Source: Museo Casa de Leon Trotsky, Mexico City.

Ávila Camacho. Born of a modest family, the eldest of nine children, his deprivations in childhood seemed to have fueled a lifelong hunger for money and power. Ironically, as a teenager he hauled coal for a copper mine owned by Lombardo Toledano's grandfather. As a Singer sewing machine salesman at the outset of the revolution, he sought to capitalize on his connections (his uncle was a general) and obtained an officer's commission. Seeing little in the way of combat, he instead chased political opportunity among different warring factions, uncannily selecting the emerging winners each time.

Ávila Camacho became governor of his home state of Puebla in 1937 and quickly consolidated tight control. He cajoled, pressured, threatened, and brazenly used political patronage to elicit obedience. He paid close attention to the press, which within months began to sing his praises. In 1939, when his most vociferous journalist-critic was murdered, the state police quickly reported that communists from out of state had committed the crime, and there was no hope of ever solving the case. Ávila Camacho often prepared to levy steep taxes on business enterprises, only to suddenly cancel them when some last-minute deal was struck. He got rich. By the time he left office, the governor was a multimillionaire. Days before his term ended, he ordered all of his administration's documents destroyed. Trucks rolled up to state buildings, clerical workers dumping hundreds of boxes out of windows. Needless to say, archival records about the inner workings of his governorship are in very short supply.

Puebla and the Gulf coastal states had seen relatively little fighting during either the 1910s or the Cristero rebellion. They participated unevenly in Cárdenas's aggressive land reform. These were the more industrialized states, though, and they had some upstart labor organizations. Ávila Camacho brooked no serious unrest in factories whose owners were "friendly." Strikes were often savagely repressed, and it was not uncommon for union leaders in Puebla to turn up dead. Cárdenas and Lombardo Toledano could not provide safety for unions in the east short of challenging powerful men like Ávila Camacho. And after the CTM's stark failure in Monterrey, the president chose his battles with great caution. In exchange for labor's surrender and political acquiescence to his rule in Puebla, he received Ávila Camacho's support.

Even after purging Callistas from its ranks, Cárdenas faced considerable danger from the army, led by some high-ranking officers increasingly influenced by anti-communism and uneasy about rising tensions with the United States. With good army contacts, as well as links to other powerbroker governors, Ávila Camacho played a critical role in keeping everyone faithful—his younger brother Manuel becoming minister of war shortly after the oil nationalization. But standing on such thin ice, Cárdenas could not hope to appoint another idealist like himself to the presidency; he was indebted to Maximino and other conservatives who had sustained his unpopular administration for the duration of its six-year term. Thus, he designated Manuel as his successor, the elder Ávila Camacho brother rallying contacts high and low to his candidacy, with the state of Puebla delivering unbelievable electoral support in the balloting. Fraud was rampant, and it is possible that the official candidate in actuality lost the 1940 election. Monterrey's industrialists bankrolled the candidacy of an army general commanding their local garrison (to whom they had also given a lucrative business—he owned a construction company linked to the Zambrano family's cement conglomerate). Urban riots erupted nationwide when official returns showed that Ávila Camacho had won, most Mexico City newspapers having first reported an opposition victory.

The Ties That Bind

The capitalists of Monterrey were not terribly disappointed by Ávila Camacho's win. Manuel had come to quietly visit them during the campaign, and they were content enough to forego contesting the outcome. In public, Ávila Camacho appealed to Catholics with the statement "I am a believer"—a stunning repudiation of anti-clerical government policies over the past two decades. He later called Cárdenas's agrarian communes a "cardinal sin." By disposition, Manuel was generally low-key with an unassuming presence—a contrast to his high-strung elder brother. Mexicans mockingly called him the "Unknown Soldier" because, like Maximino, it was hard to figure out what exactly he did in the so-called revolution, save obtain easy promotions. But like his brother, he enjoyed the good life. The main focus during his presidency was wooing back U.S. investors. He frequently hosted American businessmen at his Cuernavaca home south of Mexico City, which featured a nine-hole golf course. He developed a close relationship with the U.S. ambassador.

For his part, Maximino insisted on becoming the new minister of public works, where he oversaw contracts for road-building and other big projects. His office helped construct a natural gas pipeline from Texas to Monterrey, to the benefit of that city's industrial elite and their energy-hungry factories. With American help, he undertook construction of a massive hydroelectric dam in

Figure 16.3. One of the great public works projects in Mexico in the 1940s was the System Lerma, a daunting feat of hydraulic engineering that rerouted a river in order to supply water to a burgeoning Mexico City. The project took nearly the entire decade to complete. The Río Lerma naturally flowed into the Pacific, but after completion, it flowed into the Gulf of Mexico.
Source: Museo Archivo de la Fotografía, Mexico City.

The Limits of Idealism   175

Puebla. The ministry's budget tripled in his first year, and during a four-year tenure Maximino's wealth soared from millions into tens of millions of dollars (contractors called him Mr. Fifteen Percent in reference to his standard cut). To this day, the Ávila Camacho family is among Mexico's super-rich.

For the United States, the political shift rightward in Mexico was a godsend. And momentum toward outright collaboration quickened in the context of World War II, as the United States coveted raw materials and surplus workers to drive its wartime economy. In this context, the political naiveté of the Marxist Lombardo Toledano fit nicely. Sympathetic to the Soviet Union, he swung the CTM into line after Hitler's Germany warred on Russia. In May 1942, Mexico (at the encouragement of the United States) declared war on Germany. Though most of Mexico's roughly twenty-three million people were likely ambivalent about the war, a general sympathy for the Allied cause arose over time, in part through propaganda films and the reorienting of journalism via the U.S. Office of Inter-American Affairs.

Figure 16.4. During World War II labor shortages prompted the Bracero Program, whereby Mexican workers received legal entrance into the United States. Nearly 220,000 participated in the program, while even more came without permission. Working in agriculture, the Braceros sent money home and later brought back tales of racial discrimination. The state of Texas was officially banned from participation because of its racist tradition. Here, Mexican workers await their entry visas at Ciudad Juárez.
Source: Museo de la Revolución en la Frontera, Ciudad Juárez.

Mexican military participation in the war was all but symbolic, though the nation's economic contributions to the Allied cause were considerable. Even more important were the lasting consequences of (again) linking up with the Colossus of the North. An entirely new political class in Mexico was learning to speak English and befriend the Americans who, unlike in the Porfiriato, now had such overwhelming capital and such enormous businesses that they could lock their weak southern neighbor into a fixed orbit.

For most Mexicans, the Ávila Camacho presidency yielded mixed results. Though far less polarizing and more attuned to dominant cultural values than Cárdenas, Ávila Camacho undid some programs that in fact could have helped many poorer Mexicans in the long term. He halted land reform and reduced the education budget. Gains in literacy slowed considerably, a much-celebrated "each one teach one" program amounting to little more than a publicity stunt. American philanthropies arrived and initiated immunization programs that spurred population growth. The nation that would one day give the world progesterone (from a wild desert yam)—the basis of the birth control pill—was about to experience a dangerous growth spurt that would see its population more than double by 1970. Emphasis on industrialization drew the poor into urban areas ill-equipped to house and feed them, while it triggered an inflationary cycle.

As World War II ended and the 1946 election approached, Manuel's elder brother Maximino anticipated the presidency. But the high-strung political boss succumbed to a massive heart attack at age fifty-three, and the question of succession suddenly became a bit more complicated. Cárdenas and the nationalists around him longed to shift the political gears into reverse, but the ascent of the United States and its newfound influence in Mexico (and the world) was difficult to resist. Ávila Camacho turned to his faithful minister of the interior, Miguel Alemán, who as governor of Veracruz in the late 1930s had already proven himself nearly as unscrupulous as the deceased Maximino. The president's and minister's wives were best friends, and most cabinet officials and governors were at peace with continuing on the same ideological and political course. Popular opposition to the government came as much from the political right as from the left. When anti-government protests rocked the devoutly Catholic city of León, in the Bajío, the army slaughtered seventy-four people as it suppressed them. Caught up in personal rivalries, a clueless Lombardo Toledano further undercut an idealist-nationalist candidacy by endorsing Alemán. With the weight of the media and official party, though also with a modicum of genuine popular support (including from the industrialists of Monterrey), forty-six-year-old Miguel Alemán won the presidency. His time in office would prove momentous, indeed.

PART V

STRUCTURES OF POWER

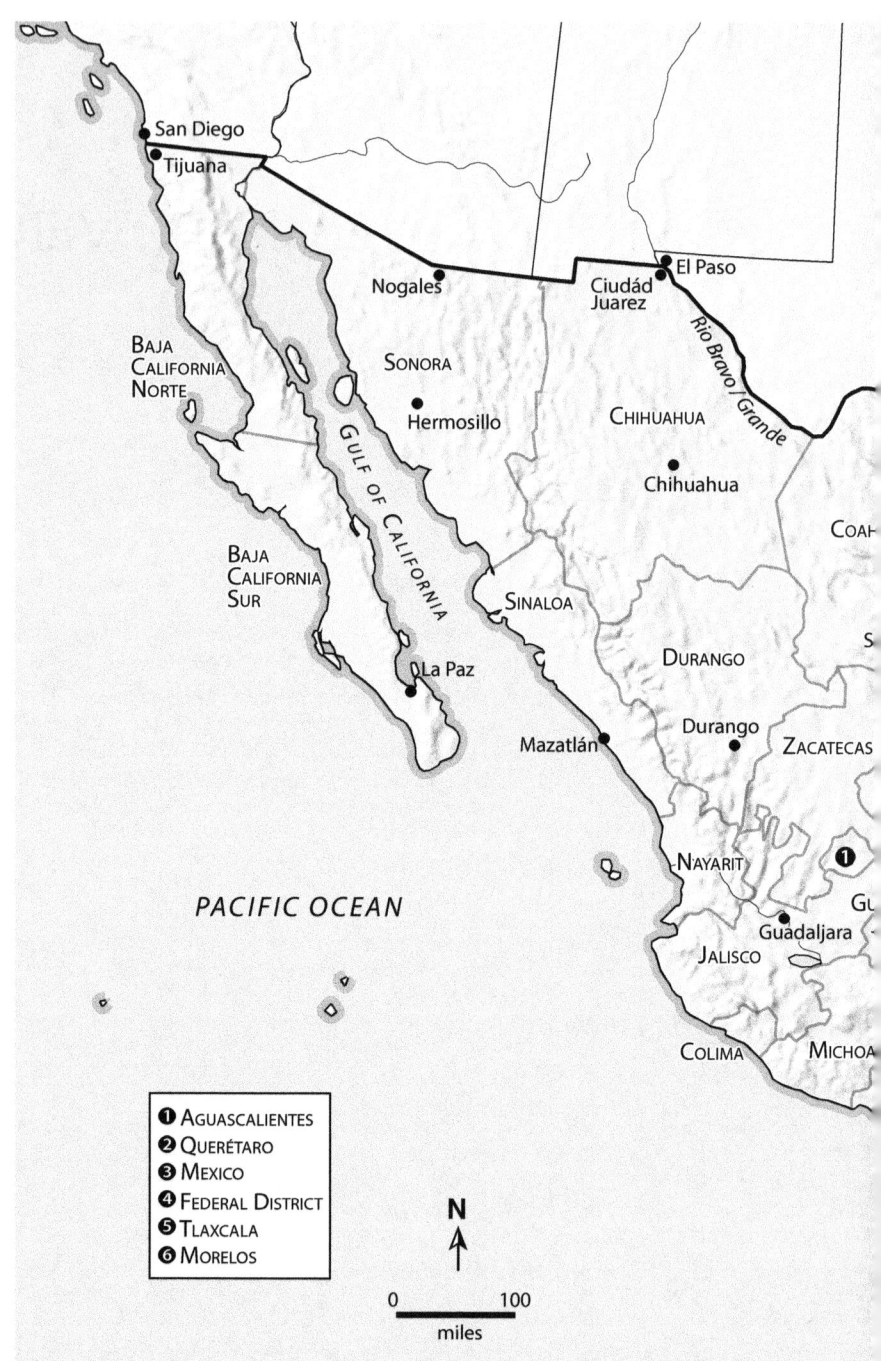

Modern Mexico

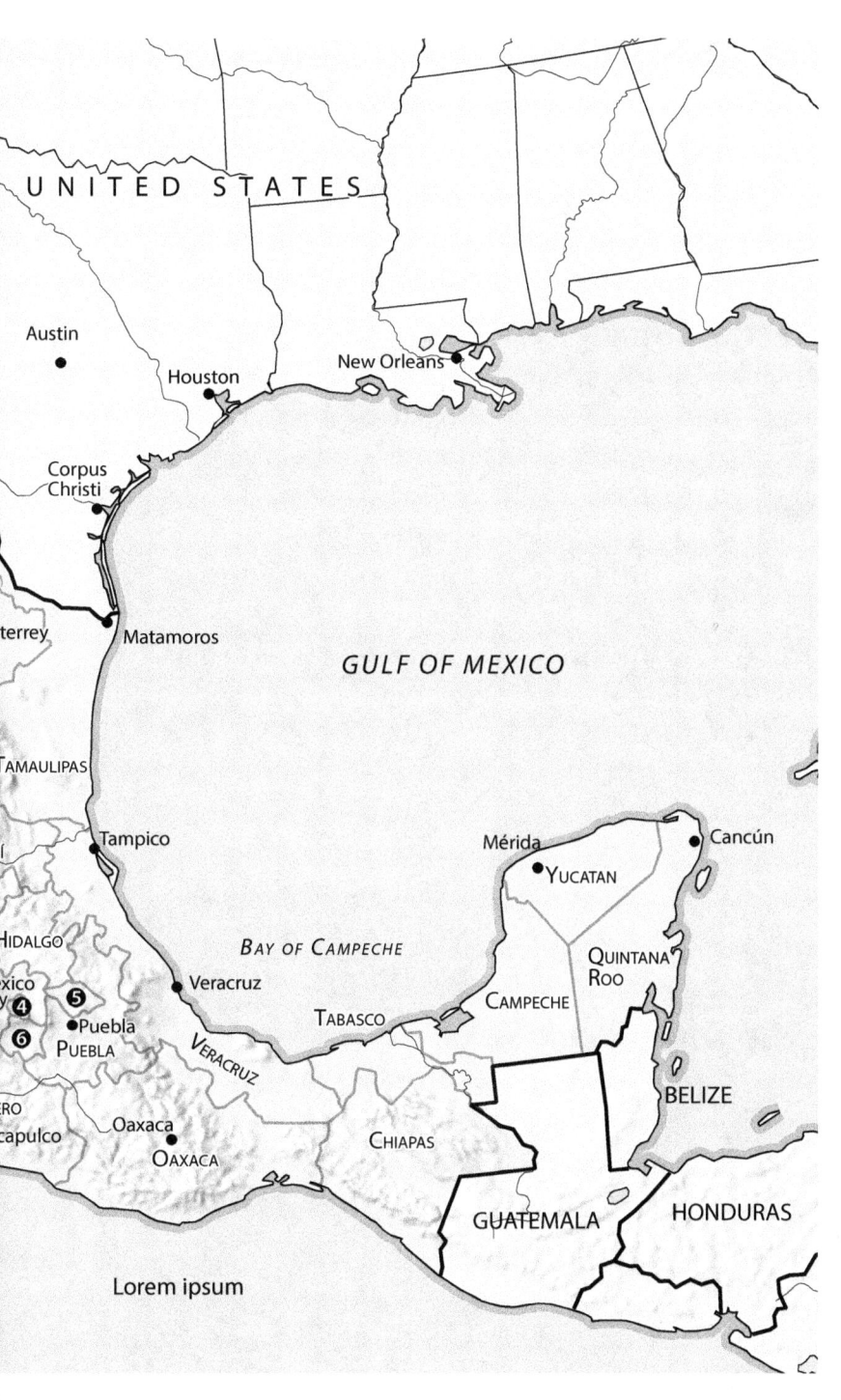

CHAPTER SEVENTEEN

Miguel Alemán—Legacy President

No place in Mexico is more readily associated with glamour, power, and hedonism than the ritzy Pacific Ocean resort of Acapulco. In colonial times a port of call for the Manila galleon, the old town had slid into a centuries-long hibernation, until it caught the unlikely attention of the swashbuckling Australian actor Errol Flynn in 1940. Soon other Hollywood stars escaped the pressures of fame by strolling its white-sand beaches, though many—like Flynn—enjoyed sexual escapades as they swam and suntanned the days away in this tropical paradise. Catching wind of their presence, Mexico's new postwar president soon began pilgrimaging to the little town, drawn by the prospect of befriending the famous and cherished. Though psychologically analyzing a historical figure is always a dubious proposition, it is fairly easy to conclude that Miguel Alemán very much wished he had not been born a Mexican. The insecurities of this man drove him on an endless quest for status and money, and above all the approbation of rich whites from America and beyond. The consequences of Alemán's political decisions in the immediate postwar period have lasted for decades.

Miguel Alemán Rewrites the Rules

Born in a small town in southern Veracruz state, young Miguel watched his father manage a modest store before the rebellion against Porfirio Díaz. By the end of the 1910s, his father was Carrancista General. Loyal to the memory of the First Chief, he made no peace with either Obregón or Calles and was gunned down during a spell of political unrest in 1929. His son seemed to have internalized a great cynicism about politics by then, just as he finished his law studies at the national university. He married a middle-class woman named Beatriz and drove her to Texas on a honeymoon—a reflection of Miguel's rising infatuation with the United States. He spent the couple's early savings on an American car, and though Beatriz grew concerned that Miguel might not be ambitious enough, other friends took note of his longing to be rich.

A former Carrancista with government influence helped young Alemán obtain a judgeship. During Cárdenas's subsequent rupture with Calles, Alemán found himself unexpectedly in a position to access power. A sharp division between political bosses in Veracruz allowed him to become governor of the state, though only as a presumptive puppet. But Alemán was determined to be his own man. With machiavellian finesse, aided by the mafia-like assassination of select opponents, he took control of the state government, much like his counterpart, Maximino Ávila Camacho, in the adjoining state of Puebla. Uncanny luck and fortuitous connections continued to unfold; Maximino's brother Manuel pegged him as his presidential campaign manager in 1940. The two men bonded as friends. Alemán was,

Figure 17.1. No figure is more important to understanding contemporary Mexico than Miguel Alemán. The man linked his nation directly to the United States and its corporations, established its myriad and formidable security apparatuses, and drew around him a cadre of opportunists who bonded like brothers in a fraternity. The closed Party of the Institutionalized Revolution (PRI) elite came to comprise a powerful oligarchy, which continues to dominate Mexican politics and economic life to the present day.
Source: Museo de Historia de Tijuana, Tijuana.

after all, much like the Ávila Camacho brothers, with a willingness to do nearly anything for power. With Maximino's unexpected death, Manuel supported Alemán as his successor, and he obtained the presidency in 1946.

Within weeks after assuming office, Alemán carried out an aggressive campaign to destroy economic nationalism in his own country. His first trip was to New York City, where he met with American bankers and businessmen. He gutted the few remaining agrarian programs, routing money and legal prerogatives into the hands of American agribusinesses—Monsanto, Quaker Oats, Cargill, and other big corporations assumed control of processing and marketing of agricultural commodities over the next decade. Alemán also quickly targeted independent, worker-based forces within organized labor. He declared a strike at PEMEX illegal and sent the army in to crush it. With a skill for divide and conquer that would have impressed Hernán Cortés, he shrewdly turned unions against one another, then destroyed his labor adversaries piecemeal. In 1947, he was able to announce that the oil workers' union had decided to *willingly* accept a pay cut and supported the elimination of several "outdated" safety regulations. The annihilation of that union so shook others that many fell quickly into line, with the remaining holdouts overwhelmed, demoralized, and then broken. In this process, Alemán found an ally in none other than Lombardo Toledano, whose CTM ultimately played the role of the Tlaxcalans in labor's demise. Money bought off most union chieftains, and the unbending were dealt with severely; abduction and torture of members of so-called "communist" unions (i.e., those that attempted to defend workers' rights) became commonplace.

Security was the centerpiece of the new Mexican state. Alemán greatly enhanced the nation's secret police. He launched a new Federal Directorate of Security (DFS), transferring this entity from executive oversight into the interior ministry at the end of his term so that he could continue to control it. He personally appointed close associates to senior DFS positions and kept close tabs on its operations. Praising the organization effusively behind the scenes, he almost never mentioned his political police in public. Very few academics have sought out information about the DFS over the years, nor has archival access been forthcoming—we do not even know the actual date of its creation or the legalities of how exactly it came about (though it was almost certainly created by executive decree). From the start, there appears to have been connections between the DFS and U.S. policing and spy agencies, in the context of Cold War fears of subversion and communism. The U.S. Central Intelligence Agency (CIA) praised the upstart organization in a since-released confidential report, noting a lack of moral inhibitions among its senior leadership and their involvement in extortion schemes and drug running—the links between illegal narcotics and Mexico's policing services appear to have begun very early.

The DFS was only one of many security apparatuses initiated or expanded by Alemán. The important General Directorate of Political and Social Investigations, also within the Interior Ministry, was in rapid ascent. The offices of the attorney general, within both the federal and federal district governments, developed investigative units. Surveillance within the capital increased with the aptly named Federal District's Secret Service of Policing. The National Security Police also began, assuming most of the duties related to guarding the president. It developed links with the U.S. Federal Bureau of Investigation, which had set up its own office in Mexico City in 1939. Agents often had somewhat awkward encounters with Alemán's myriad mistresses—his playboy reputation in newspapers well deserved (he especially savored his dalliances with white American actresses).

The main purpose of Alemán's formidable security network was to check political dissent. Equipped with the latest in technology, at his urging, much of it acquired apparently from the United States, the DFS kept close tabs on political critics. Even famous persons, such as former president Lázaro Cárdenas, were placed under surveillance, their movements monitored, their phones tapped. Evidence suggests widespread infiltration of labor, social, and political organizations. If Cárdenas gave his countrymen the gift of nationalized oil, Miguel Alemán was the great giver of gifts to the United States. His promotion of security services ensured a perpetual dirty war on union activists, peasant organizers, human rights advocates, and others who would dare to challenge the powers that be in Mexico. Empowered, independent unions and peasants were a direct economic threat to U.S. corporations operating in Mexico and, indirectly, to the U.S. middle class, which of course has come to benefit from exported commodities and the cheap labor market of its southern neighbor. We do not, however, have any conclusive evidence that the United States directly worked to set up Mexican security operations—and either way, their creation, proliferation, and eventual links with U.S. counterparts were choices the pro-American Alemán and his sidekicks willfully made.

The Emerging PRI Fraternity

Miguel Alemán rechristened the official political organ the Institutional Revolutionary Party, or the PRI by its eventually famous acronym. Around him arose a cadre of loyalists who would multiply and perpetuate their wealth, intermarry their children, and position their families to dominate

Mexico for decades. Even today, this Alemán-inspired elite, or PRI fraternity, is still decidedly in control. It is so tight-knit and enduring that it defines modern Mexican political life. Simply put, Mexico since the 1940s has been an oligarchy. One of the hallmarks of the closed PRI fraternity has been a disciplined secrecy. When Alemán died in his Mexico City mansion in 1983, the nature and location of his burial was even kept from the public—remarkable stealth for the onetime head of state of a supposed republic.

Secrecy, lies, and corruption were the hallmarks of the Alemán administration and set the precedent for decades of widespread institutionalized abuse. With tight media control, in part through a willingness to threaten or eliminate investigative journalists, Alemán and his friends were able to tarnish rivals' reputations while whitewashing their own. When two trains collided in Guadalajara in 1949 as a result of company negligence, the media blamed communist agitators, local authorities rounding up independent union activists and subjecting them to torture (under which at least one died). When hangover Cardenistas attempted to indict Alemán for corruption through the offices of the attorney general, their legal maneuvers received scant press coverage, and their legal challenges were subsequently dismissed. In May 1950, before President Alemán paid a visit to their town, the shopkeepers of Coatzacoalcos were compelled to each donate 500 to 1,500 pesos to support his visit. Alemán showed up with an entourage of well over a thousand, promising in front of fawning reporters to pave the streets and improve the sewage system. A construction company owned by one of the president's confidants received 4.5 million pesos for the contract but never did the work. As historian Stephen Niblo has shown, despite relatively paltry archival access to such materials, a deep record of corruption under Alemán is transparent, and its scope is breathtaking. Whether it be the head of his National Security Police—whose nephew was caught smuggling opium into the United States in one of his Cadillacs—or intimates who outright stole government funds (when American Airlines paid three million pesos in taxes, a treasury official simply cashed the massive check and pocketed the money), Alemán oversaw a bureaucracy of brazen and unprecedented graft.

Alemán himself acquired tens of millions of dollars by the time he left office. By the late 1950s *Fortune Magazine* identified him as one of the world's richest men. Today, his family is among Mexico's very wealthiest. He built a stylish mansion in Acapulco, where local officials divested dark-skinned poor of their lands so that PRI bosses and American rich, like oil tycoon J. Paul Getty, could build seaside estates. The one accomplishment of idealistic Cardenistas that Alemán did not reverse was oil nationalization, which might well have been preserved so as to facilitate corruption by milk-

Figure 17.2. In the 1940s the political left was frequently pilloried in the media, nearly all newspapers and radio stations owned by either the government or the wealthy. Here, caricatures of two professed Marxists, muralist Diego Rivera (seated) and labor leader Vicente Lombardo Toledano (to the right), are notably uncomplimentary in the Mexico City daily *Novedades*, a newspaper owned by Alemán's Irish friend Rómulo O'Farrill.
Source: Museo Casa de Leon Trotsky, Mexico City.

ing the healthy cow (Alemán's head of PEMEX built an Acapulco mansion catercorner to his own). Public contracts routinely included huge kickbacks, often right up to the president. One big project was an automobile-friendly, middle-class enclave on the northwest side of the capital christened Satellite City, modeled on American suburban planning. Another was the construction of a new campus for the national university. Built atop a dried lava flow that had long been neglected, the project ran inexplicably over budget. One advantage for Alemán was the consequent relocation of tens of thousands of students from downtown Mexico City, where they frequently protested his administration.

The Most Famous Mexican of All

Modern Mexico's most important president, Miguel Alemán, had a rather obvious obsession with the rich and famous. He consistently longed to be among them, though he himself did not seek the spotlight. He and his best friends were exceedingly fond of light-skinned female film stars. Alemán seemed to value white people. White skin symbolized power, cleanliness, and modernity. Thus, it is a quirky twist that Alemán's presidential term coincides with the triumph of the most famous public figure in all Mexican history. Through the silver screen a mestizo of humble origins captured the hearts of Mexico's struggling masses, even as Alemán took many steps that that helped ensure their perpetual impoverishment.

While Alemán was president, Mexican cinema reached the height of its golden age. Mexico's film industry greatly surpassed all others in Latin America; in 1947 alone, Mexicans purchased over one hundred million movie tickets. The desire of the government to influence the content of the new medium prompted tax breaks and subsidies in the 1920s, which grew under Cárdenas and continued under Alemán. Mexico's proximity to the United States, where much of the technology of filmmaking was developed, also helped the industry to thrive, especially after U.S. studios moved from New York to southern California. Cameras, film, microphones, lights, and other equipment were easily purchased in the Los Angeles area, while hundreds of Mexican Americans accessed low-level production jobs and learned the intricacies of the trade. Mexican actors and actresses were also hired early on in Hollywood, among them Dolores del Río, who became a sensation in the silent films of the 1920s. Unfortunately the advent of "talkies" ended her career, her spoken English laden with a difficult-to-understand, thick accent.

The first noteworthy Mexican film came in 1936 with *Over on Big Ranch* (*Allá en el Rancho Grande*), directed by Fernando de Fuentes, who had

Figure 17.3. While college students were the PRI's most vociferous critics, it was Alemán who, in a gradual process from 1947 to 1953, enfranchised women. Presidents Calles and Cárdenas had both been leery of giving women the vote, anticipating conservative and religious proclivities. Alemán, on the other hand, welcomed an ideological shift to the right. Enfranchisement elsewhere in Latin America also pushed Mexico forward. Here, women in Tijuana wait in line with males to cast ballots.
Source: Museo de Historia de Tijuana, Tijuana.

previously worked in Hollywood. A romance-drama with some comic relief, the story line involves a ranch owner who falls in love with a young peasant woman, Crucita, who unknowingly happens to be the fiancée of his foreman. The fallout between the two males drives the plot. Sixteen-year-old Esther Fernández played Crucita; production challenges included convincing the obsessively shy teen to kiss a man in front of the camera. After the film became Mexico's first blockbuster, Paramount Pictures contracted Fernández and brought her to Hollywood. But by this time sound had arrived and, despite intensive English-language classes, she, like del Río, could not shake a career-damning accent. After she lost the lead in *For Whom the Bell Tolls* to Ingrid Bergman, she returned to her native land, where she enjoyed considerable long-term success.

Thanks to film, del Río and Fernández became two of the most famous Mexican women of the twentieth century, but in a land of machismo it was predictably a male who garnered the most attention. Movies made Marío Moreno Reyes arguably the most famous person in Mexico's modern history. Even today, while the average citizen, when asked on the street, might be able to name one president or another, everyone knows *Cantinflas*. Born of working-class parents in the capital, Moreno was restless and poor as a teen, enlisting in the army (where he was discharged as underage), attempting to box (at which he was mediocre), and finally joining a traveling troupe. Known as *carpas*, the gypsy-like entertainers in these troupes sang lewd songs, danced, did stand-up comedy, and performed short skits and plays. Here he connected and perfected an uncanny wit while improvising and acting. Adopting a stage name that fused the word *cantina* (tavern) with the slang *te inflas* (literally, to balloon oneself—but in the 1930s meaning "get drunk"), he found his way into the budding film industry as a comic. Within just a few years, he endeared himself to Mexico's masses.

Cantinflas's appeal was actually quite formulated. In nearly every film he made, he played the role of the poor underdog, who against improbable odds trumped the powers that be and walked away victorious. Generally the plot involved winning the heart of a beautiful woman, her insistent and domineering rich lover enraged by the antics and audacity of the lowly interloper. But variations abounded, making each of Cantinflas's film (at least the earlier ones) fresh and engaging. As an unlikely police officer, he solves the crimes and befuddles the uptight commandant; as an undisciplined fireman he inadvertently saves the day; as a private in the army, he rolls out of bed long after the bugles have sounded, dressing at a leisurely pace that enrages his sergeant. In the 1941 film *Neither Blood nor Sand* (*Ni Sangre, Ni Arena*), he plays a matador who, despite obvious incompetence and a complete dis-

Figure 17.4. No Mexican has gained greater popular acclaim than Cantinflas, the mid-twentieth-century film comedian who remains broadly recognized even today. Facial expressions were key to his humor. When an aging Cantinflas had plastic surgery to remove excess facial tissue, it adversely affected this facial animation. For this and other reasons, the quality of his films declined over time. Still, when he died of lung cancer in 1993, the nation mourned.
Source: Hotel El Detalle, Ciudad Valles.

regard for all etiquette, surpasses the accomplishments of the dashing and cocksure veterans (after making the film, Cantinflas quipped to the press that only cows should really get to know bulls).

In 1944, with government help and with profits from Cantinflas's films, Mexicans built a state-of-the-art facility on the south side of Mexico City. The Churubusco Studios had a sound stage that rivaled anything in Hollywood and the very best in equipment; ironically, it was here that Cantinflas made some of his less evocative films. Part of the problem was that, after many years, the plot formula grew stale. In *Romeo y Julieta* (1944) he plays a Romeo often more inclined to eat chocolate than to kiss Juliet, much less die with her; but despite sophisticated production, the film lacks the compelling spontaneity of his earlier work. A subsequent venture to Hollywood was also critically disappointing, though commercially bright. Cantinflas costarred with David Niven (with Shirley MacLaine in a supporting role) in *Around the World in Eighty Days* (1955), a film based loosely on the popular Jules Verne novel. It won the Oscar for Best Picture and extended his fame to the United States and Europe. Little of note would follow. In his private life, Cantinflas was reclusive and balanced—he owned a ranch and often stayed out of the public eye. As a young man, he had married the daughter of the carpa's owner; his marriage with the Russian-born Valentina lasted a lifetime.

Politically, Cantinflas swam in the conservative current of the rising PRI elite. In the Cárdenas years, during a stint in Mexico City theaters, he frequently lampooned the president and playfully mocked his policies. He was fond of using the phrase "laza los cárdenos" (round up the drunks), a play on the president's name, while poking fun at his unpopular attempts to curtail alcohol consumption. He was more brazen in taunting the labor leader Lombardo Toledano. In one monologue he implied that the avowed Marxist was Stalin's passive homosexual partner. In his early film work he was predictably more discreet, but his overtly anti-Cárdenas reputation surely helped him advance as Alemán's clique rose. Cantinflas was friends with Alemán. He joined him on the campaign trail in 1946 and was undoubtedly pleased when the elected magistrate required that at least half of the films shown in theaters be Mexican-made. He bought a beachside estate in Acapulco not far from Alemán's and celebrated the chief magistrate's beloved resort (a couple of his early 1950s films are not far from amounting to advertisements for Acapulco). He spent many leisurely days on Alemán's yacht in the harbor and shared his enthusiasm for aviation, even taking flying lessons. In following decades, Cantinflas partied and mingled with the PRI rich. His films portrayed a generous spirit of identification with the poor. But when poor Mexicans wrote to him or stood outside his office or the studios in a quest for help, they were invariably ignored. His was a career that, in reality, reflected a maturating oligarchic age.

CHAPTER EIGHTEEN

PRI-Eminence

Miguel Alemán can rightly be called corrupt and opportunistic, but he was also intelligent and immensely shrewd. He understood that power need not be exercised by a high-profile, single man—that it can be perpetuated through networks and alliances best served from behind the scenes. The oligarchic state that he helped craft was far more sophisticated than anything Porfirio Díaz or Plutarco Calles had engineered. Consequently, it has lasted for decades (though in recent years it has come under considerable pressure). In the second half of the twentieth century, Mexico's PRI fraternity oversaw, in the words of Peruvian political commentator and novelist Marío Vargas Llosa, "the perfect dictatorship." Yet although quick to obliterate its unbending opponents, it also accommodated nearly anyone who was flexible. In the postwar decades, as the global economy boomed, the Mexican state had ample resources with which to buy and coopt the politically active; it also managed to nominally elevate living standards and accomplish some noteworthy goals. Mexico, for example, was the first Third World nation to host the Summer Olympics (and only one of four to do so, out of thirty-one selected venues, between 1898 and 2028).

The brilliance of the PRI's system lay in the concentrated power of a tight oligarchy. As long as a fraternity-like bond persisted among the rising super-rich, no simple or obvious one-man rule would ever be necessary. As his intelligence and media operations defeated a last-gasp challenge from idealistic nationalists in 1952, Alemán transferred the presidency to a faithful member of the club, ensuring that the PRI elite could perpetuate

Figure 18.1. Downtown Chihuahua City in the 1950s. Note the clash of old and new—the late colonial cathedral with a modern department store. In the postwar years, middle-class Mexican families bought automobiles, nearly all imported from the United States. New mid-century highways spurred growth in many secondary cities. Chihuahua, on a major route northward to Ciudad Juárez–El Paso, reached a population of nearly four hundred thousand in 1970.
Source: Museo Tarike, Chihuahua City.

political control and extract enormous amounts of money from a corruption-permeated system. His successor began an erstwhile if somewhat comical tradition of PRI governance: the fingering of corruption in the previous administration, which implicitly suggests a new respect for financial integrity. This ruse has been played over and over again, basically on cue, every six years. But neither Alemán nor any president or PRI club member has ever been meaningfully penalized in this decades-long charade. For his part, after he left office, Alemán assumed leadership of the National Tourism Council, an entity his own administration had created. He spent much of the rest of his life in his increasingly chic Acapulco, helping deepen the already formidable links between Mexican and American mega-rich, while engaging the budding industries of tourism and commercial aviation—two key businesses for Mexico's elite down to the present day.

Dimensions and Limitations of PRI Power

An astute and calculating man, Alemán understood the power of information control. Even as president, he took a keen interest in radio and the emerging technology of television. He personally invested in the expanding radio network of Emilio Azcárraga and even involved himself in some of the day-to-day operations of XEW, Mexico City's premier station, and he watched with great interest the launching by Azcárraga of Channel 2 (XEW) TV. With the help of Alemán and his American-born wife, Azcárraga effectively monopolized advertising from big U.S. corporations like Colgate and Procter & Gamble. This tactic and other pressures helped convince rivals to sell, and by the late 1950s the Monterrey-based media tycoon was well on his way to creating a TV monopoly via his *Televisa* network. The Alemán family has been one of Televisa's early, long-term, and major stockholders.

The media connection with Alemán is one of many links made between the capitalist elite of Monterrey and the PRI powerbrokers based in Mexico City. During the 1940s, the Monterrey rich were pleased with, and affable toward, the administrations of Ávila Camacho and Alemán. By the early 1950s they embraced the rising PRI fraternity, though they themselves had gained money through business enterprises rather than bureaucratic graft. Now, like the PRI elite, they were developing connections with foreign corporations and capital. Big Monterrey companies incorporated under international law in the 1950s, and many partnered with U.S. firms—Vidriera (Vitro), for example, with Owens in glassmaking. Monterrey rich built mansions in the Lomas de Chapultepec neighborhood of Mexico City, alongside the rich PRI bosses. Parties, social events, common preparatory schools and universities for their children, and eventually marriages linked the two groups over the next three decades, though a faction of the Monterrey elite kept their nominal distance and touted the small National Action Party (PAN) as an alternative to the PRI. The PAN routinely received token seats in the national congress, where it voted in harmony with the PRI—both sides routinely referring to it as the "loyal opposition."

Much of the PRI fraternity embraced a spiritual identity that repudiated both the nineteenth-century anti-clerical liberal tradition and the Calles clique's virulent anti-Catholicism. Like his friend, Ávila Camacho, Alemán identified himself as a believing Catholic. But the brand of Catholicism with which he and his associates affiliated had strong capitalist and even quasi-fascist inclinations. Though European fascism had been defeated in war, a fringe of the Roman Catholic Church had come under its spell. A Mexican priest, Carlos Cuesta Gallardo, spent most of the war years in Berlin, hobnobbing with the Nazi pseudo-philosopher Alfred Rosenberg and others who sought to define a new spiritual reality. He founded a private Catholic school, the Autonomous University of Guadalajara. Another fascist and Spanish Falange-influenced cleric, Marcial Maciel, established an organization called the Legionnaires of Christ, which in turn later spawned the club-like Anáhuac

University, its network of small branch campuses serving only well-to-do Mexicans. These and other hyper-capitalist, power-oriented Catholic entities later connected with the Spanish-created, Rome-based organization Opus Dei.

In the Catholic tradition, Alemán and his friends of course practiced traditional marriage with nuptials sealed through a religious mass (though the 1917 constitution had made marriage a civil ceremony, Mexicans who could afford it still typically had a formal though symbolic wedding in a church). In 1961 Alemán was undoubtedly delighted to see his son, Miguel, marry a foreigner, the former 1953 Miss Universe, France's Christiane Magnani, in the presence of a small cadre of friends that included Cantinflas. In 1957 one of his closest friends, Italian-born Bruno Pagliai, wed British film star Merle Oberon, who had portrayed a sensual Anne Boleyn in *The Private Life of Henry VIII*. After Oberon divorced Pagliai, the Veracruz-based industrialist married Italian fur designer Kika Viglietti, with Alemán as his best man. In 1962 Alemán and the PRI elite attended the intimate wedding of CIA station chief Winston Scott. The American spymaster in Mexico took his vows in the private home of one of the PRI's rich (Pablo Dietz), with Mexico's then president serving as his best man. Intimacy with powerful foreigners was a mark of the PRI fraternity.

A Mexican president serving as best man in the CIA station chief's wedding testifies to the exceptionally close bonds between U.S. security operatives and Mexico's super-rich. One of the more important U.S. intelligence assets in Mexico was Frank Brandstetter, an Austrian-born, naturalized U.S. citizen who managed the Acapulco Hilton in the 1960s. In such a privileged position, "Brandy," as he was known to his friends, interacted regularly with Mexico's elite. He developed a strong friendship with Alemán and his inner circle, including the elusive Carlos Trouyet, a confidant and financial advisor to Alemán who appears to have helped him skim massive amounts of money off the operations of Telmex, the nation's phone service, which had been converted into a monopoly by the Alemán administration. Brandstetter's circle also included some of the most important ex-Nazi assets of U.S. intelligence, including Walter Doraberger and others involved in the V-2 program who were brought to America and secretly given U.S. citizenship through Operation Paperclip. Many of these operatives frequented the Acapulco Hilton and in turn networked with Mexican contacts. Scores of Cuban intelligence officials from the pre-Castro Batista dictatorship also resided in Mexico and often stayed in Acapulco, while the British had a robust intelligence community in the country as well—Peter Hope, Britain's ambassador to Mexico (1968–1972), was long known to be involved in military and MI6 intelligence work.

Alongside Brandstetter in Acapulco was Alemán himself, who delighted in hosting America's political and social elite. John and Jackie Kennedy honeymooned in the upscale resort in 1953, while Hollywood's famous continued to retreat there. Alemán socialized with nearly all foreign visitors of note, with day trips aboard his luxurious yacht standard fare—he hosted Pat and Richard Nixon, Lyndon and Lady Bird Johnson, and a number of celebrities, including Frank Sinatra. He was advised by his American associates to steer clear of the heavyweight *mafiosos*, even though they shared his enthusiasm for the aviation and tourism industries as they promoted the middle-class American mecca of Las Vegas. A boon for intelligence and security forces was the election of Kennedy to the U.S. presidency in 1960. A rabid anti-communist, John, his father Joseph, and younger brother Bobby all had deep ties to the U.S. intelligence community and related anti-communist organizations (Bobby had worked as an aide to Senator Joe McCarthy during the Red Scare). Under Kennedy and Johnson, the U.S. government poured money into security apparatuses, both at home and abroad.

Figure 18.2. U.S. President John F. Kennedy, a rabid anti-communist, aggressively enhanced military and security apparatuses throughout Latin America and the Third World. The public face of the man was far more benign: hyped in the media as energetic and idealistic, his appearances often drew an enthusiastic public response. Here, inspired by New York ticker-tape parades, the Mexicans welcome him with confetti in downtown Mexico City, his Mexican counterpart Adolfo López Mateos at his side.
Source: Robert Knudsen, White House Photographs, John F. Kennedy Presidential Library, Boston.

During the 1960s, a network of anti-communist U.S. agencies rained support on select Mexican entities that could in turn feed the deepening pro-American security state. One important target was Cuesta Gallardo's private Autonomous University of Guadalajara (UAG). The Carnegie, Rockefeller, and Ford Foundations supported the UAG liberally, as did the U.S. Agency for International Development. The U.S. Consul in Guadalajara and several American academics, including Texas zoologist Oscar Wiegand, helped steer the UAG's leadership in their endeavors (Wiegand setting up its medical school). A secretive society emerged within the UAG called *Los Tecos* (The Owls—not to be confused with the present-day school's mascot), from which emerged death squads that pillaged both the Mexican idealist-nationalist left and forces deemed subversive in Guatemala and elsewhere over the next twenty years. Rich Mexicans also funded the UAG but generally favored the Ibero-American University in Mexico City, another Catholic university with overt connections to the PRI political establishment.

As academics have long realized, there is little that qualified as democratic in postwar Mexico. The PRI won 98 percent of all local and congressional elections, and every gubernatorial contest, from its founding under Alemán until the mid-1980s. Frozen out of elections, some opponents of the regime resisted in the streets. In western Chihuahua, with its revolutionary tradition, a robust movement of landless peasants, students, and some middle-class farmers launched a nonviolent agrarian and political reform movement. Rebuffed after years of agitation, a small minority of activists turned to armed insurrection, with no success. In the city of San Luis Potosí, a medical doctor named Salvador Nava scored a major upset by winning the mayoral race in 1958. His movement flourished as he ran for governor, until the PRI dispatched army troops to occupy the state capital and enforce several months of martial law. Eventually, among hundreds of students and mostly middle-class followers, Nava himself was arrested and taken off to endure torture sessions at Military Camp One, an army base in Mexico City that housed a clandestine prison filled with political activists.

The Nava movement was suppressed by the administration of Adolfo López Mateos, a man who postured publicly as an agent of progressive change and goodwill. While Televisa's fast-multiplying TV stations extolled his accomplishments, behind the scenes he brooked no dissent. In 1959 his government savagely crushed a nationwide railroad strike led by an independent-minded union. Hundreds of workers were beaten and abused, some tortured, in police stations throughout the country; the union's leaders were arrested and shipped off to an island prison in the Pacific Ocean, where some remained incarcerated for years. The union had made strategic errors, overplaying its weak hand while disrupting passenger service during the busy

Easter Holy Week. The PRI's media was able to largely turn public opinion against it, the media portraying strikers as Soviet-influenced communist dupes. When Mexico's most famous muralist at the time, David Alfaro Siqueiros, voiced criticism, he was hauled off to prison as well—though his fame and international criticism ensured a lack of physical abuse.

Spontaneity and circumstance, however, could sometimes provide an edge to popular movements. Such was the case in the summer of 1968, when the pending Olympic Games in Mexico City placed an international spotlight on the nation. Clashes between university students and riot police boiled over in what should have been a localized and apolitical incident. Instead, with increasingly political ramifications, massive protests unfolded. Hundreds of thousands of mostly middle-class Mexicans took to the streets, demanding a range of reforms. They did so in the context of worldwide events—the student-led uprising in Paris, and political violence in American cities in the wake of Martin Luther King Jr.'s assassination. Security forces smartly bided their time, while Televisa and media outlets gave the movement scant attention. After the crowds diminished, just before the opening of the Olympic Games, the state struck back: several thousand protestors were targeted at the Plaza of Tlatelolco, where Aztecs had fought Spaniards in the siege of Tenochtitlán centuries earlier. Over three hundred protestors died and hundreds were injured in a one-sided massacre. The next day, the *Excélsior* newspaper headline read "Terrible Gun Battle in Tlatelolco." The flurry of political unrest in the capital evaporated like the morning dew, with little lasting consequence.

Besides fleeting, episodes such as the violence in Mexico City and the Nava movement in San Luis Potosí were isolated. The premise that the poor and downtrodden naturally rise up against oppression is dubious. Despite remarkable wealth concentration at the top, a decisive majority of Mexicans remained politically disinterested. With its formidable security forces, Mexico's power structure could have easily become a "hard dictatorship," but in truth it did not have to. Much of the population was sedate and even content under what critics dubbed the PRI-firiato. The malcontents were mostly intellectuals, the educated, and student youth (typically from the middle class). A small, progressive, and mostly intellectual wing of the Catholic Church also raised pertinent social and political questions. In contrast, the rural peasantry remained in a political slumber, while some peasant organizations—many tied to old Cardenista *ejidos*—proactively supported the PRI. The majority of the middle class, including working adults, were also reasonably satisfied. Taxes stayed low and there was a modicum of upward mobility.

Part of the explanation for this acquiescence is the nature of the PRI's governance. Along with its formidable cooptation of mass media, the oligarchic regime broadly employed the carrot more readily than the stick. In Mexico

Figure 18.3. Though the 1968 anti-government student movement has been widely analyzed by historians, a pro-government countermovement has received relatively scant attention. Here, thousands rally against the student left, buying into the government and media line—that the reform movement was communist-inspired. Rightist rhetoric appealed to Catholics and nationalists, as reflected in banners such as "Communism No, Mexico Yes."
Source: Museo Archivo de la Fotografía, Mexico City.

(as worldwide), postwar economic growth was strong. The expanding pie allowed for co-optation of potential dissenters. Poor people are cheap to buy off. A local firebrand demanding trash pickup in an urban slum was often made a municipal official and PRI operative with a salary of a few thousand pesos. In the massive bureaucracy of governance, a pyramid structure redirected the ambitions of people—one could in fact advance and gain power, over time, by playing ball within the system. Labor unions were in particular an object of co-optation. Under a wholly compromised chieftain named Fidel Velásquez, organized labor ironically became a bulwark of the PRI system. In turn, it received incentives that made its workers relatively better-off than the general populace. The Mexican Institute of Social Security largely served it, providing modest pensions—to the delight of the business elite—at state expense. When the students were massacred at Tlatelolco in 1968, Mexico's union leadership commended the government and staged counterrallies on its behalf.

Bread and Circuses

The general public had myriad distractions in the postwar era, including that of mass media. By 1960, Mexico had 240 radio stations blanketing the entire country. Affordable televisions sold by the millions in the early 1960s; a collective addiction to TV developed in Mexico. In myriad homes the television stayed on almost constantly. Slum-dwelling poor pooled their resources, often sharing a TV set. In 1958 Televisa pioneered its first *telenovelas*, soap operas modeled on those in the United States, though most typically broadcast in the evening hours. Melodramatic, with thick plots of romance, love gone wrong, betrayal, and intrigue, they captivated the public. At first these dramas commonly ran for thirty minutes, but later most ran for a full hour. Also unlike their U.S. counterparts, they were usually designed to air for only a few months or a year, though exceptionally popular ones were sometimes re-broadcast or remade a couple of decades later. Beyond dramas, Televisa mastered live broadcasts and aired the games of the Mexican Football (Soccer) Federation, an organization it came to largely control.

Music, through mass media, entranced Mexicans. Radio and TV celebrated the nation's rich musical heritage. Mariachi bands had become much more photogenic since the early twentieth century, as they donned traditional *charro* attire like the old Porfirian Rurales, with matching uniforms—their leather trousers and short jackets often glittering with ornamentation. *Norteño*, a country genre from the borderlands defined by the accordion and an um-pah polka beat, received ample airtime as well. In urban areas, Americanized *rocanrol* took hold in middle-class homes, especially after a much-celebrated 1969 concert by The Doors in Mexico City's bullring. The first successful Mexican rock band was Three Souls in My Mind, fronted by a long-haired Alex Lora, which largely imitated the sound of the Rolling Stones and Credence Clearwater Revival. In 1971 Mexico had its own Woodstock of sorts, a similar mud-drenched organizational disaster, the crowd of tens of thousands disappointed when native-born Carlos Santana failed to appear.

For the urban poor, other distractions included *lucha libre*, or professional wrestling. Among migrants to Mexico City was a young man of limited means whose fame eventually challenged that of Cantinflas. Rodolfo Guzmán Huerta embraced the theatrics of lucha libre. From the start of his five-thousand-match career he donned a silver mask, often walking to the ring in a silver cape—a mystery man who became Mexico's embodiment of a superhero. He performed with acrobatic grace at a higher level than most, but it was his ring persona that drew the fans and made him a superstar. As *El Santo* (The Saint), he displayed an integrity that turned lucha libre into

Figure 18.4. Whether fighting the mafia or the vampire women, El Santo surely faced nearly impossible odds. A couple dozen low-budget Santo films were made in the sixties, often with some racy scenes, despite their overarching moral connotations. Studios used preexisting wrestling match footage and shoddy stage sets in order to reduce costs. Professional actors did vocal overdubs—the real Santo's voice was monotone and unconvincing.
Source: Centro Cultural, San Luis Potosí.

a morality play. Fighting the wicked *rudos*, El Santo faced difficult odds. But the cheers of fans brought down on him supernatural energy, and almost miraculously (to the incredibly naïve, at least) he triumphed over evil again and again. In the dismal lives of the struggling urban poor, this victory of the "little guy" against the corrupt and powerful engendered hope. El Santo's obvious faith in God and modesty with his fans endeared him to thousands.

Those thousands turned into millions through mass media. In the 1940s he appeared in countless *fotonovelas*—flimsy comic books that employed photographs instead of drawings. Characters changed, but the plot remained the same. Some helpless victim, a woman or child, faced an impossible, often supernatural, adversary. Seeking out El Santo, who in turn cried out to the Virgin of Guadalupe, the evil warlock, the werewolf, or the devil himself was vanquished. By the time television began broadcasting lucha libre matches in 1955, he was already well known. Films followed, first in 1959 with *El Santo versus the Evil Brain*, a production that temporarily revived the flagging Mexican film industry. Interestingly, in both fotonovelas and his films, El Santo appeared as a well-to-do businessman, complete with stylish office, modern gadgetry, a sports car, and an attractive wife. The trappings of middle-class life were no barrier to sainthood. But the worldwide boom years of the sixties masked fundamental problems in Mexico's political and economic trajectories. As the population surged to over fifty million by 1970, access to a middle class proved elusive for the vast majority. What was dubbed by ardent capitalists as the "Mexican Miracle" had, in fact, structural flaws, and those flaws soon became apparent.

CHAPTER NINETEEN

Bombast, Boom, Bust

In December 1969, Televisa, Mexico's lone TV network, aired a new variety show called *Always on Sundays* (*Simpre en Domingo*). Modeled on *The Ed Sullivan Show* in the United States, *Always on Sundays* would become a fixture in Mexican life, with 1,480 programs offering viewers over ten thousand hours of entertainment before its final broadcast in 1998. Raúl Velasco, its host, became one of the best-known Mexicans of the twentieth century. Tied to the record industry, radio, and print media, Televisa invariably helped create Mexico's pop culture stars, many of whom first rose to fame via appearances on the show. Such was the case with José José, a Mexico City nightclub singer whose father performed in operas and whose mother was an accomplished pianist. After signing with RCA in 1969, José José made multiple *Always on Sundays* appearances, which powered him to stardom. Through his *boleros*, or soft ballads, he became an international phenomenon in the Hispanic world, ultimately selling over thirty-five million records. His success was echoed in the career of Guadalupe Pineda, the Queen of Bolero, who sold ten million records while singing not only in Spanish, but also in French and English. Televisa's global reach, and the careers of these pop sensations, reflect the internationalization of Mexican life after 1970. *Bolero*, a dreamy musical genre thick with background strings, arguably provided a needed psychological escape for Mexicans, whose economic and political plight in these strange times was something many would have preferred to forget.

Two Neighbors Reconnect

The 1970s and 1980s saw a dramatic increase in interaction between working-class Mexicans and their American neighbors. A 1965 agreement between the two countries created a free trade zone along the border. Factories within thirty kilometers of the frontier were ensured duty-free transit, giving U.S. corporations direct access to cheap Mexican labor. A robust labor movement in the United States had come to demand middle-class wages for low-skill workers in the mid-twentieth century. Now, corporations could pressure those unions for wage concessions via threats to move operations into Mexico. As an added incentive, plants that shipped raw material or components into the trade zone for assembly could legally stamp their products "Made in America" if a last production step was completed on the U.S. side (a transistor radio merely needed its cover screw inserted). By the early 1970s, not surprisingly, border assembly and textile workshops were flourishing. Called *maquiladoras* in Spanish, they hired tens and eventually hundreds of thousands of poor Mexicans—a half million in two thousand facilities by 1995.

In conjunction with the maquiladoras, transportation connections between the border cities and interior Mexico improved, drawing millions of Mexicans northward in search of jobs. The population growth on the frontier was astounding: Ciudad Juárez, with a population of just forty thousand in 1945, counted 1.3 million residents sixty years later. But for Mexico's burgeoning population, there was never enough employment. Those who failed to find work in the maquiladoras often continued northward, filling service sector positions in U.S. border cities or ending up in large cities such as Los Angeles and San Antonio, which already had sizable Mexican American populations. These tended to stay among other Mexicans, often only speaking Spanish. But in the early seventies, they constituted the first big wave of an ultimately massive and controversial illegal immigration into the United States.

Above the migrating masses, in the skies, binational interaction also multiplied. Commercial aviation grew exponentially in the 1960s and 1970s, even before the Carter administration deregulated air transport and sent ticket prices plummeting. Miguel Alemán's connections to the tourist industry drew much of the PRI power elite into the business. In turn, Mexico's super-rich used their control of the government to paternalistically enhance the lucrative and booming sector. After all, Mexico had something the Americans very much wanted: sandy beaches under a warm sun. In 1970, the government selected a remote stretch of an idyllic barrier island for development. Cancún is testimony that even a planned city can turn out ugly. When the first hotel opened here in 1974, its guests survived on trucked-in water

Figure 19.1. New hotel construction in Cancún. An idyllic barrier island was transformed in the last quarter of the twentieth century into one of the world's biggest tourist draws, cruise docks and an international airport servicing nearly twenty million annual visitors by 2015. The pre-planned city of Cancún became home to the tens of thousands of Mexican workers who cleaned sheets and served food to Europeans and Americans.

and its lights were powered by a single electric generator. By 2007, Cancún's airport had become Mexico's second largest, handling over ten million passengers; by 2020, concrete-heavy Cancún was home to nearly seven hundred thousand Mexicans.

Mexican and American interaction had a seedy side as well, with the emergence of big drug cartels. Though Mexico's security apparatuses seem to have been involved in moving illegal narcotics in the previous two decades, it was the 1970s that saw the trade flourish, coming in the wake of a 1960s counterculture that embraced the exploratory use of mind-soothing and imagination-altering drugs. When the famous French Connection was disrupted in 1972, heroin rackets in Mexico stepped in to meet market demand in east coast U.S. cities. These operations grew opium high in the western Sierra Madre, in a triangle region near the borders of Chihuahua, Durango, and Sinoloa states. With over twenty-five million people crossing the U.S.-Mexican border each year, transit was easy. Drug lords made epic amounts of money. In the late seventies, however, the U.S. Drug Enforcement Agency carried out a highly successful eradication campaign, employing the controversial herbicide paraquat, which dropped the Mexican heroin market share from nearly 90 percent to just 30 percent by 1979.

In the 1980s, the vogue American drug of choice was cocaine, and this time around some of the traditional PRI power elite cut into the action—employing select security and policing forces in the process. Cocaine was routed through Mexico, from Bolivia, Peru, and Colombia, but coca paste was also frequently processed in the country as well, in part because of the availability of ether and acetone, two conversion agents. There appears to have been some resentment among Mexico's elite for having missed out on the earlier heroin boomlet (one reason why they were apparently fine with the Americans eradicating it). Such a good business opportunity would not be missed again: by the late eighties, a mini revival of heroin was also in the works, while marijuana grown in Mexico also began to penetrate the burgeoning U.S. drug market.

Though tensions periodically arose regarding Mexico's "failures" in the drug war (of course it was U.S. demand that created the market), it was illegal immigration that most annoyed the American public. In 1986, Ronald Reagan's administration responded with the Immigration Reform and Control Act (IRCA). This law gave amnesty, or a road to U.S. citizenship, to 1.2 million illegals residing in the United States, issuing them so-called Green Cards (which, in the infinite wisdom of the U.S. government, were actually pink, and later beige, in color). Otherwise, the IRCA proposed to rigorously enforce rules that prohibited the hiring of illegal residents by employers. But strangely, the Department of Labor under Reagan actually cut the number of its inspectors! It was as though the U.S. government *wanted* to encourage more illegal immigration rather than reduce it. In fact, this is exactly what happened. Amnesty prompted more Mexicans to cross the border, many drawn by the hope of one day becoming U.S. citizens (polling data in the early 1990s showed that 92 percent of Mexicans would rather be Americans). Reagan's supposed fix was profoundly counterproductive to stopping illegal immigration, something favored by a decided majority of the American people, if not by U.S. employers.

Eccentric Executives

In 1970 the PRI designated a stalwart politician named Luis Echeverría as its presidential candidate. It was in retrospect a very poor choice. Long compliant and ambitious, Echeverría carried with him a burdensome insecurity, an inner need to win the approval of the crowd (he had served as minister of the interior during the Tlatelolco massacre, and some noted that he acted like a man trying to appease his troubled conscience). His campaign for the presidency saw him crisscross the country, delivering rousing speeches and promising a new era of populist renewal. Some PRI leaders were aghast when he joined a group of university students in a moment of silence for the victims at Tlatelolco.

Once in office, Echeverría surprised with his boundless energy. He engaged meetings with zeal, while devoting much less time to reading reports or studying complex issues. When a subordinate suggested a new idea, he often pushed it ahead recklessly. On a seemingly intelligent proposal to promote the cultivation of sunflowers from his agricultural department, he scribbled "do this four-fold." He was convinced that, by decisive leadership, he could transform Mexico into a prosperous and modern country within six years. He very much wanted to be the agent of that transformation, aspiring to see grateful citizens cheer him.

Figure 19.2. Mexico City's subway system, called the Metro, opened in conjunction with the 1968 Summer Olympics but underwent rapid expansion in the 1970s. Construction digs repeatedly turned up myriad Aztec artifacts. Here, an altar to the wind god Ehecatl (note its circular shape) sits at a critical work site just south of the Zócalo. Rather than remove it, authorities incorporated the altar into the Pino Suarez station, an important Metro stop where two major lines intersect.
Source: Museo Archivo de la Fotografia, Mexico City.

Unfortunately for Echeverría, some were not inclined to cheer. Many university students in particular spurned his overtures. A few affiliated with upstart guerrilla organizations, which were subsequently savaged in a low-level dirty war by the security forces. An anti-government march in Mexico City was attacked by knife-wielding PRI-financed thugs, leaving dozens dead and hundreds wounded. When Echeverría visited the National Autonomous University of Mexico (UNAM) campus in mid-term, he was pelted with beer bottles, one striking him in the head. Nor was the timing of governance in his favor. By 1970 Mexico's booming population had finally exceeded the semi-arid nation's foodshed capacity. Grain imports from the United States widened an already considerable trade deficit. In 1974, spiking global oil prices triggered an inflationary cycle. Too proud to float the peso and allow it to find its real value on the currency market, Echeverría financed ever-growing deficits by printing money, which only served to worsen the inflation. The national debt also ballooned, while nervous middle-class families with bank accounts began converting pesos to dollars. When Echeverría finally did float the currency, just before he left office, the peso collapsed from a rate of 12.5 to just 26 to the dollar.

If Echeverría had bad timing, it appeared that his successor, José López Portillo, had the very best of luck. Shortly after taking office, he was informed of the discovery of massive oil reserves in the shallow waters of the Gulf of Campeche. Under Echeverría, López Portillo had proven himself an obedient minister of the treasury, willing to ratchet up debt without fiscal discipline on the orders of his impulsive boss. Now, as president, he proved that he truly *believed* in reckless spending. With global oil prices sky high, against better advice he ordered PEMEX to develop the fields as quickly as possible. Taking on tens of billions of dollars in debt in order to purchase drilling equipment and oil rigs at a pace faster than the industry could normally supply them (and consequently paying inflated prices), the Mexican government gambled that it could beat the market and reap enormous profits that would easily retire any short-term debt.

By 1979 it appeared that the wild scheme was working. Oil prices were still high, and several major platforms in the Gulf were pumping crude. López Portillo himself swaggered with hubris. Before a PRI assembly he boasted of Mexico's newfound wealth. He began to spend lavishly on social programs, darting across the country to dedicate new soccer fields, hospitals, and schools, some bearing his own name. Predictably, all the largesse facilitated corruption, the skimming of funds on a scale not seen since the days of Alemán (who had milked a thinner cow with more acumen). The president even spent money to make a film about himself, showing his ostensible compassion for the poor, his devotion to God, and his horseback-riding skills. In meetings with U.S. officials, he was unduly curt and dismissive, informing Americans that Mexico was about to become their material equal. Indeed, his indulgent spending had transnational implications: the PEMEX expansion helped spark an economic boom in the Texas oil-based city of Houston.

As López Portillo's boomlet unfolded, Mexico's super-rich flourished. Besides well-guarded mansions in Mexico City or Monterrey, they purchased auxiliary homes in Acapulco and in the United States (most typically in Miami and San Antonio). Some maintained weekend country estates in Cuernavaca, roughly fifty miles south of Mexico City. A few bought skiing chalets in Aspen, Colorado. Many sent their sons to Harvard. Extravagance was the order of the day. The Garza Sada family of Monterrey used their private jet to transport specialty foods from Houston; another elite family used their jet to occasionally transport just their dog. Discretion of the super-rich continued, too, with few willing to even join country clubs. Instead, most socialized privately with one another, their most powerful males still often marrying either French or American women. It was not uncommon for them to fly famous American musicians to their houses for private parties. Several families crossed the line to billionaire status.

In the midst of the boom, Televisa aired one of its most successful year-long telenovelas. *The Rich Also Cry (Los Ricos También Lloran)* was in some ways a brilliant propaganda piece, ensuring Mexico's toiling masses that those with money have no spiritual advantage over them. Its plot suggests that goodness can also be found among the rich. A poor young woman named Marianna (played by singer-actress Veronica Castro) is left in a precarious position after her loving father dies; a priest intervenes and convinces a wealthy patriarch to care for her. He is a gentleman, kind and caring, but his womanizing son tries to seduce her—the naïve Marianna is easy prey. In time, though, even this devious soul is awestruck by the woman's innocence, his heart transformed, his malicious ways put to rest. True love brought him peace . . . his riches meant nothing.

The Crash

Perhaps José López Portillo did not watch the telenovela. He, his family, and PRI associates around him amassed great wealth in the late seventies. But then, in the midst of personal and political triumph, López Portillo's own nightmare began. Oil prices began to waffle. Multiple factors accounted for this, including a production glut, a slowing global economy, and tighter U.S. fiscal policies under the incoming Reagan administration, which strengthened the dollar. As oil prices slid, López Portillo's PEMEX at first refused to cut its prices, demanding contract renewal and threatening buyers with restricted future market access. Prices slid further; buyers walked. By late 1981 oil was in free fall, and PEMEX was sitting on large stockpiles of unsold crude. The national debt, which had surged from US$17 billion in 1976 to US$80 billion, demanded servicing. Mexico's fiscal solvency was now at stake.

Rarely in history has a leader risen so high and fallen so low as José López Portillo. In the face of the crisis, he vowed to never debase the national currency, to never float the peso, to in fact "defend the peso like a dog." Mexicans began referring to his luxurious mansion, built carelessly astride a major highway on Mexico City's south side, as the "Dog House." But as oil continued its decline and the dollar its rise, the president had no choice. When he floated the currency in February 1982, it sank from 26 to 45 to the dollar within days. By August it was at 80 to 1. Mexico slid into an economic depression. López Portillo appeared before Congress, his voice choking before breaking into tears. Disgraced like no other president since Porfirio Díaz, he left the country and entered a comfortable exile in Spain, leaving a hapless technocrat to pick up the pieces.

Miguel de la Madrid's term in office (1982–1988) saw Mexicans shell-shocked by economic collapse. The peso continued its precipitous fall, eventually sinking to 800 to the dollar by 1986. Travel abroad for the middle class became next to impossible. The poor flooded into the United States in search of work. For its part, America showed little mercy for its debt-ridden southern neighbor, even after Mexico shunned attempts by Argentina to create a debtor's cartel (the entire region falling into debt) and instead willingly submitted to the demands of New York's big banks. Servicing the debt became the primary goal of the Mexican state. Ultimately, as it surpassed US$100 billion, Mexico's debt was effectively taken off the banks' ledgers and transferred to the International Monetary Fund, a preexisting, Washington-based entity that in effect became a giant global debt collection agency. Social spending ground to a halt. Reduction of subsidies on food staples drove the price of corn tortillas up 40 percent. Even corruption by Mexico's rich basically ended—there was little to scrape off the empty plate.

Grassroots activism surged in the late 1980s, with countless marches, protests, and some civil unrest, but open rebellion did not occur. De la Madrid governed cautiously and garnered at least a modicum of public support by fingering corrupt officials in the now despised López Portillo administration. Time-tested, the traditional PRI charade of supposed anti-corruption reform still had some effect. Arturo Durazo, Mexico City's police chief and a close personal friend of the former president, was very visibly arrested and prosecuted for embezzling funds totaling several hundred million dollars, some of which he had used to construct a Roman-style villa on the outskirts of the capital. Durazo was hauled off to jail in front of Televisa cameras, only to be quietly released a few years later. For the PRI fraternity, seriously disciplining anyone involved in the security state is a dangerous proposition. De la Madrid, with the IMF's blessing, maintained spending on the DFS and other policing entities. When an earthquake killed more than ten thousand in Mexico City in 1985, it leveled a secret police prison; rescuers found scores of crushed bodies bearing the marks of gruesome torture.

One of the most important political assassinations of the entire postwar era came in May 1984, when an investigative journalist named Manuel Buendia took four .38 caliber slugs in his back as he walked to his car in Mexico City's business district. Buendia was an insider of sorts, a well-known columnist for the quasi-governmental newspaper *Excélsior*, whose authentic anti-corruption revelations had for several years rocked the Mexican political establishment. Having published a book titled *The CIA in Mexico*, he was onto some of the nefarious activities of the intelligence apparatuses, including links between security forces, the CIA, and some drug cartels, most notably that of Rafael Caro Quintero, which was training Guatemalan paramilitaries on a ranch in Jalisco in coordination with Los Tecos. He had developed contacts from within government circles and even, apparently, within the ranks of the DFS. His journalistic crusade held the potential to trigger real reform in Mexico, but, predictably, he also had many powerful enemies.

Figure 19.3. The early 1980s saw horrific violence in the neighboring Guatemalan highlands, which left some two hundred thousand civilians dead—mostly young males, some mourned here by their Mayan widows. Publicly the Mexican government condemned the United States' genocidal policies in Central America; behind the scenes, Mexican intelligence and security networks helped carry the policies out.
Source: Centro Fotográfico Alvarez Bravo, Oaxaca.

First to arrive at the murder site was José Antonio Zorrilla Pérez, head of the DFS. Over subsequent years, under his supervision, key evidence was lost and critical leads left dormant. His improbable conclusion, that rogue PRI thugs had killed Buendia, eventually unraveled, and in 1990 Zorrilla himself was arrested for the murder, along with Juan Rafael Moro Ávila Camacho, grandson of the former president. Buendia's revelations never made it onto Televisa newscasts, of course, and ultimately the journalist's reach was limited. But they were enough to cost him his life. His murder sent a chill through journalistic circles, prompting other inquisitive reporters and editors to temper their activities and ask fewer questions. The most compliant and mainstream of Mexico's reporters often grew inexplicably rich, with money and possessions materializing beyond the scope of their relatively modest salaries.

As the difficulties of life in Mexico multiplied in the mid-eighties, Televisa helped launch the career of a pop icon to whom the lowly and defeated could particularly relate. Alberto Aguilera Valdez was born on a farm in 1950, the youngest of ten kids in a family trapped in acute poverty. At age fifteen he left home, living on the streets in Mexico City. He stole a guitar, and served a year in prison for the petty crime. When he made his first album at age twenty-one he adopted the stage name Juan Gabriel. After appearances on Televisa's *Always on Sundays* and the lightning success of his RCA-released *Recuerdos* album in 1984, he became forever known as simply *JuanGa*. If bolero singer José José was the "Tom Jones" of the Hispanic world, JuanGa became its Elton John. Singing a variety of simple soft rock and pop songs, his media-infused career produced record sales totaling thirty million. When he died in 2016 of a heart attack at his home in Santa Monica, California, the entire nation mourned, Televisa devoting hour-by-hour coverage of his funeral entourage as it weaved its way through the capital. Even in fame, unlike Cantinflas, JuanGa did not forget his roots, often performing for free in prisons and orphanages. His big arena shows celebrated Mexico and Mexicans, with traditional dance and *mariachis*. At the end of the twentieth century, Mexican identity was in flux, caught up in a fast globalizing world. So too, economic and political pressures defined the closing decade of the century, in an era of challenges and doubt.

CHAPTER TWENTY

Crises and Control

On a September morning in 1973, at an intersection in Monterrey, a car screeched to a halt in front of Eugenio Garza Sada's armored Ford Galaxie. Several men jumped out of another vehicle, approaching the eighty-two-year-old patriarch of Monterrey industrialists on foot. In the brief gunfight that ensued, an armed Garza Sada, along with his chauffeur and a bodyguard, perished. The press explained the event as a failed kidnapping attempt by communists. Over one hundred thousand turned out for the old man's funeral, where speakers eulogized him as a champion of Mexican capitalism and mid-century founder of the Monterrey Institute of Technology—popularly known as "El Tec"—the nation's premier engineering and technological university. Already hostile public sentiment hardened toward urban guerrillas and their leftist supporters.

A few years later, state police in Monterrey burst into a print shop and seized thousands of copies of a book. Its author was Irma Salinas, a grandmother within the Monterrey elite who alleged, among other things, that the attack on Garza Sada was in fact an assassination ordered by family insiders. She claimed that they were miffed at Eugenio for collaborating with President Luis Echeverría and for agreeing to the nationalization of Mexico's steel industry. Supposed communists, according to Salinas, were arrested and tortured until they made false confessions, then thrown unjustly into prison. Over subsequent weeks the wealthy Mrs. Salinas faced some harassment of her own and had exceptionally bad luck—an airport that she owned, for example, was suddenly found to be out of compliance with aviation laws.

Dirty Laundry and Dirty Elections

The case of Irma Salinas hints at a closeted underworld within the mansions of Monterrey's Obispado neighborhood. Historians are not in a position to determine the truth about the 1973 attack on Garza Sada, nor can we be certain about much of the internal workings of either the PRI or the Monterrey elite—who neither archive their most sensitive papers nor reveal all when they grant rare interviews. The opaque nature of Mexico's oligarchy is beyond doubt, but logic leads any disciplined mind into a nebulous unknowing, on a narrow path flanked by pitfalls of naïveté and conspiracy theory. What is certain is that an elite figure with considerable dirty laundry obtained the presidency in 1988. As a child, Carlos Salinas (no direct relation to Irma) and his older brother were playing with a loaded handgun when they killed a domestic servant. The story of this incident, and family connections to the Monterrey rich, were sequestered as Salinas ran for office in a campaign orchestrated by sophisticated public relations firms—though the effort still did not quite go as planned.

In the late 1980s, both the Mexican economy and political system were under great duress. The collapse of the peso and concomitant debt crisis had triggered years of depression; robust grassroots reform movements nipped at the PRI and revived the long-moribund political left. Its new champion was none other than the son of 1930s nationalist Lázaro Cárdenas, who was himself named after the last Aztec emperor. Though not a gifted public speaker, Cuauhtémoc Cárdenas caught the imagination of Mexico's students, intelligentsia, and disenchanted workers. On the right, whatever the circumstances of the elderly Garza Sada's death, there is no doubt that a core of Monterrey elite despised ex-president Echeverría, with whom he had parleyed. Many of them wavered in their allegiance to the PRI—even more so during the financial crisis of the early eighties that saw banks temporarily nationalized—and began to support the long-associated but tiny National Action Party (PAN). Now flush with money, the once staunchly Catholic, pro-business party gained momentum, especially in the northern states, much of its cadre graduates of El Tec in Monterrey. One of these, formerly president of the Owners' Confederation, ran for president. On the campaign trail an animated Manuel Clothier criticized Televisa, telling his supporters to abstain from watching "the lies" of the evening news.

In fact, there were many misrepresentations on Televisa. At first the network ignored both insurgent campaigns. But as Cárdenas rose in the polls, it pilloried him. One news-oriented show produced two reputed illegitimate children of his father Lázaro, both of whom robustly criticized their half brother and sang the praises of the PRI. When the fiftieth anniversary of the popular oil expropriation inconveniently occurred in the heat of the presidential campaign, the network and other media downplayed it while going to great lengths to, at the very least, never mention the name Cárdenas. As Cuauhtémoc's campaign continued to gain traction in the home stretch, Televisa hyped the PAN, clearly strategizing to divide the opposition.

The tense 1988 election culminated with enormous Cárdenas rallies in cities, some drawing over one hundred thousand participants. In the indigenous-dominated south, where his campaign was also popular, hundreds of campaign activists were disappeared and murdered. When early results poured in on election night, they suggested that the opposition left had scored a stunning victory. But then, Televisa and other media aired reports from the electoral commission that, unfortunately, the newly computerized tabulating system had broken down. After a long delay of several days, the

Figure 20.1. The most powerful and corrupt president since Miguel Alemán, Carlos Salinas benefited from a favorable media that still strained to cloak some of the more sordid details of his past. Hailing from the inner circle of the PRI fraternity, he strove to deepen already robust oligarchic links to American corporations, while privatizing public properties to the delight of Wall Street investors. Many Mexicans called him "The Bloodsucker" (*Chupacabra*).
Source: Museo de Historia de Tijuana, Tijuana.

revived computers indicated that Carlos Salinas had pulled out the narrowest of victories, winning a majority with 50.3 percent of the vote. The PRI remained in power.

In office, Salinas governed with a mentality befitting his elite Monterrey roots. A hyper-capitalist agenda saw the government re-privatize the banks and also sell off a host of money-making entities, most notably Telmex—the nation's telephone monopoly. The elite bought many of these properties, sometimes at questionably low prices, and when Salinas left office the number of Mexican billionaires rose from just a few in the late 1970s to two dozen. His close friend and associate, Carlos Slim, soon became the richest man in the world. A much-hyped free trade agreement with the United States inspired corporate America's confidence as well, and foreign capital also flowed inward. Though the peso stabilized (now reset with three zeroes lopped off), the mass of Mexicans did not greatly benefit from the sloshing billions at the top. Grassroots activism and protests largely continued, evoking considerable repression from security and police forces.

Mexico on the Brink

As the free trade agreement took effect in January 1994, a rebellion erupted in the highlands of Chiapas, in southeastern Mexico. Evoking the memory of Emiliano Zapata, the *New Zapatistas* were ironically created by middle-class mestizos, including one Subcommandante Marcos, who kept his face covered with a ski mask. Scores of reporters descended on the region, as did several hundred (mostly European) foreigners, rushing to the defense of human rights in the context of the horrific slaughters in nearby Guatemala a decade earlier. Mexican security apparatuses had long been monitoring the activists who executed the media-sensational uprising, so why did they allow it to proceed? Perhaps political considerations and timing were at play, but how could Mexican military personnel not be awed by the influx of enormous amounts of American money and arms to their counterparts, previously in Central America and presently in Colombia? A little rebellion could clearly become a profitable proposition. As if on cue, after the rebellion broke out, the United States poured several hundred million dollars' worth of military aid into Mexico, including nifty and swift Apache helicopters (poetically named after a native tribe the Americans once annihilated). And did Salinas and the PRI's leadership see promise in a controllable little fury on the eve of the next general election? The specter of a bloody revolution might sway the masses to vote for the enduring stability of the PRI.

In fact, the PRI fraternity approached the end of the Salinas term with an unprecedented degree of trepidation. Cuauhtémoc Cárdenas's 1988 challenge had nearly destabilized the system, with much of the country believing that the election had been stolen. A bout of instability in a fragile political system such as Mexico's could trigger capital flight, frighten away foreign investors, and reduce the elites' net worth by billions of dollars. Yet the inconvenient electoral process—given the weight of history and precedent—could not be evaded. For its candidate, the PRI designated Luis Donaldo Colosio, a Sonoran of relative youth and considerable energy. Perhaps he could reinvigorate the party and renew a modicum of popular faith in the system, especially as he took his campaign out to the rural hinterlands, where many poor were still apolitical and at least nominally acquiescent to the PRI's domination. Colosio certainly tried, but his campaign rallies drew thin crowds and sparked little enthusiasm. They came to an abrupt end in a Tijuana slum when an assassin placed a .38 caliber pistol two inches from the candidate's temple and pulled the trigger. Caught on video, the murder drew worldwide media coverage.

Colosio's death also spawned countless conspiracy theories. This of course is the point where a "voice of god" textbook is supposed to tell the reader, with decisiveness, what exactly happened. In truth we will probably never know. While in a pluralistic and functional democracy a web of intrigue would be almost impossible to weave and manage, in Mexico the PRI fraternity is tight enough, and its control of resources and information thick enough, that a conspiracy is plausible. Nothing really adds up about either the immediate or broader circumstances of Colosio's death—the security detail's irresponsible routing of the candidate through a jostling crowd, the removal of some state police assigned to security, the access obtained by an armed assassin, and missteps in the subsequent investigation. As she died of pancreatic cancer just months later, Colosio's thirty-four-year-old wife was clearly convinced of a plot, repeatedly demanding a more impartial and thorough investigation.

Coupled with the even more improbable murder of senior PRI party secretary (and former Salinas brother-in-law) José Francisco Ruiz Massieu as he approached his curbside limousine outside a plush Mexico City hotel six months later, enough evidence suggests some cataclysmic rupture within the ranks of the PRI's highest inner circles. Did Colosio's cadre take premature control of some money flow emanating from a PRI-aligned (most likely the Gulf) cartel? Did his sputtering campaign convince Salinas and other *jefes* that he was not the right candidate to revive the party and reassert its political control? Certainly the popular notion that Colosio was an idealistic

Figure 20.2. The Tijuana slum where Colosio was assassinated in 1994. Lomas Taurinas was a dusty hillside barrio with dirt roads and limited electricity at the time. Today it has a more permanent air, with solidly constructed houses, ample concrete, and sufficient pavement. The assassination site is now home to a modest community center. Unemployment remains sky high. This is the kind of lower-class neighborhood that still typically buys into the lofty, unkept promises of the PRI.

reformer is bunk. Nothing in his past suggests anything but party loyalty, periodic corrupt activity, and compliance; his talk of reform and social justice on the campaign trail was standard PRI claptrap. As Salinas stood solemnly beside Colosio's coffin at PRI headquarters days later, he must have suspected that the assassination would in fact evoke popular sympathy and (ironically) revive the party's fortunes—just as Garza Sada's death in 1973 maligned guerrilla movements and elicited goodwill.

In fact, Colosio's campaign-manager-turned-replacement, Ernesto Zedillo, found the political winds blowing in his direction. The assassination, coming just weeks after the dramatic debut of the Zapatistas, fed a collective sense that the nation was falling apart. Fears of instability fostered a desire for the relative safety of the known. The PRI's media machine worked overtime to hype the dangers of civil war and social unrest. Televisa aired reports from the former Yugoslavia, with graphic images of snipers and slaughter in Sarajevo, and the misery of a people caught in a political firestorm. It brought out longtime PRI supporters like the aged philosopher Octavio Paz, who bemoaned Colosio's death and the season of travail. Its newscasts gave Zedillo and the PRI overwhelming coverage, and the PAN scant but favorable reportage, while studiously avoiding mention of Cuauhtémoc Cárdenas's upstart Party of the Democratic Revolution (PRD). In a mansion in Mexico City, billionaire PRI elites gathered, and on a single night quietly pledged over $700 million to support the party.

The key PRI operative behind the scenes was Miguel Alemán Jr., son of the former president. Born in 1932, a young Miguel traveled the world to hobnob with wealthy socialites, just like his father, before marrying French Miss Universe Christiane Magnani. He of course inherited great political clout and vast sums of money. In the mid-1980s, after his father's death, he set up the Miguel Alemán Foundation, a high-publicity charity dispersing a very low percentage of the family's wealth. In the mid-1990s, as a national senator, he was in charge of PRI fundraising. His family was still vested in Televisa, and he headed its news department—the foremost source of political information in the country. No one was going anywhere within the PRI establishment without his awareness and approval. At Televisa he collaborated with an elderly Emilio Azcárraga Jr., who called himself a soldier of the PRI, until his death in 1997. His son, also named Emilio (born of his French-born third wife, Nadine Jean), then inherited leadership of the domineering and influential TV network.

Besides the billionaires and Televisa, the PRI had in its pocket the resources of the government itself. By the mid-nineties its mechanisms of control were fully intact, and yet by repeated economic dislocation and force of circumstance, the oligarchic system still wobbled. In June 1995, after Zedillo's easy win at the polls, idealist opponents rallied in Mexico City's main plaza to protest the apparently stolen gubernatorial election in the southern state of Tabasco. The aggrieved candidate, Andrés Manuel López Obrador, and his supporters were surprised when a nondescript car pulled up and its driver dumped fourteen boxes of documents into their hands. Files revealed massive payoffs throughout Tabasco—to reporters, labor unions, select church officials, and even political "opponents" (the Socialist and Workers' Parties had been long under the PRI's manipulative control). Scrutiny of the cache showed that the PRI and government had spent over $65 million clandestinely in Tabasco's election, a marginal state home to just 2 percent of the nation's population. Nationwide, clearly the establishment was dropping hundreds of millions of dollars to orchestrate and co-opt a largely fraudulent "democratic" process.

New Trends in Old Mexico

Zedillo's administration was predictably rocky. Having campaigned on the slogan "Free Trade Prosperity Is Here," the president struggled to contain disillusionment with unmet expectations. In fact, open trade with the United States both created and eliminated jobs. Auto parts and assembly factories sprouted up, one of several industrial sectors to benefit from the pact. But the much-touted "free trade" treaty actually erected new barriers with third parties—Mexico was forbidden, for example, from importing computer chips from Japan. In the service sector, the construction of hundreds of Walmart stores undercut the livelihood of myriad shopkeepers. And just three weeks after taking office, Zedillo was forced to again float the badly overvalued peso—allowing it to find its true market value. In 1995, inflation peaked at over 50 percent while real wages declined by 27 percent. The downturn came in the context of a financial panic that especially disrupted the economies of southeast Asia. Bank solvency was almost in doubt until the U.S. Treasury and IMF rained tens of billions of dollars onto the global financial system, to the relief of Banamex billionaire Roberto Hernández and other financial super-rich.

In the late 1990s, a not-too-hidden virus within the Mexican body politic—one that would soon begin to claim tens of thousands of lives—was exuding symptoms with increased regularity. In 1997 Zedillo designated an army general, Jesús Gutiérrez Rebollo, as the nation's first Drug Czar. The decision won praise among drug-fighting "experts" in the United States, U.S. General Barry McCaffrey calling his counterpart honest. Five weeks later, Gutiérrez Rebollo was arrested as an operative of a drug cartel. By Zedillo's term, realistically, the so-called drug war in Mexico had already been lost. Police and security forces had long been bought off and fully infiltrated by the cartels. When Héctor "El Güero" Palma of the Sinaloa cartel once made an emergency landing in his private jet, officials discovered that his entire security entourage was comprised of Federal Judicial Police. PRI politicians, too, were on the cartels' dole, right up the hierarchy, almost certainly into the upper echelons of the party establishment. Nevertheless, a remarkable naïveté permeated the U.S. military and Drug Enforcement Agency, neither of which could seem to grasp the nature and circumstances of Mexico's prostituted security apparatuses, while some of the exceedingly limited evidence available to investigators raises the plausibility of direct CIA links to the cartels since the mid-1980s.

Endemic police corruption deepened in the 1990s, even as the U.S. government began very dubious funding programs for select local and state

Figure 20.3. The frequently visited altar to Father Pedro de Jesús Maldonado in Chihuahua's Cathedral. Not a typical Cristero death by timing, he was beaten unconscious by a local police force in 1937 and died in a Chihuahua City hospital days later. Maldonado's murder at the height of Cardenismo made his canonization by conservative Polish pontiff John Paul II an obvious repudiation of Mexican "leftism," which had reared its head and roared loudly in the late 1980s and 1990s.

forces. California state police busted Tijuana municipal police officers while stealing vehicles in San Diego—on several occasions. A group of policemen outside of Mexico City pulled over Zedillo's own son and began to mug him, until they realized their terrible mistake (and a carload of Zedillo's bodyguards arrived, threatening to shoot them). The long-standing practice of "dirty enforcers," ex-officers and police associates who kill rival gangsters and human rights investigators, continued unabated. Abuses flourished as well with the advent of private security firms, often owned and managed by corrupt former police officials. By 1995, there were more private security officers in Mexico City than in the 25,000-strong municipal police force. New extortion and kidnapping rings began to multiply among the police as the decade wound down, setting the stage for unprecedented levels of abuse and murder in the early twenty-first century.

In the nineties the Mexican economy fundamentally changed, and not just because of the U.S. trade pact. Cartel revenue became one of the four pillars of the nation's economy, with some secondary cities, such as Culiacán, robustly prospering due to illegal drugs. Over a decade and a half of depressed oil prices, coupled with limited reinvestment, reduced the importance of PEMEX, for decades the economic centerpiece. Nearly three decades of northward immigration created a new revenue flow—that of remittances from Mexicans working in the United States. Hundreds of Western Union offices popped up on both sides of the border, allowing for tens of thousands of daily fund transfers from migrants to their families, many of whom came to depend on these payments for basic living expenses. By 1998, remittances were a larger source of revenue than oil. The tourist sector also continued to boom, though it created mostly low-paying service sector jobs, with wealth concentrated in the PRI elite. Miguel Alemán Magnani, grandson of the president and graduate of a branch of the Legionnaires of Christ's elitist, club-like Anáhuac University, founded and chaired a new discount air carrier called Interjet, while Carlos Slim launched Volaris, both billionaires benefiting from a deregulation of the airline industry that undercut one of the two longtime national airlines, Mexicana.

Implicitly endorsing the economic and political state of affairs was the conservative Polish-born pontiff, John Paul II, who made three media-hyped visits to the still overwhelmingly Catholic country. Marcial Maciel, founder of the Legionnaires organization, traveled with the pope and helped arrange private services for the oligarchs, saving them the inconvenience of rubbing elbows with the unwashed throngs at the vast open-air ceremonies. In exchange, many of Mexico's super-rich made large donations to the Vatican via Maciel, who eventually retired to Florida amidst sexual misconduct allegations

Crises and Control 223

Figure 20.4. Though notoriously stingy with their money, on occasion Mexico's billionaires have engaged in highly visible acts of philanthropy. The most famous example is that of the Soumaya Museum, a gift of the Carlos Slim family, which opened its doors in 2011. A stylish building houses a pretentious collection, with names like Degas and Renoir well represented, though in works that are generally small and of lesser import. It is, nevertheless, Mexico's best art museum.

(which the church was exceedingly slow to investigate). While a traditional and politically conservative Catholicism persisted in the heart of Mexico, an often apolitical and prosperity-oriented Protestantism—benefiting from radio and TV broadcasts with the advent of cable television—made inroads, especially in the northern and southeastern peripheries of the country.

Myriad forces thus played upon Mexico as the new millennium approached. Cable TV allowed for an apparent cacophony of journalistic angles and voices, though Televisa remained the preeminent player, alongside its U.S.-based Univision network, an NBC-linked Telemundo, and an elite-financed upstart called TV Azteca. Polling data showed that the vast majority of Mexicans perceived newscasts as reliable, and as the economy stabilized in the late 1990s long-stormy grassroots activism subsided. Cuauhtémoc Cárdenas and the political left stood atop a shrinking base; the political right, in contrast, received more openly favorable media coverage.

Carlos Salinas's presidency and prosperity at the top helped mend Monterrey elite–PRI divisions, while the PRI fraternity came to understand that it had nothing to fear from the trade pact–supporting, corporate-friendly PAN. It is not surprising, then, that in the year 2000 the PAN was able to edge the PRI and win the presidency, even as the genuine opposition languished. Vicente Fox, the PAN's candidate, had close ties to the glassmaking Garza Sadas and other Monterrey rich, as the onetime head of Coca-Cola in Mexico. Portrayed as a Reaganesque, Western-style maverick, Fox rode to victory, creating the illusion that real democracy had arrived. In truth, as Mexico entered the twenty-first century, it was striking how very little had changed.

Afterword

Present-day demographics diminish the meaning of Mexican history, as a surging population takes us into uncharted waters. In 1940 Mexico had 20 million people; today it has nearly 130 million. More Mexicans have lived at least part of their lives in the last fifteen years than the number who were born between the mid-seventeenth century and 1925. The nation's population reached fifty million around 1969 and (though census data is notoriously unreliable) doubled to one hundred million sometime around 1999; thus, though present numbers are daunting, the actual rate of population growth has slowed considerably—a reflection of increased access to birth control and family planning, as life expectancy has broadly remained stable. Yet Mexico is simply not geographically endowed to sustain 130 million or more human beings. Importing grain since the early 1970s, the nation has now decisively exceeded its foodshed and sits atop a demographic time bomb. In the event of a structural economic failure, tens of millions of its citizens would go hungry. As is, though, death tolls by malnutrition and related causes has been strikingly small, numbering only in the low hundreds of thousands each year. Fond of high-fat-content foods while eating limited amounts of green vegetables, Mexicans have a paradoxical problem with obesity—the nation's rate is actually as high as that of the badly overweight U.S. population. The seemingly sold-on-every-street-corner *gordita*, a tortilla-like shell stuffed most typically with cheese and often deep-fried, is not the Mexican's dietary friend.

Mexico's demographics are alarming, while Mexico City's physical condition continues to be perilous. In a seismic zone and within range of four potentially active volcanoes, its setting has never made sense for a great metropolis. At 7,400 feet elevation, with terrible pollution and thin air, the modern city has never been a salubrious place to live (in the 1970s U.S. embassy staff received one year of retirement credit for every two years served here—the assumption being that they would suffer chronic health problems later in life). Atop a dried lakebed that shakes like a bowl of jelly when the earth trembles, the capital is fast running out of water. Tapping deeper and ever-more-distant aquifers aggravates a problem with sinking subsoil in a city that moves millions of people via underground subway lines each day. Visitors now step *down* to enter Mexico City's cathedral, rather than ascend into its nave. The good news is that, over the past three decades, great strides have been made in smog reduction, while the urban area's population has stabilized at twenty-one million. But these and other successes are barely keeping pace with one of the greatest urban management challenges on the planet.

Yet despite these formidable problems and disconcerting trends, the early twenty-first century has been relatively good to Mexico. The nation's economic fate is largely tied to that of its powerful neighbor, the United States, the two countries now generating nearly US$700 billion in annual trade. As the United States has prospered, Mexico has done well. Higher oil prices have fattened government coffers, while fluctuating but still robust numbers of foreign (mostly American) tourists have pumped additional capital into the economy. By the early 2000s, Mexicans working in the United States were remitting over US$25 billion each year—an annual influx of roughly $240 per person in a nation where nearly thirty million live on less than four dollars a day. Finally, the forth pillar of the modern Mexican economy, that of illegal narcotics, has generated considerable wealth. The lean and difficult period from 1982 to the year 2000 has been followed by two decades of relatively good years, with the peso declining steadily but not sharply since being allowed to freely float against the U.S. dollar.

The violence of Mexico's drug cartels and the drug war, pursued vigorously by the PAN administrations of Vicente Fox (2000–2006) and especially by his successor, has rightly captured international headlines. From 2004 to 2017, some 125,000 Mexicans were murdered. By way of comparison, police terror and dirty wars against political opponents from the mid-forties to the year 2000 likely killed somewhere in the range of eight thousand to fifteen thousand. In 2005, Ciudad Juárez had a murder rate surpassing that of Baghdad, Iraq, making it the most dangerous city in the world. While we have only fleeting glimpses of security operations and political violence over the course of the past several decades, our understanding of this great bloodletting is even more uncertain. Most academics have declined to take risks and interact with the violent or their victims; journalists have been braver, with roughly 150 murdered since 2000 in the context of cartel and drug war investigations. The U.S. government, on paper, is committed to the eradication of drugs, but the assumption by U.S. agencies that Mexico's power structure is clean has been damning. When Mexican police investigator Guillermo Calderoni fingered the presidential family of Carlos Salinas in drug running, an incredulous FBI apparently went to the Salinases and talked to them—only to have the Mexican government then order the arrest of Calderoni. He survived, but how many other courageous Mexicans have perished because of the persistent naïveté and general dullness of U.S. authorities?

By the 2010s the cartels—and associated criminal gangs such as the Zetas (which emerged from within the Mexican Army's Special Forces)—branched out from drug running into a range of activities, including widespread kidnapping and extortion. With horizontal depth and hierarchy, thick penetration of all levels of Mexican security and policing apparatuses, and a continually clueless American intelligence community, Mexico's now highly sophisticated crime syndicates cannot be stopped. They will, like Mexico's oligarchy, likely persist for decades. Conversely, the common American perception that all of Mexico is swimming in blood is categorically false; the violence has been geographically uneven, primarily along the coasts and near the U.S. border. Entire swaths of central Mexico (and Yucatán) have remained largely unaffected by cartel-related violence.

The Outsider President

Any aspiration by Mexico's elite to create a two-party, PRI-PAN system of artificial political choices was dashed with the dismal presidency of Enrique Peña Nieto (2012–2018), a PRI clone whose poster-boy good looks could not hide a juvenile and opportunistic disposition. The continuation of the drug war by the PRI was immensely unpopular, while the partial privatization of PEMEX enraged nationalists. Transparent corruption was reported in quasi-independent print media, the newsmagazine *El Proceso* and newspaper *La Jornada*, while compliant network news at Televisa and TV Azteca could not cloak the fact that the economy flatlined after the 2008 U.S. financial crisis. The election of Donald Trump further complicated politics. The jarring American president, who regularly disparaged Mexicans as criminals and rapists, greatly offended national sensibilities and—as Peña Nieto and the PRI establishment failed to confront him—helped shift public sentiment in the direction of a political outsider.

Andrés Manuel López Obrador, popularly known as AMLO, was a maverick long waiting in the wings. He had previously run for the presidency in 2006 and 2012, and had staged massive street protests in Mexico City (where he had served as mayor) after each defeat. His campaign spawned a formidable grassroots organization of mostly urbanites and students, but the TV networks still downplayed his efforts and disparaged his performance in televised debates. A PRI–PAN combination could have probably stopped him, but the two very similar parties failed to unite—their candidates and staffs harboring deep animosities toward one other. With 52 percent of the vote, the grandfatherly AMLO swept into the presidency as the head of a new political party christened MORENA, the Movement for National Regeneration.

At his inauguration, AMLO received an incense-laden purification by Native Americans, an image that caught the imagination of Mexicans and subsequently made the ritual a tourist activity on Mexico City streets. To the chagrin of U.S. investors and the PRI elite, he promptly canceled the construction of a new Mexico City airport in Peña Nieto's nearby home state, an extravagant $6 billion project that was running over budget. Wall Street ratings agencies subsequently downgraded select public entities, foremostly PEMEX, even though its deficits and liabilities had grown more rapidly under the previous administration—a clear indication that politics interfaces with the supposedly objective economic analysis of big U.S. financial institutions. In a range of symbolic acts, the new president shunned the prestige and trappings of his office. He converted "The Pines," Mexico's opulent presidential residence since the days of Alemán, into a museum. He declined the traditional protection of hundreds of secret service–like musclemen, opting instead for a personal entourage of twenty unarmed MORENA activists, half of them women. He drove to work in his own modest sedan and sold the presidential jet, instead opting to travel aboard commercial airliners.

Early in his administration AMLO bemoaned the atrocities of the conquests, insisting that the Vatican and Spain issue public apologies. That he was looking into the distant past, instead of the future, arguably reflects a lack of answers for Mexico's daunting present-day problems. Criminal activity and cartel-related killings rose during his first year in office, homicide rates hitting a record high in 2019, with 17,600 murders in just six months. The creation of a National Guard continued the process of militarizing Mexico—yet cartels have been able to consistently infiltrate and compromise whatever new security apparatus the state throws at them. Other AMLO reforms are certainly logical and significant: devolving government offices away from Mexico City might lead to a much-needed population decline in the capital, while changes in labor laws and union governance (with, among other features, secret ballots in leadership elections) could empower workers. AMLO has threatened to rupture security links with the United States, but he has not done so—and it is a fair question to ask if he even can. He has astutely avoided head-on debate and even much direct interaction with Donald Trump, while collaborating with U.S. authorities to stem Central American migration through Mexico. Austerity in government spending appears poised to keep the peso stable, though it will also likely lead to a continued low-growth economy.

Whether the 2018 election of López Obrador signals a political transformation of Mexico is uncertain. Indicators thus far suggest not, and the oligarchs—while quieter than usual—are economically healthy and in position to again wield power. At the outset of the 2020s, like all the world, Mexicans are experiencing sweeping change. Ubiquitous cell phones are diminishing traditional face-to-face interaction; recognition of a global, cultural modernity makes some reluctant to sing a folk song or strum a guitar. But technology and time have yet to eradicate that which makes Mexico *Mexico*—the distinctiveness of a great people born of Native American glory, shaped by European conquest and colonialism, and defined by a dramatic national history, remains.

Suggestions for Further Reading

Most of the following fifty books address political and/or economic aspects of Mexican history, thus effectively expanding upon the major themes presented in this book. Some social histories are included—but only those relating to the few topics addressed (most very lightly) herein. All are written in English, and the vast majority are in accessible prose easily digested by the non-specialist, unless noted. Ten suggestions are provided for each corresponding part in this book, and all are listed in roughly corresponding and chronological order.

Hundreds of additional works on Mexican history exist, including a large corpus in Spanish. In the last two decades, scholars have developed an engaging array of social and cultural histories, along with a rising number of excellent studies relating to women and gender. Others have undertaken micro-histories and regional studies. A vast number of unlisted works also address the much-celebrated Mexican Revolution (corresponding to chapter 14, *The Season of Rebellions*), most of these written between 1950 and 1980, often in an engaging narrative style. In sum, there is published material on Mexico that can reach anyone's conceivable interest, and this list is merely a cursory invitation for further study.

Part I: Ancient Civilizations

George L. Cowgill, *Ancient Teotihuacan: Early Urbanism in Central Mexico* (Cambridge, UK: Cambridge University Press, 2015). A rather weighty but thorough examination of Teotihuacán, including the process of archeological investigation at the premier site—though it is not terribly up to date (in defense of the author, work at Teotihuacán is progressing at a rapid pace, with new findings almost yearly).

Richard E. Blanton et al., *Ancient Oaxaca: The Monte Albán State* (Cambridge: Cambridge University Press, 1999). There is much technical writing here, but a casual reader can still glean basic material about the early phases of the Zapotec site of Monte Albán and its surroundings in this short book.

Michael Coe and Stephen Houston, *The Maya*, 9th ed. (London: Thames & Hudson, 2015). Clarity issues abound in this, the standard and regularly updated work on the Maya. The book's uneven prose arguably has a salutatory effect in a field so rife with debate and speculation, but it can make for tedious reading. Much of the organization is centered around various archeological sites, which is helpful for tourists visiting Yucatán.

Christopher A. Pool, *Olmec Archaeology and Early Mesoamerica* (New York: Cambridge University Press, 2007). A solid overview of the Olmec and the Pre-Classic, demonstrating the lasting influence of this early culture; detailed, but not overwhelming.

Michael Coe and Rex Koontz, *Mexico: From the Olmecs to the Aztecs*, 7th ed. (London: Thames & Hudson, 2013). Arguably Coe's best book, it provides an all-encompassing sweep through the pre-contact era, with insightful material on the earliest hunters and the Archaic Period (before the Pre-Classic). It is particularly thorough on the Late Classic (Epiclassic) and Post-Classic, with a chapter-long analysis of Aztec society and life. A wonderful array of photographs and apropos illustrations complement the prose throughout.

Richard A. Diehl, *Tula: The Toltec Capital of Ancient Mexico* (London: Thames & Hudson, 1983). Though decades old, this is still the best source on the Toltecs' demographic heart. There have not been many new discoveries at Tula that alter or contradict Diehl's interpretations.

Bernal Díaz, *The Conquest of New Spain* (New York: Penguin Books, 1963 [or any edition]). The classic firsthand account of the conquest of the Aztecs by a foot soldier under Cortés has inspired history lovers for centuries. Díaz wrote his memoir in old age, but it is flush with energy and captures the spirit of fascination with which the Spaniards first beheld Mexico.

Ida Altman, *The War for Mexico's West: Indians and Spaniards in New Galicia, 1524–1550* (Albuquerque: University of New Mexico Press, 2010). This largely narrative history of the Western conquest confirms the importance of indigenous allies to the Spanish cause, while drawing some important distinctions between semi-nomadic and nomadic peoples. Two chapters document early settlement and extensive Spanish abuses.

Barbara E. Mundy, *The Death of Aztec Tenochtitlán, the Life of Mexico City* (Austin: University of Texas Press, 2015). Mundy finds many continuities before and after conquest of the great Aztec-Mexica city. Her work is also sensitive to environmental and ecological issues, including the importance of water to life in Tenochtitlán.

Matthew Restall, *Seven Myths of the Spanish Conquest* (New York: Oxford University Press, 2003). An easy-to-read evaluation of how Spaniards triumphed over native civilizations, built around debunking falsehoods. It is a little messy because the author frames the debates from the negative, while the "divide and conquer" factor does not receive nearly enough attention.

Part II: Colonial Centuries

Inga Clendinnen, *Ambivalent Conquests: Maya and Spaniard in the Yucatán, 1517–1570* (Cambridge, UK: Cambridge University Press, 1987). A beautifully written, sophisticated work on the Franciscans and their savage 1560s inquisition under fanatical Bishop Diego de Landa. Clendinnen's audacious psychoanalysis of Landa has since been called into question, but her command of sources and thoughtfulness is all too evident. A classic book and must-read for those interested in early Church-Indian relations.

Miguel León-Portílla, *Bernardino de Sahagún: First Anthropologist* (Norman: University of Oklahoma Press, 2002). A prominent historian analyzes the life of Franciscan Friar Sahagún, calling him the "first anthropologist" and focusing on his work in understanding native cultures. Sahagún spent a formative thirty years in Spain, before residing in Mexico for two-thirds of his long life. This is an erudite biography, concerned mainly with tracing his scholarship.

Kelly S. McDonough, *The Learned Ones: Nahua Intellectuals in Postconquest Mexico* (Tucson: University of Arizona Press, 2014). A literary study of major indigenous writers, such as the Tlaxcalan lord and convert Juan Buenaventura. McDonough's lucid ethnohistory extends into the national period as well.

Jonathan Truitt, *Sustaining the Divine in Mexico Tenochtitlán: Nahuas and Catholicism, 1523–1700* (Norman: University of Oklahoma Press and Academy of Franciscan History, 2018). A complex book, its sophisticated overarching arguments might well escape the casual reader. But as Truitt looks at how religious devotion among natives both persisted and changed after the conquest, he reveals much visual and interesting anecdotal material along the way.

Dana Velasco Murillo, *Urban Indians in a Silver City: Zacatecas, Mexico, 1546–1810* (Stanford, CA: Stanford University Press, 2016). The diversity of subcommunities in the town of Zacatecas was great, while indigenous peoples maintained their languages and customs through social means and institutional venues such as parish brotherhoods (*cofradías*).

Arturo Giráldez, *The Age of Trade: The Manila Galleons and the Dawn of the Global Economy* (Lanham, MD: Rowman & Littlefield, 2015). Giráldez provides great detail about the galleons, including their construction in the Philippines, composition of their crews, navigational routes, and cargoes. He then ties them to the emergence of a global economy—the galleons were a critical early link between East and West.

Patricia Seed, *To Love, Honor, and Obey in Colonial Mexico: Conflicts over Marriage Choice, 1574–1821* (Stanford, CA: Stanford University Press, 1988). A much debated but still seminal study of marriage patterns and the role of the church in the colonial era. Seed finds that Catholicism often supported marital choice among youth who were in conflict with their parents.

Irving A. Leonard, *Baroque Times in Old Mexico* (Ann Arbor: University of Michigan Press, 1959, reissued 1990). An exceptional history book can stand the test of time; such is the case with Leonard's brilliant work. Though he overplays the Inquisition's significance, most of his material is still apropos, including with regard to *máscaras*. Chapter 7 biographic material on Sor Juana and Sigüenza y Góngora comes from Leonard, who devotes entire chapters to each.

Javier Villa-Flores, *Dangerous Speech: A Social History of Blasphemy in Colonial Mexico* (Tucson: University of Arizona Press, 2006). Building upon the work of Leonard and early Inquisition scholar Richard Greenleaf, Villa-Flores examines some of the several hundred cases of blasphemy tried before the Holy Office, which often makes for entertaining reading. He perceives significant social trends and implications in the process.

Charles H. Harris, *A Mexican Family Empire: The Latifundio of the Sánchez Navarro Family, 1765–1867* (Austin: University of Texas Press, 1975). A thorough and incisive narrative history of the rise and fall of the powerful Sánchez Navarro clan in Coahuila, one of the greatest landowning families in the history of the world. Social and political continuities of the late colonial and early national periods are evident in this masterful study.

Part III: Independence and Modernity

Matthew D. O'Hara, *A Flock Divided: Race, Religion and Politics in Mexico, 1749–1857* (Durham, NC: Duke University Press, 2010). Drawing on ecclesiastical documents, O'Hara uncovers tensions within the church and broader society. He finds that village priests were losing political and social control over time. This book can be rather challenging for non-specialists.

Timothy J. Henderson, *The Mexican Wars for Independence* (New York: Hill & Wang, 2009). A basic history of the 1810–1821 period, with solid introductions to major figures and a grounded narrative of political and military affairs.

Donald Fithian Stevens, *Mexico in the Time of Cholora* (Albuquerque: University of New Mexico Press, 2019). Drawing on parish church records, Stevens engages 1830s Mexican society amid a terrible cholera epidemic, with many intimate and human stories interlaced with the broader narrative of this thoughtful study.

Will Fowler, *Santa Anna of Mexico* (Lincoln: University of Nebraska Press, 2007). Fowler resuscitates Santa Anna, debunking myths of pure opportunism and buffoonery. At a little more than five hundred pages, with extensive back matter, it is weighty, with relentless detail on the twists and turns of politics from the 1820s through the mid-1850s that will likely overwhelm the casual reader.

Mark Wasserman, *Everyday Life and Politics in Nineteenth Century Mexico* (Albuquerque: University of New Mexico Press, 2000). Almost a textbook, this work provides a solid overview of social conditions by gender and class, interfacing it with the sweep of an 1810–1910 political history that includes short biographies of major figures.

Timothy J. Henderson, *A Glorious Defeat: Mexico and Its War with the United States* (New York: Hill & Wang, 2007). A sweeping account of Mexico's struggles with the United States in the mid-nineteenth century, with ample context and detail on both the U.S. War and the earlier loss of Texas.

William H. Beezley, *Judas at the Jockey Club and Other Episodes of Porfirian Mexico* (Lincoln: University of Nebraska Press, 1987). A brief, fun book on sports and society by one of the pioneering social historians of Mexico.

Paul J. Vanderwood, *Disorder and Progress: Bandits, Police, and Mexican Development* (Lincoln: University of Nebraska Press, 1981). The tumultuous mid-nineteenth-century countryside is the focus of Vanderwood's study, which is also the best source on the Rural Police (*Rurales*)—and revealing with regard to their considerable limitations.

Stephen B. Neufeld, *The Blood Contingent: The Military and the Making of Modern Mexico, 1876–1911* (Albuquerque: University of New Mexico Press, 2017). A scholarly yet lively examination of the army in Porfirian Mexico, with a focus on the lives of enlisted draftees and junior officers, and closing chapters that examine the internal wars against the Yaqui and Maya Indians.

One chapter addresses the role of women, who lived alongside their soldier-husbands; barracks life, including its social dimensions, is discussed in depth.

Jonathan Brown, *Oil and Revolution in Mexico* (Berkeley: University of California Press, 1993). A thorough examination of the upstart oil industry, its weathering of the 1910s turmoil, and some of the political and legal dynamics it faced in the early 1920s. It is particularly good in its chronicling of how companies parleyed and dealt with various armed factions in the 1910s. Concluding chapters wrestle with the deeper question of the lasting benefits and downsides of foreign industrial penetration into an underdeveloped and structurally weak nation.

Part IV: The Age of Rebellion

Martín L. Guzmán, *The Eagle and the Serpent* (Garden City, NY: Doubleday, 1965 [or any other edition]). A Mexican literary classic on the revolution—see chapter 15.

Friedrich Katz, *The Life and Times of Pancho Villa* (Stanford: Stanford University Press, 1998). At 818 pages of prose, Katz's authoritative biography is both exhaustive and exhausting. Partly chronological, at times thematic, and always thick on context, every possible known angle of the revolutionary leader (but not his childhood) is explored. Skillfully researched and readable.

Joseph A. Stout Jr., *Border Conflict: Villistas, Carrancistas and the Punitive Expedition, 1915–1920* (Fort Worth: Texas Christian University Press, 1999). One of the better books on violence in the borderlands and the U.S. hunt for Pancho Villa after his 1916 New Mexico raid.

Jürgen Buchenau, *Plutarco Elías Calles and the Mexican Revolution* (Lanham, MD: Rowman & Littlefield, 2007). A highly readable and insightful biography of Calles, addressing his background and activities during the decade of rebellion but focusing primarily on his actions and opportunism as president. Buchenau gives a realistic assessment of this domineering man.

Luis González, *San José de Gracia: A Mexican Village in Transition* (Austin: University of Texas Press, 1974). This is a classic account of life in a small Jalisco village. The "revolution" completely bypasses it; the Cristero Rebellion shakes it to the core. A little stiff in prose (this is a translation from the original Spanish), it makes a vital point by downplaying the 1910s period.

Graham Greene, *The Power and the Glory* (New York: Penguin/Random House, 2015). A stunning novel about the nature of martyrdom and faith, set in Mexico during the 1920s Cristero rebellion. Like most of his works, Greene's book starts out a bit slow, but then it becomes so engaging that it is difficult to put down. A twisting plot complements the author's astounding depth of perception about human nature. A travel-addicted Greene spent time in 1930s Mexico.

Dudley Ankerson, *Agrarian Warlord: Saturnino Cedillo and the Mexican Revolution in San Luis Potosí* (DeKalb: Northern Illinois University Press, 1984). The astute reader of this book will have detected a disproportionate number of references to San Luis Potosí, where I have spent quite a bit of time. Ankerson's book is one of the very best ever written on Mexico. Masterfully researched, beautifully penned, and—though a regional history—one with excellent context and significant national implications.

Aaron W. Navarro, *Political Intelligence and the Creation of Modern Mexico, 1938–1954* (University Park: Pennsylvania State University Press, 2010). A detailed but exceedingly worthwhile study of the mid-century era, focusing mainly on the elections of 1940, 1946, and 1952, and the concomitant role of the intelligence services that spied on and worked to undermine the opposition at the behest of Miguel Alemán and his friends.

Jeffery M. Pilcher, *Cantinflas and the Chaos of Mexican Modernity* (Wilmington, DE: Scholarly Resources, 2001). This short biography served as the basis for the section about Cantinflas in chapter 17. Its chronological treatment of this world-renowned Mexican includes the political dimensions of his life, which made him a PRI party stalwart.

Alejandro Quintana, *Maximino Ávila Camacho and the One-Party State: The Taming of Caudillismo and Caciquismo in Post-Revolutionary Mexico* (Lanham, MD: Lexington Books, 2010). Despite the convoluted title and its dissertation origins, this is a short accounting of the important governor. That the author was able to produce a biography off such paltry archival sources is impressive, and Quintana does not wince in mentioning the ugly features of this narcissistic, power-hungry man.

Part V: Structures of Power

Roderic Ai Camp, *Memoirs of a Mexican Politician* (Albuquerque: University of New Mexico Press, 1988). This is a fictional autobiography of a politically ambitious man who becomes an operative of the PRI in postwar Mexico. Camp shows the benign face of the PRI, how at times it could be flexible and co-opt potential opponents into its power structure.

Renata Keller, *Mexico's Cold War: Cuba, the United States, and the Legacy of the Mexican Revolution* (Cambridge, UK: Cambridge University Press, 2015). Perceptions of revolutionary Cuba and the context of the Cold War weighed heavily on postwar policy makers in Mexico and the United States.

Keller's examination of this is especially strong with regard to the early 1970s guerrilla movements and their eradication by the state.

Stephen R. Niblo, *Mexico in the 1940s: Modernity, Politics, and Corruption* (Wilmington, DE: Scholarly Resources, 1999). Niblo was one of the first historians to discern the significance of Miguel Alemán's presidency. His analysis of Ávila Camacho's term is good, but his study of Alemán's "counter revolution" is incisive and pathbreaking, in part because he taps into the few intelligence and security services records that are available to researchers. Niblo also addresses society and culture, with particularly important analysis of radio and other media. This is one of the most important books available for understanding Mexico over the past eighty years.

Elena Poniatowska, *Massacre in Mexico* (New York: Viking Press, 1975). A Mexican journalist's compilation of material on the October 1968 killing of protestors. Poniatowska's critique of the media is particularly insightful and damning.

Eric Zolov, *Refried Elvis: The Rise of Mexican Counterculture* (Berkeley: University of California Press, 1999). The authoritative account of postwar (middle-class) youth culture, especially *rocanrol* in the 1960s and 1970s.

Alan Riding, *Distant Neighbors: A Portrait of the Mexicans* (New York: Alfred A. Knopf, 1985). A *New York Times* correspondent who lived in Mexico for several years in the late 1970s and early 1980s offers a broad introduction to Mexican politics, life, and society. The prose is wonderfully smooth, and the firsthand stories are evocative and insightful. Riding stays close to history as well, providing context to his analysis of (at the time) contemporary issues.

Ruben Martínez, *Crossing Over: A Mexican Family on the Migrant Trail* (New York: Picador USA, 2001). A beautifully written account of a family making its way to the United States by a journalist and creative writer. This book is in two parts: the first shows life in Mexico, complete with its dismal economic prospects; the second brings the family into the United States, with a mind to all the challenges and barriers that must be overcome.

Andres Oppenheimer, *Bordering on Chaos: Mexico's Roller-Coaster Journey Toward Prosperity* (Boston: Little, Brown and Company, 1996). A revealing examination of Mexico's corruption and dirty politics in the mid-1990s by a well-connected journalist before he went on to a high-powered and highly compromised corporate career at the *Miami Herald* and beyond.

Nick Henck, *Subcommander Marcos: The Man and the Mask* (Durham, NC: Duke University Press, 2007). A rather long-winded and sympathetic biography of the leader of the Zapatista rebellion in Chiapas, focusing primarily on the mid-1990s.

Ioan Grillo, *El Narco: Inside Mexico's Criminal Insurgency* (New York: Bloomsbury Press, 2011). A gritty journalistic account of Mexico's ongoing drug war, and arguably the best so far of a plethora of similar general readership books. Grillo follows changes in cartel methods and activities, focusing much of his attention on President Felipe Calderón (2006–2012) and his (ultimately vain) counter-cartel efforts.

Index

Note: Page references for figures are *italicized*.

academe and academics (in study of Mexico), 183, 196, 226
Acapulco, 66, 181, 185, 190, 192, 194, 195, 209
adobe, 9, 12, 56
advertising, 190, 193
agrarian reform, 154, 163, 167, 169, 173, 174, 176, 183, 196
agribusiness, 183
Aguayo (family), 84
El Águila Oil Company, 140
Aguilera Valdez, Alberto. *See* Gabriel, Juan
Agustín I (Mexican emperor). *See* Iturbide, Agustín de
Ahualulco (battle), 117
airlines. *See* aviation industry
Alamo (mission), 103–104
alcohol and alcoholism, 9, 54, 57, 125, 131, 151, *164*, 166, 188, 190. *See also* máscaras; pulque
Alemán (family), 185, 193
Alemán, Beatriz, 176, 182

Alemán, Miguel, vi, 176, 181, *182*, 183–187, *187*, 190, 191–193, 194, 195, 205, 208, *215*, 228
Alemán (Alemán Velasco), Miguel, Jr., 194
Alemán III (Alemán Magnani), Miguel, 222
Alfonso (of Castile), 37
Allende, Ignacio, 85–86
Allies (World War II alliance), 175–176
Almohads, 36–37
Alvarado, Pedro, 155
Always on Sundays (TV show), 203, 212
Americans (U.S. citizens). *See* United States (of America)
AMLO. *See* López Obrador, Andrés Manuel
amnesty (U.S. immigration policy), 206
Anáhuac University, 193–194, 222
Andalucía, 36, 37, 65
The Angel (Mexico City monument), 141

Ángeles, Felipe, *153*
animals, 21, 56, 65, 73, 84, 85, *139*. See also cattle; horses
anthropology, 3, 4, 5, 23. *See also* National Museum of Anthropology; National Institute of Anthropology and History
anti-clericalism, 94, 98, 116, 141–143, 160–161, 170, 174, 193
anti-communism, *195*, 196, *198*
anti-Positivists, 144–145, 160
Apaches, 84, 85, 103, 216
archbishop, 78, 100
archeology and archeologists, 3, 4, 5, 6, 9, 13–15, 17, 21, 23, 28, *207*
architecture, 36, 49, 54, 63–64, *132*, 133, *223*
archives, 133, 173, 183, 185, 214
Arizona, 56, 83, 115, 137
army and armies, 86, 91, 93, 95, 96, 98, 161, 172, 173, 188, 196, 216, 220, 227; in Texas filibuster and U.S. war, 102, 104, 106, 107–111; during War of the Reform and Porfiriato, 117–118, 123, 125–126, 140; in 1910s' rebellions, 149, *151*, 152. *See also* battles; cavalry; militias; war and warfare
Army of Three Guarantees (independence wars), 91
Arriaga, Camilo, 142–143
art, *30*, 50, 51, 67, 83, *121*, *142*, *143*, 158, *223*. *See also* biombos; murals and muralists; retablos; Soumaya Museum; *and* specific names of artists (e.g., Rivera, Diego)
Article 123 (of 1917 constitution), 154, 166
artillery, 81, 86, 103–104, 109, 148, 152, 153
artisans and craftsmen, 7–8, 12, 19, 32, 36, 59–60, 64, 124
Asia (and migration to Americas), 4

astrology, 76
astronomy, 6, 20–21, 72, 74
audiencias, 48, 53
Augustinians, 52
Austin (Texas), 105
Austin, Moses, 101
Austin, Stephen, 101–102
Austria, 119, 122
automobiles, 182, 185, *192*, 220
Autonomous University of Guadalajara (UAG), 193, 196
Avenue of the Dead (at Teotihuacán), 6–7
aviation industry, 185, 190, 192, 195, 204–205, 213, 220, 222, 228. *See also* tourism and tourist industry
Ávila Camacho (family), 175, 183
Ávila Camacho, Juan Rafael Moro, 212
Ávila Camacho, Manuel, 173, 174, 176, 182–183, 193
Ávila Camacho, Maximino, 171–173, 174–175, 176, 182–183
Azcárraga, Emilio, 163, 193
Azcárraga, Emilio (Azcárraga Milmo), Jr., 219
Aztecs, vii, 4, 22, 26, 27, 28, 42, *207*; conquest of, 38–41, *43*; cosmology and religion, 30–32; origins and rise to power, 29–30; society, 32. *See also* Jaguar Knights; Tenochtitlán
Azuela, Mariano, 159, 160

Badiano, Juan, 75
Bajío, 59, 60, *61*, 85, 99, 117, 128, 176
banks and finance, 95, 96, 118, 126, 138, 139, 144, 154, 183, 208, 220, 228; crises in late twentieth century and, 210, 214. *See also* coins and coinage; debt; devaluation; investment; peso
baptism, 50, 62, 116
baroque (architecture), 64, *73*, 81, 82
Barreda, Gabino, 132, 142

baseball, 131
Batres, Leopoldo, 5, 6
battles and battlefields, 86, 88, 96, 104, 108–109 , 110–111, 114, 117. See also war and warfare
Beauregard, P. G. T. de, 110
beef. See cattle, haciendas
beer and breweries, 129
bicycles, 131, *143*
bigamy, 70
billionaires, 209, 216, 219, 222, *223*
biombos, 67
birth control, 176, 225
bishops, 51, 52, 53, 73, 84, 141, 142, 161
Black Jaguar (Maya Lord), 16–17
boleros, 203
Bolívar, Simón, 111
Bonaparte, Napoleon, 85, 87
books, 71, 85, 88, *119*, 138, 141, 159, 211, 213
Bourbon dynasty (of Spain), 79–80, 81, 87
Bourbon Reforms, 79–81, 83
Bracero Program, *175*
Brandstetter, Frank, 194–195
Bravo, Nicolás, 95,
brigandage, 95, 113, 123, 126, 152
buccaneers, 65
Buena Vista (battle), 108–109, 113
Buendia, Manuel, 211–212
bullfighting, 131, 188–189
burials. See death and funerary rituals
business, 126, 129, 132, 133, 137, 139, 156, 165, 166, 168, 172, 176, 183, 193, 204, (U.S.) 206. See also corporations; oligarchs and rich; trade; unions
Bustamante, Anastasio, 96, 98, 102, 106

cabildos, 54
Cabo San Lucas, 66
cacao, 16, 21

Cacaxtla, xi, 10
Caldroni, Guillermo, 227
calendars and time (Native American), 23, 28, 31, 42. See also Maya, calendars
California, 66, 67, 83, 106, 107, 111, 187, 212, 222
Calleja del Rey, Félix María, 87–88
Calles, Plutarco Elías, 160, 161, 163, 164, 165, 167, 169, 170, 181, 182, *187*, 191, 193
Cananea, 137
Canary Islands, 83
Cancún, 13, 204, *205*
Cantinflas, 188–190, *189*, 194, 212
Cárdenas, Cuauhtémoc, 214-216, 217, 219, 223
Cárdenas, Lázaro, vi, 167, 168–169, 170, 171, *172*, 176, 182, 187, 190, 214
Caribbean (Sea), 35, 49, 65, 66
Carlota, 119, 120, *121*, 122
Carmelites, 71
Caro Quintero, Rafael, 211
Carranza, Venustiano, 150, 151, 152, 154, 155
cars. See automobiles
Carta Blanca (beer), 129
cartels. See drugs and drug cartels
Caso, Alfonso, xi, 11–12
Castro, Veronica, 209
Catholic Church and Catholics, 9, 48, 53, 54, 62, 70, 74, 76, 99, 100, 101, 107, 111, 132, 163, 97, 219, *221*; church buildings and construction, *43*, 50, 60, *63*, 64, *73*, 74, 83, 85, *192*; clergy (*see also* specific clerical orders, e.g., Franciscans), 62, 81, 120; conversion of Native Americans and, 49–51, 62, 76, 77, 83; friars and Maya, 13–14, 20, *49*, 51–52; nineteenth century ideologies and,

94, 95, 96, 98, 116–118, 120, 123, 140–142; Mexico City cathedral, 64, 95, 100, 119, 141, 226; nuns and convents, 71–72, 81, 116; power and wealth of, 62–64, 77, 81, 117, 118, 222–223; relations and attitude towards government since 1920, 160–162, 169, 170, 171, 173–174; relations with and connections to PRI elite, 193–194, 198; saints and, 52, 64, 74. See also anti-clericalism; archbishop; Augustinians; baptism; bishops; cofradías; convents; Cristeros; Dominicans; Franciscans; Inquisition; Jesuits; Legionnaires of Christ; National Defense League for Religious Liberty; priests; retablos; sacraments; Virgin of Guadalupe
cattle, 59, 84, 85
cavalry, 84, 86, 92, 103, 109, 153
Cavendish, Thomas, 66–67
Cedillo, Saturnino, ix, 170, 171
Celaya (battle), 153
cement and CEMEX (corporation), 165
Cempoala, 5, 38
cenotes, 18, 44, 114
Central America, 15, 42, 211, 216, 229
Central Intelligence Agency (CIA [of the United States]), 183, 194, 211, 220
centralism (of state authority), 102, 117, 124
Cerro Gordo, 109–110
Cervecería Cuauhtémoc, 129, 138, 166
Chaac (Mayan deity), 18
Chapultepec, 111, 120, 152. See also Lomas de Chapultepec
Chiapas, 216
Chichen Itzá, 13, 16–20, 19
Chichimecs, 29, 56
Chihuahua (city or state), 87, 95, 128, 141, 192, 196, 205, 221; in 1910s' rebellions, 145–146, 149, 153, 154, 157

Chilam Balam, Books of, 15
children and childbearing, 32, 44, 52, 70, 71, 99, 133, 138, 159, 184, 193, 201
cholera, 99, 133
Cholula, 8–9, 10, 12, 38–39, 40
Christians and Christianity, 36–37, 49, 50, 79. See also Catholic Church and Catholics; Protestants
churches. See Catholic Church and Catholics
Churrigueresque, 63, 64, 82
Churubusco (battle), 110
Churubusco (film) studios, 189
Cinco de Mayo, 118
cinema. See film and film industry
Cipac, Marcos, 50
The Citadel (at Teotihuacán), 7
cities. See urbanization *and* specific names (e.g., Mexico City)
Ciudad Juárez, ix, 128, 139, 146, 175, 204, 226
Civic Action, 168
Classic Period, 8, (Mayan) 16–17, 23
cloth and clothing. See textiles
Clothier, Manuel, 214
Clovis (and theory of Native American origins), 4
Coahuila (and Coahuila y Tejas), 84, 85, 101, 102, 103, 107, 144, 145
Cobá, 16
cocaine, 206
codices, 10, 14–15
Coe, Michael, 13–14
cofradías, 72
coins and coinage, 58, 59, 62, 130,. See also banks and finance; peso
Colombia, 111, 115, 206, 216
Colorado, 83, 209
Colosio, Luis Donaldo, 217–219, 218
Columbus, Christopher (Cristóbal Colón), 21
comic books, 201
commerce. See trade

communism, 164, 168–169, 171, 172, 173, 183, 185, 213
Confederates (U.S.), 122, 129
congress (national), 92, 93, 96, 98, (U.S.) 107, 116, 124, 193, 210. *See also* government
conquests. *See* Spaniards *and* specific Native American cultures (e.g., Aztecs)
conservatives and conservatism, 94, 96, 115, 116–118, 120, 122. 123. 140, 169
Constant, Benjamin, 94
Constitution of 1917, 154, 155-156, 160, 162. *See also* Article 123
constitutions, 92, 94, 95, 102, 114, 116, 124
convents, *49*, 63, 64, 71, *110*
copper, 42, 126, 137
Córdoba (Spain), 36
corn. *See* maize
corporations, 183, 184, 193, 204, *215*, 216
corregidores, 53, 58
corruption, 80, 81, 129–130, 142, 155, 172, 174–175, 185–186, 191–192, 201, 208, 219; in police and security forces, 183–184, 220, 222; symbolic probes of, 192, 210–211
Cortés, Hernán, 5, 37–41, *40*, 41, *43*, 47, 48, 49, 126, 158, 183
Cos, Martín Perfecto de, 103–104
Cosmic Race (concept), 158
cotton, 101, 107, 131
coyotes (animal), 85, 86
creoles, 57, 58, 78, 80, 81, 85; in early nationhood period, 91, 92, 93, 95
crime and criminal activity, 85, 149, 157, 162, 172, 182, 183–185, 211-212, 213, 214, 215, 217, 226, 228; among police and security forces, 183–184, 217, 220, 222, 227. *See also* brigandage; corruption; drugs and drug cartels

Cristeros, 160-162, 169, 173, *221*
CROM. *See* Regional Confederation of Mexican Workers
Cruz, Sor Juana Inés de la, 71–72, 73, 74
CTM. *See* Mexican Workers' Confederation
Cuauhtémoc, 41, 214,
Cuba, 35, 37, 40, 44, 48, 94, 107, 115, 194
Cuernavaca, 48, 174, 209
Cuesta Gallardo, Carlos, 193
Culiacán, 222

danzantes, 12
Davis, Jefferson, 109
Day of the Dead, 74, *143*
death, 7, 12, 18, 31, 32, 57, 58, 62, 70, 86, 124, *143*, 154, 155, 157, 176, 217; funerals and funerary practices, 74, 99, 116, *119*. 133–134, 141, *170*, 185, *189*, 212, 213, 218
Debs, Eugene, 144
debt, 59, 63, 96, 99, 116, 118, 120, 126, 208, 210, 214
debt peonage, 84, 124
Decena Trágica. *See* Tragic Ten Days
de la Madrid, Miguel, 210
de los Santos, Pedro, 148, 149
del Río, Dolores, 187, 188
department stores, 129, 138
devaluation (of peso), 208, 210
Díaz, Bernal, 38
Díaz, Félix, 148,
Díaz, Porfirio, 124–125, *125*, 137, *139*, 140, 147, 154, 181, 191; as president, 124–125, 139, 140–141, 144–146
Diego, Juan, 50
Díez Gutiérrez, Carlos, 130
disease and epidemics, vii, 41, 48, 50, 57, 58, 62, 74, 76, 81, 99, *119*, 125–126, 133
divorce, 70
Doheny, Edward L., 139

Dolores Cemetery (Mexico City), 133–134
Dolores-Hidalgo, 85, 141
Dominicans, 49, 50
Don Quixote, 69
dowries, 71
draft (military levy), 103, 107, 113, 151
Drake, Francis, 65, 66
Dresden Codex, 14–15
drought and famine, 83, 85
Drug Enforcement Agency (U.S.), 205, 220
drugs and drug cartels, 183–184, 185, 205–206, 220, 222, 226; violence and, 211, 226–227, 228. *See also* Drug Enforcement Agency; marijuana; *and* specific names of drugs (e.g., heroin) and cartels (e.g., Gulf cartel)
Durango (city or state), ix, *142*, 149, 205
Durazo, Arturo, 210–211

The Eagle and the Serpent, 159–160
earthquakes, 15, 211, 226
Echeverría, Luis, 206–208, 213, 214
education, 71, 76, 81, 98, 124, 132, 145, 154, 170, 176. *See also* schools; universities; *and* specific institutional names (e.g., UNAM)
Ehecatl, 28, *207*
Ek Balam, 16, *17*, 18, 22
elections, vi, 96, 98, 124, 144, 166, *187*, 196, 224; presidential, in twentieth century, 145, 148, 162–163, 167–168, 173, 176, 214–219, 228
electricity, 132, 140, 174, 205, *218*
elites. *See* nobility, oligarchs and rich
El Paso (Texas), 122, 128, 146
El Proceso (newsmagazine), 227
El Santo, 199, *200*, 201
El Universal (newspaper), 163
encomienda, 48, 51, 53, 58, 62, 77

The Enlightenment, 3, 79, 81, 94
engineering, 142, *174*, 213
England. *See* Great Britain
epidemics. *See* disease
Excélsior (newspaper), 163, 197, 211
exports. *See* trade

family, 70, 171, 184. *See also* children and childbearing; marriage; women
famine. *See* drought and famine
Feathered Serpent God (and prince), 7, 10, 18, 42
Federal Bureau of Investigation (FBI [of United States]), 184, 227
Federal Directorate of Security (DFS), 183–184, 211–212
federalism, 94, 101, 102, 114. *See also* liberalism
Federal Judicial Police, 220
Fernández, Esther, 188
filibustering, 101, 102–105, 106, 113. *See also under* Texas, United States
film and film industry, 187–189, 194, 200, 201, 208
floods and flooding, 85, 93, 99, 129, *174*
Flores Magón, Ricardo, 142–143, *146*
Florida (La Florida), vii, 65, 73, 222
flowers, 32, 74, 76, 94
Flynn, Errol, 181
food, 21, 25, 27, 32, 42, 54, 59, 77, 83, 99, 100, 107–108, 115, 208, 210, 225. *See also* alcohol and alcoholism; animals; haciendas; wheat and grain; *and* specific foods and drink (e.g., maize)
forts. *See* presidios
Fox, Vicente, 224
France, 65, 79, 83, 85, 106, 120, *132*, 146, 194, 197, 205; invasion of Mexico and, 118–120, 122, 123, *125*, 142
Franciscans, 13, 49, 50, 51, 77, 81, 83

friars. *See* specific orders (e.g., Dominicans)
de Fuentes, Fernando, 187–188
fútbol. *See* soccer

Gabriel, Juan, 212
Gadsden Purchase, 115
galleons, 65, 66–67, 181
Gálvez, José de, 81
gambling, 131
Garza Sada (family), 129, 155, 165, 209, 224
Garza Sada, Eugenio, 155, 213–214
Germany, 122, 129, 166, 171, 175, 193, 194
Getty, J. Paul, 185
gold, 35, 41, 42, 44, 48, 60, 65, 82, 111, *121*, 126, 154, 160
Gold Shirts, 168
Gómez Farías, Valentín, 98, 102, 106
Gonzales, Texas, 103
González, Abraham, 146, 149, 150
González Ortega, Jesús, 117, 118
government (national), 51, 53, 65, 93, 94, 98, 113, 118, 120, 124, 143, 161, 162, 163, 164, *165*, 171, 197–198, 208, *211*, 226, 227–228; colonial, 48, 53–54, 78, 80–81; during 1910s' rebellions, 148, 149; media and, 163, 176, *186*, 187, 189, 197, 211; organized labor and, 164-166, 183; relations with business and elite, 129, 130, 156, 166, 168, 193, 204, 219; rhetoric of "The Revolution" and, 158, 167, *198*. *See also* Catholics and Catholic Church, relations and attitude towards government since; 1920; congress; constitutions; federalism; oligarchs and rich; National Action Party; Institutional Revolutionary Party (PRI); unions, labor policies and; *and* specific offices (e.g., viceroy)

governors, 53, 94, 124, 144, 147, 148, 149, *170*, 172, 173, 176, 182, 196. *See also* specific states (e.g., Veracruz) *and* specific persons (e.g., Cedillo, Saturnino)
grain. *See* maize, wheat
Grand Canyon, 56, 83
Great Britain, 62, 65, 67, 80, 118, 126, *132*, 139–140, 141, 194
Green Cards (U.S. immigration), 206
Guadalajara, 42, 131, 160, 185,
Guadalupe Hidalgo, Treaty of, 111, 113
Guanajuato, 60, 61, 80, 85–86, 87
Guatemala, 8, 25, 42. 113, 196, 211, *211*, 216
Guerrero, Vicente, 91, 93, 96, 98
guerrillas (in the 1970s), 208, 218
guilds, 64, 84
Gulf cartel, 217
Gulf of Campeche, 208
Gutiérrez Rebollo, Jesús, 220
Guzmán, Martín, 159–160
Guzmán, Nuño de, 42, 44
Guzmán Huerta, Rodolfo. *See* El Santo

haciendas and land, 59, *60*, 63, 71, 84, 85, 98, 99, 111, 124, 130, 131, 138, 157; disputes over (in early twentieth century), 148, 149, 169, 170
Harvard University, 19, 209
henequen, 114, 131, 144, 169
heresy, 51, 76
Hernández, Roberto, 220
Hernández de Córdoba, Francisco, 35
heroin, 205–206
Hidalgo, Miguel, 85–86, 87, 88, 91; honoring memory and body of, 95, 140–141, *142*
history (approaches to) and historians, v–vi, 214
Hollywood (California), 187, 188, 189
Holy Week, 72, 100, 197

horses, 37, 38, 44, 69, 84, 85, 109, (racing) 131, 149, *150*, 208
Houston (Texas), 105, *105*, 209
Houston, Sam, 104, 105
Huasteca. *See* Téenek
Huasteca Potosina, 25, 27
Huehueteotl, 8–9
Huerta, Victoriano, 148–149, 150, 151, 152
Huitzilopochtli, 29, 31, 32, 39, 41
humanism, 52, 62, 132
human rights, 184, 222
human sacrifice, 6, 7, 18, 20, 31–32, 39, 50, 51

Iberia. *See* Spaniards and Spain
Ibero-American University, 196
ideology. *See* Catholic Church and Catholics, nineteenth century ideologies and; conservatism; liberalism
immigrants and immigration, 101, 124, 155, 166, *175*, 204, 206, 210, 222, 226, 229. *See also* United States, border and immigration
independence: Mexican, 87–88, 91, 93, 95, 96; Texas, 105, 118, 122
industry, 126, 128–129, 137, 138, 144, 153, 168, 173, 176, 204. *See also* banks and finance; smelters and smelting; tourism and tourist industry
inflation, 77, 83, 176, 208, 220
Inquisition, Holy Office of, 51–52, 76–77, 85, 87
Institutional Revolutionary Party (PRI), 184, 191–193, 196, 197–198, 207, 214, 215, 216–218, *218*, 219, 224, 227
intelligence and security apparatuses, 154, 162, 171, *182*, 191, 194, *195*, 197, *211*, 216, 220, 226, 227, 228, 229. *See also* Federal Directorate of Security; police; surveillance

intendants and intendencies, 80, 81, 85–86, 88
Interior, Ministry of, 176, 183, 184, 206–207
Interjet (airlines), 222
International Monetary Fund (IMF), 210, 211, 220
internet, 85,
investment, 95, 126, 129–130, 137, 138, 139, 140, 144, 149, *215*, 216, 217, 228; by United States after 1920, 155–156, 171, 174. *See also* banks and finance
Ireland and Irish, 65, *110*
iron and iron ore, 11, 62
irrigation, 28, 32, 84, 144
Isabella (Spanish queen), 37, 77
Islam, 36, 37
Iturbide, Agustín de (Mexican emperor), 91, *92*, 93, 95, 96, 141

Jackson, Andrew, 94, 105
jade, 25
Jaguar Knights (of Aztecs), 32, 41
Jaguars, 6, 10, 25, 32
Jalapa. *See* Xalapa
Jalisco, 117, 160, 211
Japan, 67, 220
Jesuits, 73, 81, *82*, 87, 98
Jews and Judaism, 36, 76, 160, 163
John Paul II (pope), *221*, 222
Johnson, Lyndon B., 195
José, José, 203, 212
journalism, 73, *150*, 172, *175*, 185, 211–212, 223, 227
Juárez, Benito, 111, 116, 117, 118, 119, 122, 141; as president, 123–124

Kardec, Allen, 145, 147
Kennedy, John F., 195, *195*
Kennedy, Robert (Bobby) F., 195
King, Martin Luther, Jr., 197
Kino, Eusebio, 73

Kulkulkán, 18, *19*
Kurikaweri, 42

labor. *See* artisans and craftsmen; encomienda; guilds; slavery; Spaniards and Spain, and Native labor and; tribute; unions
ladinos, 114, 115
La Jornada (newspaper), 227
land. *See* haciendas *and* specific geographic entities (e.g., Yucatán)
Landa, Diego de, 13, 51
language and languages, vii, 13, 25, 27, 36, 38, 50, 51, 54, 59, 64, 102, 176, 187–188, 203
LaSalle, Sieur de, 83
La Valenciana, 60, 80
La Venta, 23
Legionnaires of Christ, 193, 222
León (Guanajuato), 176
Lerdo de Tejada, Miguel, 116, 117
liberals and liberalism, 94, 95, 96, 98, 102, 114, 120, 140–143, *146*; The Reform and, 115–117, 120, 123, 124. *See also* anti-clericalism; Catholic Church, nineteenth century ideologies and; conservatism
Lincoln, Abraham, 107
Lomas de Chapultepec, 193
Lombardo Toledano, Vicente, 168, 172, 173, 175, 176, 183, *186*, 190
López Mateos, Adolfo, *195*, 196
López Obrador, Andrés Manuel, 219, 228–229
López Portillo, 208–210
Lora, Alex, 199
Los Angeles, 138–139, 187, 204
Los Tecos, 196, 211
Louisiana, 83, 88, 101, 104
lucha libre, 199, *200*, 201

Maciel, Marcial, 193, 222–223
Madero (family), 144; Madero, Francisco, 145, 146, 147, 148, 149, 154

maize (corn), 8, 15, 17, 20–21, 27, 32, 44, 50, 77, 99, 115
malaria, 76
Maldonado, Pedro de Jesús, *221*
(La) Malinche, 38, 39
Manila Galleon. *See* galleons
maquiladoras, 204
markets, 39, 54, 70, 99
mariachis, 79, 163, 199
marijuana, 125, 206
Márquina, Ignacio, 9
marriage, 62, 69, 70, 76, 99, 116, 140, 155, 182, 189, 193, 194, 209
máscaras, 69, 131
massacres, 39, 40, 42, 86, 176, 197, 208, *211*
Matamoros, 129
Maximato, 163, 166
Maximilian, 119–122, *121*, 123, 124
Maya, 7, 11, 13–22, *17*, 23, *24*, 25, *26*, 27, *49*; calendars, 20–21; contact with Spaniards, 13, 35, 38; conquest of and war against, 44, 114–115; elite and lords, 16, 21–22; hieroglyphs of, 13, 15, 17, 21; religious beliefs, 15, 18, 20, 22, 51; sources about, 13–15; stelae, *14*, 15, 21. *See also* Chichen Itzá; Yucatán
media, 185, *186*, 189, 191, 193, 197, 199, 203, 212, 213, 215, 217, 218, 223. *See also* film and film industry; journalism; newspapers; radio; Televisa; television;; *and* specific names of media outlets (e.g., *La Jornada*)
medicine and medicinal procedures, *10*, 32, 126, 133, *189*; in colonial times, 72–74, *75*, 76. *See also* disease and epidemics
Mendoza, Antonio de, 53, 54, 56
mental illness and disabilities, 133, *165*
merchants. *See* trade
mercury, 62, 74, 80
Mérida, 114

mestizos, 23, 57, 59, 78, 96, 186. *See also* ladinos
metallurgy. *See* gold; mines and mining; silver
Metro (Mexico City subway), 207
Mexica, 47, 50
Mexicana (airlines), 222
Mexican-Americans, 187, 204
Mexican Central Railroad, 128, *128*, 139, 146, 151
Mexican Football Federation (FMF), 199
Mexican Institute of Social Security (IMSS), 198
Mexican National Railroad, 128, 129
Mexican Petroleum Company, 139
Mexican Revolution. *See* The Revolution (of 1910, and concept of); rebellion and revolt, in the 1910s
Mexican Telephone & Telegraph Company, 169
Mexican Workers' Confederation (CTM), 168–169, 173, 175, 183
Mexico City, ix, *14*, *24*, 31, 59, 60, 64, 72, 77, 81, 99–100, 116, 117, 118, 120, 124, 128, 131, 161, 188, 193, *195*, 199, 203, 209, 210, 212, 222, 225–226, 228, 229; in wake of Aztec conquest, 47, 48, 49, 50, 53; 1692 rebellion in, 77–78; during independence wars, 86, 87, 91, *92*; in early national period, 94, 96, 98, 102, 107, 109–111; economic development of (after 1867), 129, *130*, 133, 140, *174*, 189; in 1910s' rebellions, 148, 153, 154, 155; modern political violence in, 184, 186, 197, 208, 211–212, 217. *See also* Chapultepec; Churubusco; Lomas de Chapultepec; Tenochtitlán; Tlatelolco
Miami, 209

Michoacán, 42, 52, 116
middle class, 124, 141, 142, 144, 152, 155, 163, (U.S.) 184, 196, 197, 201, 204, 208
Mier, Servando Teresa de, 94
Miguel Alemán Foundation, 219
military. *See* war and warfare
Military Camp One (Mexico City), 196
militias, 84, 95
Millon, René, 6
mines and mining, 60–61, 80, 85, 95, 126, 129, 137, 138, 141. *See also* silver
Miramón, Miguel, 117, 118, 120, 122
missions. *See* Catholic Church and Catholics, *and* specific Orders (e.g., Franciscans)
Mixtecs, 12, 42
Moctezuma (II), 33, 38, 38n, 39, 40, 41, 49
Molina Enríquez, Andrés, 144
monasteries. *See* convents
money. *See* banks and finance; coins and coinage; investment; peso
Monte Albán, xi, *11*, 12
Monterrey, 107, 113, 128–129, 138, 145, 165, 168, 174, 193, 209, 213
Monterrey Institute of Technology, 213, 214
Montes de Oca, Ignacio, 141–142
Moon pyramid (at Teotihuacán), 5, 6
Moors, 36
Mora, José María Luis, 94
Morelos, José María, 88
MORENA. *See* Movement for National Regeneration
Moreno Reyes, Marío. *See* Cantinflas
Morones, Luis, 164-165
Movement for National Regeneration, 228
mules, 84, 100
municipios, 54, 55

muralists (of twentieth century), 158, 159
murals and muralists (twentieth century), 9–11, 197
music, 72, 79, 131, 199, 203, 212
muskets and musketry, 66, 86, 106

NAFTA (North American Free Trade Agreement). *See* trade, 1994 pact with the United States
Nahuatl, 38, 51, 59, 75
Napoleon III (French Emperor), 118, 119, 122
National Action Party (PAN), 193, 214, 215, 219, 224, 228
National Defense League for Religious Liberty, 161
National Guard, 228
National Institute of Anthropology and History (INAH), 5
nationalism, 97, 107, 111, 116, 176, 183, 191, 196, 198, 227
National Museum of Anthropology, 14, 24, 31
National Preparatory School, 132, 159
National Revolutionary Party (PNR), 162, 167
National Security Police (PSN), 184, 185
National Tourism Council, 192
National University of Mexico (UNAM), 182, 186, 208
Native Americans. *See* specific cultures or tribes (e.g., Aztecs)
natural gas, 140, 174
Nava, Salvador, 196
navy and naval vessels, 64, 65-66, 67, 81, 114, 152. *See also* galleons
Neo-Classical, 64
Nevada, 83
New Mexico (Nuevo México), vii, 29, 56. 77, 106, 107
New Orleans, 115, 116

newspapers, *143*, 163, 168–169 , 173, 184, *186*. *See also* specific names (e.g., *El Universal*)
New Zapatistas (EZLN), 216, 218
Nezahualcóyotl, 30
Niblo, Stephen, vi, 185
Niños Héroes, 111, 120
nobility (Spanish and colonial), 48, 53, 57
Norteño (music), 199
Novedades (newspaper), *186*
novels, 159–160, 189
Nueces River, 103, 107
Nueva Vizcaya, 56, 59

Oaxaca (city or state), ix, 11, 42, 88, 111, 116
Oberon, Merle, 194
Obregón, Álvaro, 152–153, 154, 155, 156, 157, 160, 162, 170, 181
obsidian, 7, 8, 32
Ocampo, Melchor, 116, 117
O'Farrill, Rómulo, 186
Office of Inter-American Affairs (U.S.), 175
oil. *See* petroleum
Ojinaja (Chihuahua), *150*
Old Spanish Trail, 83
oligarchs and rich, 63, 69, 70, 83, 86, 100, 118,131, 144, *186*, 194, 196, 209, 216, 220, 229; land concentration and, 84, 95, 114, 116–117, 123, 130-131, 137; links to government and corruption, 172–173, 174–175, 184–185; in Monterrey, 129, 138, 144, 145, 163, 165, 166, 168, 173, 174, 176, 193, 213–214, 224; 1910s' rebellions and, 147, 155. *See also* billionaires; oligarchy; PRI elite; *and* specific names (e.g., Garza Sada)
oligarchy, vi, 183, 191, 194, 209, 214, 217, 222, 227

Olmecs, 16, 23, *24*, 25, 26
Olympic Games (of 1968), 191, 197, *207*
opium, 205
Opus Dei, 194
Orozco, José Clemente, 158, *159*
Ortiz Rubio, Pascual, 162, 163
Owners' Confederation (COPARMEX), 166, 168, 214

Pachuca, 80
Pagliai, Bruno, 194
Palafox, Juan de, *73*
Palma, Héctor "El Güero," 220
PAN. *See* National Action Party
Paramount Pictures, 188
paraquat (herbicide), 206
Parral, *128*, 157
Party of the Democratic Revolution (PRD), 219
Paz, Octavio, 219
Pearson, Weetman, 140
peasants and peasantry, 59, 60, 126, 133, 138, 140, 160, 184, 196, 197; in 1910s' rebellions, 147, 148, 149, 152. *See also* haciendas
PEMEX (Petróleos Mexicanos [national oil company]), 171, 183, 185–186, 208–210, 222, 227, 228
Peña Nieto, Enrique, 227
Peru, 53, 62, 206
peso (Mexican currency), 123, 208, 210, 214, 216, 220, 226, 229. *See also* devaluation
Petén, 15, 16, 25
petroleum, 139, 140, 156, 171, 173, 183, 185, 208, 209–210, 215, 222
Philip II (Spanish king), 65
Philippines, 53, 66, 88
Pineda, Guadalupe, 203
Pipila, 86
pirates, 65, 66
Plans (formal political pronouncements), 93, 145

plants and plant life, 54, 55–56, 73, 74, *75*, 99, 138, 176, 207. *See also* flowers; maize
poetry, 71
Poinsett, Joel, 94
police, 133, 143, 145, 149, 172, 183–184, 188, 196, 197, 210, 211, 213, 216, 220, *221*, 227. *See also* Federal Judicial Police, intelligence and security apparatuses, private security; firms
politics. *See* elections; plans; *and* specific political parties (e.g., PRI)
Polk, James K., 107
pollution, 226
Popé (Pueblo shaman), 77
popes and papacy, 53, 76, 81, 118, 141, 222–223, 228. *See also* John Paul II
Popocatepetl, 9, 41
population, 47–48, 54, 57, 58, 60, 62, 78, 83, 99, 101–102, 114, 129, 138, 165–166, 176, 201, 204, 225, 226, 229
Popul Vuh, 15
Porfiriato, 125, 128–133, 138, 140–145, 148, 176
Posada, José Guadalupe, *143*
Positivism and Positivists, 132, 144, *159*
Post-Classic (period), 9–10, 12, (Mayan) 21, 29, 30, 44
pottery, 8–9, 12, 25, 31
poverty, 78, 99–100, 137, 138, 186, 190, 197, 201, 209, 210, 212, *218*, 226
Pre-Classic (period), Maya, 15–16, 24, 25
presidios, 83, 104
PRI. *See* Institutional Revolutionary Party; PRI elite
PRI elite (or fraternity), vi, *182*, 184–186, *187*, 190, 191, 193–194, 196, 197, 204, 206, 211, *215*, 217, 219, 220, 222, 224, 228. *See also* oligarchs

and rich; oligarchy; Institutional Revolutionary Party
priests (Catholic), 49, 66, 74, 77, 83, 84, 87, 117, 118, 161, 170; nineteenth century privileges and, 95, 116. See also Catholic Church and Catholics, priests
prisons, 94, 133, 143, 148, 149, 196, 197, 211, 212, 213
private security firms, 222
privatization, 216, 227
prostitution, 72, 125
Protestants, 62, 65, 66, 102, 124, 129, 133, 223
protests, 186, 196, 197, 208, 228
public opinion and polling, 167, 168, 171, 176, *195*, 197, (U.S.) 206, 213, 214, 223, 227
public relations firms, 214
Public Works, Ministry of, 174–175
Puebla (city or state), ix, 73, 96, 111, 116, 118, *119*, *125*, 172–173, 175, 182
Pueblo (Natives of New Mexico), 56, 77
pulque, 9, 131
Purists (liberals), 116–117, 120
Pyramids, 3–9, *11*, 27, *28*, *30*, 31. See also Teotihuacán

Querétaro (city and state), 113, 122
quinine, 76
Quiroga, Vasco de, 52
Quiroz, Eleuterio, 113

race. See creoles; mestizos; whites; Yucatán, race war in; *and* specific Native cultures and tribes (e.g., Aztecs)
radio, 163–164, 168, 192-193, 199, 223
railroads, 115, *127*, *128*, 129–131, 138, *139*, 140, *153*, 154, 160, 161, 185, 196

Ramos Arizpe, Miguel, 94
Reagan, Ronald, 206
Real del Monte, 80
rebellion and revolt, 42, 77, 85, 88, 93, 96, 102, 113, 116, 117, 161, 169, 171, 216; in the 1910s, 145–146, 151, 154. See also protests
Reconquest (in Spain), 37, 49, 53
Refugio (Texas), 104
Regeneración (publication), 143
Regional Confederation of Mexican Workers (CROM), 164–166, 167, 168
Regla, Conde de, 80
religion. See Aztecs, cosmology and religion; Catholic Church and Catholics; Maya, religious beliefs; Protestants
remittances (from immigrants), 222, 226
Rentoy, 131
repartimiento, 58
Republic of the Sierra Madre, 113
The Restoration (1867–76 period), 123–124
retablos, 64, *82*, 95
The Revolution (of 1910, and concept of), vi, 145, 152, 157–159, 167. See also rebellion and revolt, in the 1910s
Reyes, Bernardo, 138, 144, 145, 148
Riaño, Juan Antonio de, 85–86
rich. See nobility, oligarchs and rich, PRI Fraternity
The Rich also Cry (telenovela), 209
Río Bravo/Río Grande (river), 107, 128, 129
Rivera, Diego, 158, *186*
rock music, 199, 212
Rocky Mountain Council of Latin American Studies (RMCLAS), viii
Rodríguez, Abelardo, 163, *164*
Roman Catholic Church. See Catholic Church and Catholics

Romero Rubio, Carmen, 140
Roosevelt, Franklin D., 171
Royalists (in independence wars), 86–88, 91, 92
royal patronage, 53, 64
Ruiz Massieu, José Francisco, 217
Rurales, 126, 137, 145, 199
Russia and Soviet Union, 59, 99, 124, 171, *172*, 175

sacraments (Catholic), 50, 116, 161
Sahagún, Bernardino de, 51
Saint Patrick Brigade, 110
saints. *See* Catholic Church and Catholics, saints and
Salinas (family), 129, 138, 165
Salinas, Carlos, 214, *215*, 216, 217–218, 227
Salinas, Irma, 213–214
Salinas & Rocha (department stores), 129
Saltillo, 55, 108, 129
San Antonio (Texas), 103–104, 106, 142, 145, 204, 209
Sánchez Navarro (family), 84, 123
San Diego (California), 169, 222
San Jacinto, battle of, 102, 104, *105*
San Lorenzo, 24
San Luis Potosí (city, intendency, or state), ix, 56, 60, 61, 87–88, 107, 124, 130, 138, 145, 196, 197; anticlerical movement in, 141–143; (early twentieth century) rebellions and turmoil in, 147–148, 149, *170*
Santa Anna, Antonio López de, 93, 94, 97, 98, 113, 114, 116, 124; as president, 102, 106, 115–116; in military command, 96, 102–104, *105*, 106, 107–111
Santa Cruz de Tlatelolco, 51
Santa Fe (Nuevo Mexico), 77
Santana, Carlos, 199
Sarmiento, Domingo F., 123

Satellite City, 186
Sayil, *14*
science, 74
schools, 52, 81, 98, 124, 158, 161, 170, 193, 208
Scott, Winfield, 109, *109*, 110
security services. *See* Federal Directorate of Security; intelligence and security apparatuses
Semana Santa. *See* Holy Week
sewage, 99, 185
sheep, 84, 85
shipping. *See* galleons; navy and naval vessels; trade
Sierra Gorda, 113
Sierra Madre, 27, 29, 38, 113, 129, 155, 205
Sierra Nevada, 83
Sigüenza y Góngora, Carlos, 72–74
silk, 66
silver, 42, 48, 126; mines and production of, 60–63, 80
Sinaloa, 205
Sinaloa cartel, 220
Siqueiros, David Alfaro, 197
Sisal, 114
slavery, 12, 22, 44, 51, 61, 71, 102, 107, 115, 122
Slim, Carlos, 216, 222, *223*
smallpox. *See* disease and epidemics
smelters and smelting, 62, 129, 144
Smith, Joseph, 4
soccer, 199, 208
soldiers, 76, 81, 83, *92*, 104, 114, 117, 123, 125–126, *151*. *See also* army and armies; war and warfare
Sonora, 73, 137, *164*
Sor Juana. *See* Cruz, Sor Juana Inés de la
Soumaya Museum, 67, *223*
South America, 91, 111, 115, 187
Soviet Union. *See* Russia
Spaniards and Spain, 9, 13, 29, 30, 32, 38, 48, 51, 53, 60, 64, 66, 69, 74,

75, 77, 78, 94, 118, 158, 171, 197, 210; background, 36–37; crown (king, or state), 47, 53, 54, 58, 59, 62, 65, 79–81, 88; exploration and conquests, 35, 38–44, 47, 51, 56, 83, 228; Mexican independence and, 85, 86, 87, 88, 91, 92, 96; Native labor and, 57, 58-59, 61, 62
Spanish Armada, 65
sports. *See* specific activities (e.g., baseball)
steel, 138, 213
stele. *See* Maya, stele
students. *See* schools, universities
Subcommandante Marcos, 216
Sun pyramid (at Teotihuacán), 5, 6, 7
surveillance, 88, 142, 154, 168, 184, 216
syncretism (religious), 50, 74
System Lerma, *174*

Tabasco, 140, 219
Taft, William, 139
Tampico, 96, 139, 171
Tamtoc, ix, 27, 28
Tarascans, 26, *42*, *43*, 52, 56
tariffs, 80, 117, 118, 126, 129, 139. *See also* taxes
Tariq, 36
Taxco, 60
taxes, 53, 62–63, 80, 84, 93, 96, 98, 124, 126, 129, 147, 161, 172, 197. *See also* tariffs
Taylor, Zachary, 107–109
technology, 125, 130, 137, 184, 187, 229
Téenek, 25, *26*, 27–29, 44
Tehuantepec, 129, 140
telegraph, 124, 137
Telemundo (TV network), 223
telenovelas (soap operas), 199, 209. *See also* The Rich also Cry
telephones, 132, 162, 184, 229. *See also* Mexican Telephone & Telegraph Company; Telmex

Televisa (TV network), 193, 196, 197, 199, 203, 209, 210, 212, 227; elections and news coverage of, 214–215, 223–224, 228
television, 193, 196, 199, 223, 228. *See also* specific names of networks (e.g., Univision)
Telmex (Teléfonos México), 194, 216
Tenochtitlán, vii, 29, *30*, 32, 39–40, 41, 47, 49, 197
tequila, 131
Teotihuacán, 3–9, 29. 31. *See also* specific features, .e.g., Sun pyramid
Texas (Tejas), vii, 27, 83, 88, 107, 119, 122, 128, 129, 150, 174, 175, 182; U.S. filibuster of, 101–102, *103*, 104-106, 113
Texcoco and Lake Texcoco, 30, 32, 39, 41
textiles, 44, 54, 84, *130*, 138, 204
theater, 72, 79, *132*, 188
Third World, 191, *195*
Thompson, Edward, 19
Tijuana, ix, *164*, *187*, 217, *218*, 222
Tikal, 16
Tlaloc, 6, 8, 31, 42
Tlatelolco (plaza and massacre), 197, 198, 207
Tlaxcalans and Tlaxcala, 38–39, 41, 42, *43*, 44, 48, 56, 183
Toledo (Spain), *30*
Tolentino, Nicolás, *52*
Toltecs, 18–19, 22, 29, 31
Tonantzin, 50
torture, 49, 183, 185, 196, 211, 213
tourism and tourist industry, 6, 192, 195, 204–205, 226, 228
trade, 8, 21, 54, 58, 62, 64-66, 69, 71, 80, 95, 99, 114, 128–129; 1994 pact with the United States, 216–218, 222, 226. *See also* markets; United States, trade and economic links with Mexico

Tragic Ten Days, 148
transportation, 100, 126, 133, 140, 204, 207
Traven, B., 160
The Treasure of the Sierra Madre (novel), 160
Treasury, Ministry of, 116, 185, 208
tribute, 30, 48, 58. *See also* encomienda
Trotsky, Leon, 171, *172*
Trouyet, Carlos, 194
Trump, Donald, 227, 229
Tula, 19–20, 29
Tulum, 13, 21
Turner, John Kenneth, 144
turquoise, xi, 12
TV Azteca (network), 223, 227
Tzompantli (at Chichen Itzá), 18, *19*

UNAM. *See* National University of Mexico
The Underdogs (novel), 159
unemployment, 86, 100, *130*, 204, *218*
unions, 164, 173, 183, 184, 185, 198, (U.S.) 204, 219; and labor policies (in twentieth century), 152–153, 163, 164, 166, 167–169, 183; strikes and stoppages of, viii–ix, 137, 147–148, 168, 173, 183, 196–197. *See also* guilds
United States (of America), vii, 29, 56, 73, 80, 83, 94, 122, 123, 152, 154, 163, 169, 173, 176, 182, 195, 197, 203, 205, 220, 227, 229; American Revolution in, 81, 85, 93; border and immigration, 122, 145, 146, 153, 155, *164*, 166, 204, 210, 222; embassy and ambassador to Mexico, 139, 148–149, 161, 174, 196, 226; filibustering activities of, 101–102, *103*, 105–106, 115; Mexican War and, 106–107, *108*, *109*, 110–111, 113; relations with Mexico since 1940, 174–176, 183, 184, 194, 208–209; trade and economic links with Mexico, 129, 133, 137, 139, 171, *175*, 187, 192, 204, 205,; 206, 208, 216, 220, 226. *See also* Central Intelligence Agency; Federal Bureau of Investigation; immigrants and immigration; investment, by United States after 1920; USAID; tourism and tourist industry; trade, 1994 pact with the United States
universities, 71, 72, 193-194, 197. *See also* specific institutions (e.g., National University of Mexico)
Univision (TV network), 223
urbanization, 138
Urrea, José de, 104
USAID (United States Aid for International Development), 196
Utah, 83
Uxmal, 16

Valladolid (Yucatán), 114
Vasconcelos, José, 158, 162–163
Vatican. *See* popes and papacy
Vázquez de Coronado, Francisco, 56, 77
Velasco, Raúl, 203
Velásquez, Fidel, 198
Veracruz (city or state), 5, 40, 49, 66, 69, 81, 88, 96, 107, 117, 118, 123, 124, 131, 140, 181; Santa Anna and, 93, 95, 98, 106, 109; in 1910s' rebellions, 146, 152, 153, 154; twentieth century politics in, 176, 182, 194
vice presidency, 95, 96, 98, (Texas) 105
viceroy, 53, 69, 77, 86
Victoria, Guadalupe, 88, 93, 95, 99, 106, 120
Vidaurri, Santiago, 113, 117
Vidriera (corporation), 168, 194
Villa, Francisco "Pancho," 59, 149, *150*, 151, 153, 154, 155, 157, 158, 160
Villarreal, Antonio, *146*

Virgin Mary. *See* Virgin of Guadalupe
Virgin of Guadalupe, 50–51, 81, *82*, 85, 88, 100, 141, 201
visitas (audits), 80–81
Vizcaino, Sebastián, 66–67
Volaris (airline), 222
volcanoes, 9, 226. *See also* Popocatepetl

Walmart, 220
war and warfare (*and* warriorhood), *19*, 21–22, 29, 30, 32, 35, 37–38, 42, 44, 48, 56, 57, 175, 176; Mexican independence and, 86–88; Mexico versus Americans, 102–104, 106, 107–111, 113; Mexico versus the French, 106, 118–120, 122. *See also* army and armies; artillery; battles and battlefields; cavalry; militias; muskets and musketry; presidios; rebellion and revolt; soldiers; Spaniards and Spain, exploration and conquests; War of the Reform; United States (of America), Mexican War and
War of the Reform, 116–118, 123
water, 27, 28, 32, 44, 54, *55*, 62, 80, *105*, 114, 133, 140, *174*, 204, 226. *See also* floods and flooding, irrigation, sewage
Western Union, 222
wheat and grain, 59, 77
whites, 33, 47, 57, 58, 78, 87, 98, 124, 181, 184, 186. *See also* creoles
widows and widowhood, 71, *211*
Wiegand, Oscar, 196
wine, 84

witchcraft, 76
Woll, Adrián, 106
women, vi, 28, 32, 39, 42, 52, 57, 93, 99, 100, 108, 125, 133, 134, 161, *165*, 176, 188, 201, 228; in colonial times, 70–72, 74, 76, 83; suffrage and, 163, *187*. *See also* Catholic Church and Catholics, nuns and convents; widow and widowhood; *and* specific names (e.g., Pineda, Guadalupe)
wrestling. *See* lucha libre
Wright State University (Ohio), viii

Xalapa, 93, 109
XEW (TV station), 193
Xultún, 14–15

Yucatán, ix, 13, 15, *17*, 18, 21, 26, 35, 37, 44, *49*, 144, 160, 169, 227; race war in, 113–115. 117
Yugoslavia, 218

Zacatecas, *55*, 60–61, 63, 82, *132*, 151, 152, 153
Zambrano (family), 165, 173
Zapata, Emiliano, 149, 150, 151, 152, 154, 158, 160, 216. *See also* New Zapatistas
Zapotecs, 11–12, 26, 124
Zaragoza, Ignacio, *119*
Zavala, Lorenzo de, 96, 105
Zedillo, Ernesto, 218–219, 220, 222
Zetas (gang and cartel), ix, 227
zócalo, 54; in Mexico City 207, 219
Zorrilla Pérez, José Antonio, 212

www.ingramcontent.com/pod-product-compliance
Lightning Source LLC
Chambersburg PA
CBHW070025010526
44117CB00011B/1709